A MANIFOLD VOICE

STUDIES IN COMMONWEALTH LITERATURE

A
MANIFOLD VOICE

Studies in Commonwealth Literature

WILLIAM WALSH

PROFESSOR OF EDUCATION
AND DOUGLAS GRANT FELLOW
IN COMMONWEALTH LITERATURE
IN THE UNIVERSITY OF LEEDS

BARNES & NOBLE, Inc.
NEW YORK
PUBLISHERS & BOOKSELLERS SINCE 1873

PUBLISHED IN GREAT BRITAIN BY
Chatto & Windus Ltd.
42 William IV Street
London, W.C.2
★
First published in the United States of America, 1970
by Barnes & Noble, Inc.

SBN 389 01332 3

TO
THE UNIVERSITY OF LEEDS
AND
THE AUSTRALIAN NATIONAL
UNIVERSITY

Acknowledgments

I am indebted to the following for permission to quote from work protected by copyright: to R. K. Narayan, William Heinemann and David Higham Associates; to Nirad C. Chaudhuri, John Farquharson and Chatto & Windus; to the literary estate of Olive Schreiner and Hutchinson & Co.; to Chinua Achebe, William Heinemann and Heinemann Educational Books; to V. S. Naipaul and André Deutsch; to Patrick White and Curtis Brown; to A. D. Hope and Hamish Hamilton; to the Katherine Mansfield estate and The Society of Authors; to Morley Callaghan and Mac-Gibbon & Kee.

Contents

Preface

IN this book I start from an assumption of the intimacy of language and literature, an intimacy so close and active that I see language as the co-partner with the author in producing a given work. The existence of a work of literature depends not on the writer alone but also on the degree of maturity the language it is written in has attained to, just as its complexity and fineness depend on the range of resources within that language. The practice of criticism, consequently, is not limited to the immediate analysis of the work in question but it also involves a telling-over of the powers latent in the language. A belief of this kind is the ground of the double intention in *A Manifold Voice*. First, I seek to explore some of the less familiar resources—less familiar to the British reader, that is—existing in the English language by pointing, as precisely and concretely as I can, at a number of writers who have worked in traditions outside those of Britain and the United States. The amazing capacity of English to express such a span of sensibility, whether West Indian, Canadian, Australian, African, New Zealand, Indian, testifies not only to the gifts of individual authors but to the genius of the language.

Secondly, my intention is to offer an answer to a question implicit in this undertaking: which of the authors writing in English outside Britain and the United States of America have made a significant use of the resources of the language? Which of them are of more than simply local importance? My answer is my choice. These are the writers who, judged by appropriate standards, have added to the canon of literature in English: who have realised, that is, in a creative way capacities implicit in the language. I do not claim for all these writers an equal significance. Some are without doubt more important than others. All are serious writers, all are genuinely representative; but there are some who are more important representatively than intrinsically. In fact, in one or two—as, I hope, my treatment shows—the representative quality, the capacity to embody a national identity and sensibility, shades and limits the pure literary worth. Nor can one overlook the great differences in context in which these writers operate. Patrick White, for example, writes straight from the heart of the British tradition, even though it may be given his own national modification and even though he may do it at immense physical distance; R. K. Narayan and Nirad C. Chaudhuri work against the background of their own powerful and very different civilisation and in a second language learnt at school; Chinua Achebe also writes in a second language but against a much more strongly oral tradition; the Canadian, Morley Callaghan, works under the influence, and suffers the pressure, of both English and American literature; much of the best work of Katherine Mansfield and V. S. Naipaul was actually composed in England although the life it deals with may belong to remote and different worlds.

I speak of this book as a set of studies in Commonwealth Literature, and I am very much aware how much this is a term of art. I have no desire to justify my use of it by arguments which it would take a constitutional lawyer to appreciate and probably to frame. I use the term because it is short, much employed and useful. It may be objected to by those who take a more exact political view of the Commonwealth than I do here, and, more strongly, by writers who rightly feel themselves to be Australians or New Zealanders or Canadians, writing against a particular historical tradition and in a particular national context, and not writers contributing to the literature of an amorphous Commonwealth. I sense the justice of these feelings, but I still use the term, which has now become widespread in Britain, the United States and other countries, as a convenient, shorthand indication and because it represents, in a reasonably uncontentious though perhaps clumsy way, a fact of history and substance about the situation of the writers I have chosen to consider.

I owe much to conversation on these subjects with three close friends: Professor D. J. Enright of the University of Singapore, Professor George Russell of the Australian National University, and the late, and deeply lamented, Professor Douglas Grant of the University of Leeds. I am greatly indebted to the University of Leeds which enabled me to undertake this work and the Australian National University which made it possible for me to complete it in Canberra.

CHAPTER I

1 R. K. NARAYAN

INDIANS were writing in English before Macaulay's Minute. There has always been a remarkable quantity of first-rate Indian work in English in scholarship, philosophy, autobiography, religion, and especially in politics. Gandhi and Nehru themselves were both in their different styles masters of an oratorical idiom. And, of course, the Indians have had, and still have, their poets. But it was not till the 1930's that a number of novelists began to write in English—genuine novelists, that is, for whom fiction is an end in itself and not a means for communicating other kinds of truth. Some thirty years later it is clear that this was a form peculiarly suited to the Indian sensibility, and one to which Indian writers have made a distinct and significant contribution. So significant, indeed, that it is odd at a time when we give more and more attention to Commonwealth writers that a group like this should have received so little notice. Odd, too, that writers should have appeared during the years when the place of English in India as well as its condition should have been the occasion of endless, intense disagreement.

Without question the most individual and remarkable of these writers is R. K. Narayan. Narayan's preoccupation is with the middle class, a relatively small part of an agricultural civilisation, and the most conscious and anxious part of the population. Its members are neither too well off not to know the rub of financial worry nor too indigent to be brutalised by want and hunger. They may take their religion more easily than the passionately credulous poor, but even in those with a tendency towards modernity one is always aware under the educated speech of the profound murmur of older voices, of 'Lakshmi and Vishnu, the protector of creatures'. It is the members of the middle class who are psychologically more active, in whom consciousness is more vivid and harrowing, that Narayan chooses for his heroes—modest, unselfconfident heroes, it is true. They have some reason for independent existence; but there is always a tension between this and that deep source of power, the family where the women rather than the old represent 'Custom and Reason' and know 'what is and what is not proper'. The family is the immediate context in which his sensibility operates, and his novels are remarkable for the subtlety and conviction with which family relationships are treated—that of son and parents and brother and brother in *The Bachelor of Arts*, of husband and wife and father and daughter in *The English Teacher*, of father and son in *The Financial Expert*, and of grandmother and grandson in *Waiting for Mahatma*.

The action of Narayan's novels is centred in the small town of Malgudi in Mysore—small by Indian standards, that is—and one comes to have a strong feeling for the place's identity. The detail suggests, surely and economically, the special flavour of Malgudi, a blend of oriental and pre-1914 British, like an Edwardian mixture of sweet mangoes and malt vinegar. It is against the presence of this town and amid a net of family relationships that Narayan's heroes engage in their characteristic struggles. The conditions of the struggle vary from novel to novel. One still discerns beneath the diversity a common pattern. What is so attractive about it is the charm and authenticity of its Indian colouring; what makes it immediately recognisable is that it seems to belong to a substantial human nature. The primary aim of these characters is to achieve what Chandran in *The Bachelor of Arts* calls 'a life freed from distracting illusions and hysterics'. At first the intention is obscure, buried under the habits of ordinary life, personal responsibilities and—since this is India—a heavy, inherited burden. The novels plot the rise of this intention into awareness, its recognition in a crisis of consciousness, and its resolution, or resolutions, since there are more often than not several mistaken or frustrated efforts at a resolution. If the analysis of the subject's struggle to extricate himself from the habitual, dreamy automatism of his Indian past shows Narayan's gift for serious moral analysis, then the various solutions adopted by his *personae* in the search for another, more conscious life, exhibit his marvellous comic talent. (Not of course that the fiction offers a neatly logical division just like this. The serious and the comic flow in and out of one another throughout in an intricate, inseparable alliance.) Tracts of human experience are looked at with an affectionately ridiculing eye, and with that kind of humour in which the jokes are also a species of moral insight. Such treatment brings out the note of the bizarre, of human queerness, in the activities of many sorts of people, business men, printers, teachers, holy men, press agents, money-lenders. At our most commonplace we are all exotic if scrutinised by a fresh eye. The range is impressive but it follows naturally on Narayan's reading of the key experience at the heart of his novels. It is always a meeting which precipitates the crisis of consciousness. It is the intervention of human difference, human otherness, into the hero's narcissistic world which shatters it for him, and he feels in response that he has to break out of his solipsistic circle into a new, better still an alien, field of action. To evoke so much variety with such casual, convincing authority and to make it also organic and functional testify to an original talent of the finest kind.

I have written at length on Narayan's fiction elsewhere[1] and I will concentrate here on two novels which appeared since I wrote that essay, *The Man-Eater of Malgudi* (1961), and *The Sweet Vendor* (1967). *The Man-Eater of Malgudi* begins on a note of modest self-mockery. The protagonist, Nataraj, runs a seedy print-shop in Kabir Street next to—in fact almost in an ante-room of—the prosperous Star Press where there is an amenable proprietor as well as a large staff and 'an original Heidelberg' printing press, with groaning double cylinders. Nataraj, with the help, or really under the direction, of his one member of staff, the learned Mr Sastri, does pretty well everything in the shop, from printing on an ancient treadle machine to sewing up the sheets; he is particularly expert in printing coloured labels for lemonade bottles, the ink of which in his view is often much more drinkable than the contents of the bottle. He keeps the line between his own place and the Star Press deliberately vague and has a habit of passing through importunate and curious customers to the more important establishment, particularly if they want to be assured about the machinery on which their orders are to be printed. This is one of his ways of

[1] *A Human Idiom*: Literature and Humanity. Chatto & Windus, London, 1964

conserving his privacy and liberty even at work and enables him
to go on using one of his rooms, with its roll-top desk, Queen Anne
chair and deep cane basket-chair, as a local club where his friends,
the journalist and the poet, can endlessly analyse the state of the
town and the nation. Nataraj is both a gay and melancholy man,
protected by routine which he can slough off at a moment's notice.
He is nervy, imaginative, friendly, unambitious in external things
but with a vivid inner life. He, his family, his friends, the district,
the enveloping tissue of history and the delicate film of relations
among them all, are established by means of a patient accumulation
of detail, each point of which, whether common or odd, is seen with
a child's freshness of eye and organised with an adult's experienced
subtlety. Everything is concrete, manifold, multiplying backwards
and forwards so that the reader has a sense of life elaborated with
infinite patience and completeness. The society is formal but the
relations are quick and spontaneous. Into this world composed of
shades and subtleties of relationships, of traditions, of complex
feelings, of hallowed objects, of modes of conduct and habits of
thought which are both ritualistic and homely, there intrudes the
abstract and brutal will of 'H. Vasu, M.A., Taxidermist' as he is
described on his card.

So easily and fully is this Indian world summoned into existence,
so delicately are its primary assumptions insinuated and their
intrinsic worth indicated, that the reader, like Nataraj and his
friends, feels the affront of Vasu's intervention and the way in which
his words and actions violate both accepted manners and every
tradition implicit in them. 'The man's curiosity was limitless and
recognised no proprieties,' Nataraj says of him; and 'proprieties'
in Nataraj's phrase mean more than the small-town blenching at
anything outside the accepted canon of monogamous chastity
which is shown in, and shown up in, Nataraj's own blend of puritan
horror and sensual attraction towards the prostitute Rangi. 'Proprieties' here also mean a style of life and a whole habit of sensibility
sanctioned by the experience of generations, the whole complex of
practice, feeling and memory which makes Nataraj a person who
is a product of history. It is this propriety which is abolished by the
presence of Vasu. His will is unqualified by any impersonal past.

It simply, absolutely, initiates action. He is a form of abstract causality, and he is maddened by any whiff of what is established or unquestioned because that makes him to some degree an effect.

Vasu's self-exclusion from the world of familiar intercourse—invitation after invitation is extended to him but always abruptly rejected—gives him a nihilistic and menacing air which becomes, in the Indian context, somehow ominously superhuman—a force not negotiable on human terms. This is how he bursts into the novel:

> Now an unusual thing happened. The curtain stirred, an edge of it lifted, and the monosyllabic poet's head peeped through. An extraordinary situation must have arisen to make him do that. His eyes bulged. 'Someone to see you,' he whispered.
> 'Who? What does he want?'
> 'I don't know.'
> The whispered conversation was becoming a strain. I shook my head, winked and grimaced to indicate to the poet that I was not available. The poet, ever a dense fellow, did not understand but blinked on unintelligently. His head suddenly vanished, and a moment later a new head appeared in its place—a tanned face, large powerful eyes under thick eyebrows, a large forehead and a shock of unkempt hair, like a black halo.

This quiet passage represents Narayan's manner very well. He is an even writer, not much given to the purple passage or the set piece. The basic unit of his narrative, if one can use the term, is the incident, the event happening, and this accounts for the impression of mobility his novels invariably give. Complex action, even if it is of the most muted kind, goes on all the time. The exploitation of incident, a blend of event, action, motive, memory, feeling, cause and effect, is a perfect strategy for Narayan. Its mobility conveys that sense of flux in human life which he is so conscious of, and the transparency of surface which is characteristic of his writing draws the reader's attention down to deeper levels, a middle level of motivation and individual psychology and a deeper level of poetic myth and communal awareness.

In the description of Vasu's entry the reader will be struck by the concreteness of the whole undertaking, by the sharp sensory observation upon which it is based, the simplicity of the line and the delicate focussing upon significant points of motion in the incident. The effect of these and of the extreme clarity of the language is to bring home to the reader the silky, on-going suppleness of any human action. It carries with it, too, a sense of its complexity in that it glancingly suggests the nervy, responsive psychology of Nataraj and the unclogged, custom-free directness of Vasu. The symbol of the denying curtain means nothing to him. More than this, the last phrase, 'a black halo', a submerged almost silent paradox, hints that Vasu may constitute a more obscure and profound threat to the system by which Nataraj and his neighbours live. It is a hint taken up at other sensitive places in the novel and it gives the tale of the taxidermist-hunter, who goes from stuffing dead animals to killing live ones, a more general and religious significance.

Narayan has a special gift for pressing a mild significance from the common events of ordinary life without puffing into the ineffable or collapsing into the wambling because he works with the lightest of touches and because of the discipline and accuracy of the detail. Each incident is presented with the firm objectivity produced by intimate familiarity. And all the incidents together, each smoothly articulated with the next, glide into an elegant comedy— in *The Man-Eater of Malgudi*, a comedy of contrast. The movement is so natural and living that the various incidents—the details of the printing trade, Vasu's harassing of Nataraj, Vasu's preying on the domestic animals in the town and the wild ones in the jungle, Nataraj's mission to cure and then to protect the sick temple-elephant and Vasu's own grotesque self-destruction while he waits to destroy the sacred beast—all these incidents carried on an unbroken buoyant current become a mobile pattern or dance; and the almost dialectical opposition of character and significance posed by the antagonism of Nataraj and Vasu appears as the necessary outcome of the material, offering that combination of logic and indeterminacy we are used to in everyday life, but also hinting at the presence of obscurer and greater forces than we are normally aware of.

So that Narayan's fiction operates at one level by the candid reproduction of surfaces and manners and behaviour, the consequence of direct and unfaked perception, while at a much deeper level, because his sensibility is saturated with the Indian tradition and sensitive to the experience implicit in the Indian myth, it operates through an oblique and tentative poetry. Each of these is an effect of the receptive part of his talent, its capacity to register the outward world and what is latent in it. In between there is another area in which he brings to bear a more active and analytic talent for psychological dissection and moral analysis.

It is his nimble curiosity in this sphere together with his unruffled acceptance of what it discovers ('discovers' because what is seen is there, happening in front of one) which exempts Narayan from the charge levelled at Indian writers by V. S. Naipaul. 'There can be no effective writing. The ritual of Indian life smothers imagination, for which it is a substitute, and the interpretation of India in the Indian novel, itself a borrowed form, is at a low, unchanging level.'[1] It is true that Narayan writes within a settled scheme. The mode of belief, the pattern of life, the method of thinking and feeling, the historical inheritance and the characteristic reaction to the social and physical environment—all these recur in his novels. But why not, since they are the conditions of the civilisation which Narayan seeks to interpret? It is true, too, that the central predicament of his characters re-appears in novel after novel, the subject struggling to extricate himself from the dreamy automatism of his past. But the solution adopted by his protagonist, and by 'solution' I mean the concrete escape and the specific conditions in which it takes place, is different from novel to novel, and continually exhibits the shock of self-discovery, an experience which is inexhaustible in its content and endlessly capable of suspense and surprise.

The crisis of consciousness which extricates Nataraj from his tranquil routine, the odd humanity of which is observed with Narayan's characteristically detached and tolerant eye, is precipitated by the violent taxidermist-hunter, Vasu, who is not so much a character as the other half of a collision. His motiveless enmity towards Nataraj leaves the latter distraught. Nataraj was not constructed to sustain hostility. 'I could never be a successful enemy to anyone. Any enmity worried me night and day. As a schoolboy I persistently shadowed around the one person with whom I was

---

[1] *Magic and Dependence*, V. S. Naipaul, *Weekend Telegraph*, 18th August 1967

B

supposed to be on terms of hate and hostility. I felt acutely uneasy as long as our enmity lasted.' Nataraj had been brought up in a house where he had been taught never to kill, where his grand-uncle gave him a coin every day to buy sugar for the ants, and where he even swatted flies secretly so that the elders wouldn't know. In any event, Vasu's effect is too absolute and negative to allow a purely personal response. He is terrifying because he abolishes, by brutally refusing to acknowledge their existence, the values implicit in the life which Nataraj and his friends live. To detonate the spiritual ground in this way, and Vasu has all the impact of a bomb, is to apply an annihilating force precisely at the point on which Nataraj most depends for ultimate support.

Some of the best of the spry and mellow comedy of *The Man-Eater of Malgudi* depends on Nataraj's increasingly frantic effort at rendering the oppressive presence of Vasu at least tolerable. On the face of it he is working purely in the field of action to circumvent Vasu's persecution of the animals and the harassment of himself. But these external acts, which anyway fail in their direct purpose, are hopelessly inadequate to effect the deeper reconciliation that Nataraj's nature and indeed the character of the community call for. Nataraj cannot convert Vasu into a friend, and he finds open hostility insupportable. Both his friends and the community at large blench at the effort to enfold in an acceptable embrace the malevolently unclaspable Vasu. Men as tough as the police inspector and the game-warden, strong voices of the community's outraged authority, recoil at Vasu's combination of ferocity and legal know-how. All his friends can do is to copy the poet and develop 'the art of surviving Vasu's presence'. The problem is to assimilate a wholly alien force, and neither Nataraj himself nor his immediate circle nor the community, whether in the town or the village, is capable of solving the problem. As a result they all feel to some degree what becomes almost unbearable in Nataraj, the emotion of panic, that special resonance of disordered feeling which accompanies the disintegration of the premises of thought and action.

The climax of the comedy and the resolution of the problem of assimilation come together in Vasu's grotesque death. He has an overwhelming loathing for mosquitoes and he has made himself over many years a man of superhuman strength, with hands trained to batter thick panels of teak and iron. In crushing a mosquito on his forehead with his own fist while he waits in the dark to shoot the sacred elephant, he slaughters himself. The fantasy of this has been carefully prepared for and it fits without friction the final 'explanation' of Vasu. He becomes explicable, as well as dead, when it is realised that he is really somebody for whom 'the black halo of hair' was wholly suitable. The Maneater of Malgudi finally takes his place in the community as a 'Rakshasa', a demon, the other side of life. All his enormities now fall into place; his absolute rejection of everything Nataraj and his friends live by now makes sense and indeed testifies to the sanity of the assumptions they had begun to doubt; and everyone takes comfort, especially Nataraj, from grasping that even had he not died he could be certainly relied upon to bring about his own destruction. That it was the frailest of animals, the mosquito, which helped him, the exterminator of animals and the eater of men, to his own death clinches the lightly drawn parable.

> 'He had one virtue, he never hit anyone with his hand, whatever the provocation,' I said, remembering his voice.
> 'Because,' said Sastri puckishly, 'he had to conserve all that might for his own destruction. Every demon appears in the world with a special boon of indestructibility. Yet the universe has survived all the *rakshasas* that were ever born. Every demon carries within him, unknown to himself, a tiny seed of self-destruction, and goes up in thin air at the most unexpected moment. Otherwise what is to happen to humanity?'

Sastri's remark, contingent, interrogative, plaintive but not querulous, offering a modest word of hope about the possibilities of human survival, indicates the quality of the quietly complex tone of Narayan's fiction. His novels make no large claims, assert no tremendous faith. Sastri's words indicate pretty well its measure and character. But as Narayan's work has matured, or perhaps simply as he has grown older, the manner in which he expresses his belief in the nature of whatever it is that supports a hope for humanity becomes less diffident. What at the end of *The Guide* is only the most feathery intimation has become in *The Man-Eater of Malgudi*, in spite of the fantasy of its context, a less oblique statement of his belief in the sustaining role of some other influence—the blessings of the gods or just the stubbornness of life itself. Certainly an explicit notation of this kind appears in the conclusion of *The Sweet Vendor* where Jagan, the protagonist, suddenly determines to detach himself from 'a set of repetitions performed for sixty years' in order to spend the rest of his life helping a stonemason to carve a pure image of the goddess for others to contemplate. His decision, which is of course in the classical Indian line, requiring that 'at some stage in one's life one must uproot oneself from the accustomed surroundings and disappear so that others can continue in peace', is in Jagan's case charmingly blemished with an appealing human flaw. He doesn't neglect to take with him his cheque book. This touch is characteristic of Narayan's sensibility. His concept of spirituality is as precise and as stained with human fallibility as is his notion of the rest of life. The servant of the goddess with whom Jagan proposes to finish out his days explains that the perfection in stone which he is aiming at must still contain a deliberate fault.

> 'I always remember the story of the dancing figure of Nataraj, which was so perfect that it began a cosmic dance and the town itself shook as if an earthquake had rocked it, until a small finger on the figure was chipped off. We always do it; no one ever notices it, but we always create a small flaw in every image; it's for safety.'

Jagan's decision to retire from the world is not only part of the national tradition: 'It would be the most accredited procedure according to our scriptures—husband and wife must vanish into the forest at some stage in their lives, leaving the affairs of the world to younger people'. It also follows the bias of his own nature. He is high-minded, pious, attentive to the scriptures, observant of custom, scrupulous about ritual, a follower of Gandhi, and he has evolved a number of prim theories about diet, footwear, toothbrushes and hygiene. But his character also includes the 'small flaw' making for safety. The largeness of his spiritual ambition is clipped a bit by a measure of mercantile flexibility which enables him to count some of the money taken over the counter 'as free cash . . . a sort of immaculate conception, self-generated, arising out of itself and entitled to survive without reference to any tax'. Moreover, he is—

'protected' is the word Narayan's account suggests—protected from too much voyaging into the ineffable by a certain appealing simplicity of intelligence. ' "Conquer taste, and you will have conquered the self," said Jagan to his listener, who asked, "Why conquer the self?" Jagan said, "I do not know, but all our sages advise us so." '

Jagan's renunciation of the world, then, is of a piece with the Indian tradition and the radical disposition of his own character in so far as it is a reflection of that tradition. But, of course, for Jagan himself his renunciation is a very big decision, too big in some ways for his surface or immediate personality which is dry, fussy, narrow, commercial and self-regarding. What is necessary to make this Jagan into the world-renouncing Jagan is supplied by the Indian religious tradition. Even a nature as thin as Jagan's, it becomes clear, is able to be fed from deep and more than personal sources. Part of Narayan's gift as a novelist of a more inclusive life is the delicacy and firmness with which such depths are convincingly implied in the structure of his characters. This gift depends partly upon the power and inclusiveness of the Indian tradition, partly upon Narayan's own profound acceptance of it, partly, and as far as the reader is concerned, most, on Narayan's beautifully executed evocation of the actual presences and concrete specifications of the life of the town. The suggested halo of significance follows naturally on the meticulously defined detail.

Three areas of the life Jagan is to renounce are drawn with the crispest line and shade in *The Sweet Vendor*. First the steady encircling routine of the community of Malgudi which laps Jagan round with the certainties of history and the stability of current relationships, and which, while testing and proving him in a dozen ways, still validates his function and confirms his identity and value. Next, there is his work as the proprietor of an establishment making and selling sweets. Narayan is much drawn to the truth of character shown in a person's work in which the stretched personality submits itself to impersonal ends and he describes with tender and precise care the style and method, the rituals and satisfactions of Jagan's work. Then there is the ambiguous and dangerous ground of his relations with his son, the sullen Westernised Mali whose

American-Korean wife turns out to be—dumbfoundingly to the conventional Jagan—only his mistress, and whose contemptuous explanations to his bewildered father of a scheme for manufacturing a fiction-writing machine include all the divisions which so maddeningly separate the two of them, the division of East and West, of young and old, of child and parent.

This triple structure makes a composition marked by the combined ease and authority of an artist in full control of his instrument; and it supports a world which has a background, a context, an immediate presence and a nervous individual centre, a world which impresses the reader with the quality of its completeness. Whatever happens in India, the reader feels, happens in Malgudi, and whatever happens in Malgudi, he is persuaded, might well happen in his own life. Malgudi is an image of India and a metaphor of everywhere else.

When Jagan retires from life—'I am going to watch a goddess come out of a stone'—he does so unromantically, practically, like a sound business man, arranging for his shop to be open and deciding where he should leave his keys. He seems to be doing so for comparatively external reasons because of the hell which his son Mali has made of his life at home, or because he can no longer face the incomprehensibility of action deriving from motives beyond his grasp. 'Puzzling over things was enervating. Reading a sense into Mali's actions was fatiguing like the attempt to spell out a message in a half-familiar script.' But the real reason is a more inward one. His life, or that part of it, he realises is complete. It has achieved whatever shape it is capable of. Enlightenment means realising that one has come to the point at which struggle, and all the comedy of friction, are irrelevant: it means recognising and accepting the bitter conclusion of an early novel, *The English Teacher*, that, 'a profound and unmitigated loneliness is the only truth of life'. This 'law' comes home to one with force and clarity as one shares in a life like Jagan's, so warmly surrounded by a community and so totally involved in work and family. Mobility, shape and the significance of completeness—these are the values—and they are not only Indian ones—which animate Narayan's pure, disinterested art.

As readers of the Indian novel we in this country have our deficiencies. It is hard for us to take up the references—to the Indian scene, the agricultural tradition, the vast distances, the terrible poverty, the profoundly significant religion. We live in utterly different conditions where nobody's grandmother could hand down to her grandchildren as a legacy an image of the god Nataraja, which had been found in a packet of saffron—as happens, for example, in Narayan's novel *Mr Sampath*. As readers we are almost certainly in the position of the young man Srinivas in the same novel and 'grasp the symbols but vaguely'. And yet as we read these novels, as we contemplate the proportions of the god Nataraja and think of the packet of saffron, we are not deceived, I think, in detecting through all the appearance of strangeness a familiar rhythm, the common and extraordinary rhythm of life.

II   NIRAD C. CHAUDHURI

I want now to turn to a writer of a wholly different kind from any I have so far considered in this chapter. As I remarked early on, it is in fiction that Indian writers have shown themselves peculiarly gifted, and to the novel that they have made a significant contribution, particularly through the work of Narayan, a writer of exceptional quality. The fact that these writers worked in English is admittedly a large, though implicit, recognition of the fact and influence of British civilisation in India; but it is remarkable how little the explicit recognition of the British connection counts in them. Nirad C. Chaudhuri is not a novelist. His work evinces a most conscious and detailed recognition of the fact and consequence of Britain in India and he contrasts strikingly with many of the novelists, with the self-effacing Narayan in particular, in displaying with outrageous frankness the structure and qualities of a personality which is confidently positive to the point of arrogance and cracklingly irascible to the point of bloody-mindedness. Not, as his work reveals, that he has not a good deal to be irascible and bloody-minded about. Chaudhuri is the author of *A Passage to*

England,[1] *The Continent of Circe*[2] and *The Autobiography of an Unknown Indian,*[3] the book on which I shall concentrate.

A Passage to England is the record of Chaudhuri's first, short visit to Britain. It shows a learned, lively mind, steeped in European culture, a vivid personality of distinct and unaffected charm—the violently aggressive side of Chaudhuri's nature gets little provocation in this visit—remarkable freshness of response and acuity of sense impression, together with some highly subjective analysis of the British Welfare State. It is a graceful, unusual travel book, though slight by the standard of *The Autobiography*. Its main interest for the English reader lies in its being an Indian version of that sensibility of *recognition*, which one sees in Henry James's autobiographical writings, by which something known in literature is now known in life, by which life, in fact, verifies literature and corroborates imagination.

First the travel book, next the thesis. The core of the doctrine of *The Continent of Circe* is that the Hindus are of European stock, immigrant Aryans from Mitannian-Mesopotamia, who colonised the Indo-Gangetic plain and parts of South India. The Aryans were a complete society originally with a triple structure: an aristocracy composed of priests and fighters and then the general body of the community carrying on normal economic activities as peasants, traders, cattle-raisers, artisans, to which they added a caste of workers, the Sudras (who were not however the primitive dark autochthonous population) to make the four-caste society the Hindu community has remained ever since—at least in theory. The Aryan settlement was complete in its essential form by the end of the seventh century B.C., and with it the basic ethnic pattern of India firmly established—the outstanding feature of which is the ferocious opposition between the civilised community of the Aryans and the indigenous dark population or any other which threatened it. This Aryan civilisation was affected by later invasions of Persians and Greeks, which were culturally though not ethnically important, and later by incursions of barbarian nomads from

[1] Chatto & Windus, London, 1960
[2] Chatto & Windus, London, 1965
[3] Macmillan, 1951

Central Asia. These latter invasions meant that the Hindus had to fight for the survival of their society on two fronts, against the internal proletariat of the indigenous, 'the primitive darks' (Chaudhuri's term) and an external proletariat of Asian nomads. The Hindus in consequence became a closed society based on birth, aggressively self-conscious, violently xenophobic and intensely colour-conscious—as, Chaudhuri claims, they remain today.

The evidence for, or perhaps I should say the source of, Chaudhuri's theory or conviction or intuition about the immigrant Aryan civilisation is first the undoubted fact of the diffusion of Indo-European languages, and secondly his own interpretations of the early Indian epics, supported thirdly by a method of extrapolating backward into history and pre-history the logic of his observations of contemporary Indian society. It will not be necessary, I am sure, for me to explain that I am not qualified as a scholar to have a view on Chaudhuri's theory on the origins of Indian civilisation. But what strikes me as a reader is the intensely personal and even passionate quality of his doctrine, scholarly in material, fanatic in manner. He hurls idea after idea with tumultuous vitality and he has the disconcerting habit of attaching to some abstract conception or erudite theory a petty personal irritation like a slight he received at a concert or a women's club. He is a man lacerated by the present, scalded by scorn for the misery, poverty, degradation and inner and outer disorder which he observes in every corner of contemporary society and powerfully impelled to find in the past a coherent explanation for the chaos and despair which surround him.

The Islamic expansion in India, gradual in its first phase, overwhelming in the second, brought into India the propagators of a new aggressive culture who had both an absolute conviction of the superiority of their culture and a religious duty to spread it. It was a well established and mature society with a fully developed way of life. In the North it displaced the Hindu ruling class and lodged in the Indian consciousness the conviction of an irreconcilable conflict between Hindu and Muslim. There could be no question whatever of absorbing the Muslims, and Hindu Society on its side lost whatever power of assimilating and adaptability it had once possessed. The bulk of the new Islamic population were Hindu converts but this fact made no difference at all to their sense of solidarity among themselves and their feeling of oneness with the Islamic world outside. 'Here is the case,' says Chaudhuri, 'of a true ethnic relationship being completely broken by a new cultural and social association.'

The psychological experience of the British in India closely repeated that of the Hindus. A people of a temperate climate, at a period of great vitality in their national life, with a strong disposition in favour of the fascinating, richly promising East, became, under the brutalities of a tropical climate and among a potentially hostile population, horribly denatured. Their sense of proportion broke down. They lost their usual equability in human relations. They became extreme and strident. They were outraged by the lack among the Hindus of the European virtues of 'reason' and 'measure'; everything appeared inconsistent and extravagant, lush and awry. They were continually oppressed by the possibility of submergence in a lower culture. Their pride in race intensified. They became increasingly unwilling to share their culture and they became neurotically arrogant. '. . . The British in India . . . paraded a racial arrogance whose mildest form was a stony silence. . . .'

In mirroring the psychological development of the Hindus, the history of the British in India helped to harden the Hindus in their own radical bias as confirmed believers in blood and birth. The repetition strengthened the original disposition. The Hindus remain a people divided against themselves, suffering an exhaustion of vitality and an ever-present maladjustment with the tropical environment. What had happened to the Hindus happened to the British, and what had happened to the British made any modification of the Hindu nature still more unlikely. It was the excruciatingly cruel country which had the same effect on both people. 'Western scholars have sometimes made Buddhism or Vedanta responsible for the apparent indifference of the Hindus to the things of the world, especially for their disinclination to mental and bodily exertion, and attributed to us a world-negation which we never had. The philosophies did not make our life what it is, it was the life which made the philosophies what they are.'

A Passage to England showed Chaudhuri as a writer with a gift for registering fresh and exact impressions of what he observes about him. *The Continent of Circe* shows him as a social analyst who has evolved, as much from imagination as from history, a theory of Indian development which provides him with a causal explanation for the failures of his society. He can therefore with a steady mind and complete conviction, as well as a high degree of Bengali fury, mercilessly expose the wounds of India. Whatever one may think of his fairness, no one can question his courage. No subject is too delicate or too sacred to be attacked, whether it is Indian mysticism or Indian militarism or the Indian attitude to sex or colour or religion, or Indian relations with China or Pakistan or the West, whether it is political or social or individual morality. If we add to the sharp eye and natural audacity a buoyant intellectual vivacity and an intense fascination with himself, we can see that gifts which might not qualify him to be an impartially objective critic of national life might help to make him an autobiographer of a rare kind.

Which indeed they do. *The Autobiography of an Unknown Indian* is one of the finest examples of this *genre* to appear in English in this century, and the most significant, single discursive work to be generated by the love and hate of Indian-British relationships. I have spoken of Chaudhuri's fascination with himself in *The Continent of Circe*. Naturally, the same thing appears in *The Autobiography* but, paradoxically, in a much more disciplined way. Here Chaudhuri sees himself as an object in a landscape or as an impulse in a more inclusive and controlling rhythm, and the whole presentation of the self is impressively tranquil and objective. Chaudhuri was born in 1897, and the book which begins in the early nineteen hundreds takes him to the end of his university career, its substance being the treatment of his childhood and youth. It is written in a masculine, confident English of long, balanced sentences, which combine a degree of formality with considerable ease and lissomness, and its only oddity is a curiously Celtic use of continuous tenses. It is an idiom which is distinctly late-Victorian in flavour, with all the positive strength and assurance of that, and it is wholly consistent with the period and sensibility of the writer.

The Autobiography is organised round a conception of place, which is shown as the great means by which embodied history is

brought to bear upon growth. The significance of place in Chaudhuri's life is the principle of composition in *The Autobiography*, and
its development through the sequence of places, Kishorganj his
country birthplace, Banagram his ancestral village, Kalikutch his
mother's village, Shillong the Assam hill station, an imagined
England and a more than actual Calcutta, is handled with imaginative tact which makes the book a genuine composition obeying an
inward initiative: except for the final part where it comes to an
end in a huddled and clumsily inappropriate conclusion in a long,
theoretical essay on the course of Indian history.

The life of the places Chaudhuri lived in is revived with a kind of
creative thoroughness. There is, to begin with, the fully pictured
actuality of the town, the villages, the hill station, the city of
Calcutta—everything in their physical presence from the quality of
the dust and the shape of the trees, to the design of the houses, the
material of the roof, the layout of the neighbourhood, the character
of the rivers and the configuration of the land; next, displayed with
lucidity and warmth, there is the intense, enfolding family life with
its routine, stresses and rituals; and then the complications of the
social world outside the family with its severely functional divisions
and its absolutely arranged organisation; and all of these are
supported and surrounded by a massive fund of anthropological
and historical learning and penetrated by sensitively intelligent
sociological speculation. This intricate treatment gives the reader a
double insight. He has a sense of the young Chaudhuri's life picking
its way through a variety of densely detailed locations and assuming
definition and individuality as it goes; and he catches, too, glimpses
that steady into a vision of an extraordinary society, which combines something from the Victorian past of our own history, a
high-minded, ethically serious, self-improving middle class with
another universe as old and strange as *Lear*, in which priests with
scimitars sacrifice goats and garlanded buffaloes to the music of
drums, cymbals and gongs while the worshippers smear themselves
with the animals' blood and pelt each other with a dough made of
blood and dust.

Each of the places Chaudhuri lived in has a particular meaning
in his development—not meaning in the sense of anything emblem-

atic or mystical but, more straightforwardly, meaning as a special and precise twist in the shaping of his character. The town of Kishorganj, which came into existence as a municipal township in the 1860's, was the constant in the family existence. Life there was solidly based, plain, industrious, but also on occasion exciting, when enlivened by feasts, fairs, gypsies and the attractions of the river and the rains, or perilous during the season of cholera, when a workman would pass along the road swinging a censer full of sulphur. The family house stood on a plot of two acres and was composed of an intricate collection of buildings around an inner courtyard. It was furnished with beds and chests, baskets, books and trunks. The simplicity of furniture and the complexity of structure of the house corresponded to the life lived in it. There were innumerable traditions and customs, a whole complex of habits, rituals and disciplines but at the same time great simplicity and directness of feeling. The father was a liberal 'protestant' Hindu, monotheist and enlightened and mainly concerned with educating his children in a rational way of life and encouraging them in what were thought of as the English qualities of energy and self-reliance. It was a calm, regular life for the elders absorbed in their profession and for the children occupied in learning. Colour and movement broke into it only at rhythmic intervals. There was a remarkable feeling of equality among the citizens but, of course, the idea of citizenship was a restricted one, excluding the workers and peasants and indeed government officials and wealthy landowners. It was a town ruled by some hundred families. There were few old people in the population of the citizens and a large number of children. Profession and education were two serious concerns of these people and they all worked unremittingly at them. The children were in touch through their father and his clients (as well as being vice-chairman of the municipality he was a lawyer with a wholly criminal practice) with the world of human violence. Murder, robbery, rape, arson were common events in the town and outside it. But these things were balanced by two other forces. Around them there seemed to be an immutable sphere of justice and order presided over by an organisation the ordinary people still called the 'company' and the educated the 'government'; and underneath they felt the unquestioned foundations of

religion and morality, 'things in which everyone believed and
things to which in the last resort everybody returned'.

Life in Kishorganj made for a rational habit of mind. It offered
stability but it also encouraged, largely because of the influence of
an admirable, level-headed father, moral and intellectual independence. Parental connections led back to the villages, the ancestral
village of Banagram and the mother's village of Kalikutch—'so
self-effacing in bamboo and cane greenery'. Here the children's
experience fed a rich emotional life. The rhythms of the country,
the feeling for blood and family, the living Bengali tradition of
drama and folk-poetry, the intimate connection of family life and
art deepened and refined the children's feelings. *The Autobiography*
presents, through the minutely detailed round of daily life, a portrait
of a highly civilised society, in which drama, poetry, religion and
ordinary life were intimately united.

> We always had these plays at the time of religious festivals and
> weddings, and at times also for their own sake. The repertory, though
> large, was almost exclusively drawn from either of the great epics, the
> *Ramayana* or the *Mahabharata*, and the stories were thus familiar to the
> audience. From this followed that the watching of the plays was even
> for young people like us not a passive gulping down of a story but an
> appraisal, in the light of a critical code which was never crude, of
> points of composition and acting, and, at times, even of doctrine.[1]

At the same time this is not an idyll of lyrical nostalgia. Chaudhuri
makes very clear the claustrophobic atmosphere, the suspicions and
distrusts and the envies and meannesses which this patrician society
was capable of, particularly for women. His mother felt imprisoned
in it and she was sure that her own health—she was subject to some
pathological, mental condition—was ruined by her sojourn in
Banagram. His father felt that to live permanently in the way the
gentry did in the villages would be to live without work and without purpose. He had the deepest possible conviction of the sanctity
of the present and the future and he hated the spirit of Byzantism
that he saw expressed in this society.

Shillong, the paradisal Assam hill station, with its pure, cool air
and pine trees, where the children visited an uncle who collected

---

[1] *The Autobiography of An Unknown Indian*, p. 60

orchids, makes a natural bridge to another place which exercised a profound influence on Chaudhuri's nature—England—for it was in Shillong that the amazed children saw the English in the flesh, men and women and doll-like babies. England had been a living presence in Chaudhuri's imagination from his early days, partly because of his father's care that he should learn English and the good sense of the teaching methods he adopted to this end, partly through the books and pictures in the house, and partly through the poems he read and the history he studied. Nor could any educated person escape the influence of England that came through the political administrative system imposed on India by the British, an influence which was recognised and supported (even if it was rejected on patriotic grounds) by great names of Hindu and Bengali thought like Michael Dutt, Bankim Chandra Chatterji, Tagore, Rammohun Roy. Chaudhuri's feeling for England was a more explicitly conscious attraction than any English boy could have had, but it was added to a personality which had the strongest natural affinity for English civilisation. He saw it vaguely at first and more precisely as he grew older as a necessary penetration of the East by the West in one of its most beautiful and worthwhile forms. It was of course England and the English civilisation, it should be stressed, which influenced Chaudhuri, not the English in India. He was the last person alive to be impressed by colonial insolence. If one asks why Chaudhuri should have had this extraordinary understanding of and sympathy with English civilisation, the answer seems to be that he saw in it an essential corrective to certain Indian qualities. He was fascinated by the vitality and pragmatism of English character, by the genius for the concrete shown in English art, by the English capacity to give form and solidity to its insight, and by the English gift evident at every point and in all its production for the differentiated and particular.

Chaudhuri, himself a man with a relish for the specific, loved the quality of concreteness in English civilisation. And it was the absence of this in Indian civilisation to which he gave a measured philosophic expression towards the end of *The Autobiography*.

I think there is even in the highest and most characteristic teaching of Hinduism (apart from the layer on layer of infinitely varied primi-

tiveness which constitutes its buried foundation), something impelling
a Hindu towards the simpler in preference to the more complex,
towards the unemerged in preference to the emergent, and towards
the general in preference to the particular. According to some of the
noblest teaching of Hinduism, the manifested universe is an illusion,
the ultimate reality attribute-less, and man's supreme happiness lies in
putting an end to the cycle of births and deaths, or, in other words,
in eliminating precisely those particular forms possessing sensible
attributes which confer qualities and values on reality, and clothe it
with attractiveness for us. With such a philosophical background it is
not surprising that a Hindu should tend to ignore distinctions. To me,
however, Hinduism appears to be swimming against the current.
Although its penchant for the undifferentiated and attributeless is
undoubtedly due to its anxiety to bite on the rock of truth and reality
lying underneath the flux of changes, I would still say that in actual
fact it is retrograde and out of sympathy with reality. For I believe in
change and hold all reality to be a process, a process which is justifying
itself, as well as making itself more significant, by becoming more
particular and differentiated and by endowing itself with ever more
new values.[1]

Kishorganj, Banagram, Kalikutch, Shillong and the implied
presence of England, together with the vast and terrible city of
Calcutta, which I shall come to in a moment—these, with one
exception, complete the pattern of influences which inaugurated
Chaudhuri's fundamental sensibility and fixed the scale and organisation of his interests. The exception is his parents. The Chaudhuri
family was a real family in the Western sense and not, as was
common form in Bengal, a joint family. It enjoyed its own forceful
identity and not merely the passive existence of a cell in an amorphous clan. Chaudhuri's father and mother asserted their parental
authority and responsibility against their relatives so that their
children were brought up by them and not by a set of surrogates
in some vague, impersonal community crèche, a system which
eliminates the influence of mother and father by abolishing parental
exclusiveness, and one which in Chaudhuri's view Plato would
certainly not have recommended so strongly had he seen the results
it produced in Bengal. The father was physically robust, conscientious in his work in court and afterwards in business, liberal, intelli-

[1] *The Autobiography of an Unknown Indian*, p. 439

gent, disinterested, concerned to develop the initiative and the independence of his children, and a solicitous nurse of his wife during her bouts of melancholy madness. The mother was ferociously honest and emotionally grasping, at once intensely self-centred and cool and objective towards the children, and deeply afflicted by her mental disease. Chaudhuri shows himself to have the courage, the ethical and intellectual values of his father and the honesty and the impassioned egocentricity of his mother. The life of the family in the places he lived in as a child was the source of everything positive and committed in Chaudhuri's nature. Calcutta, when he came to it as a student and undergraduate, opened to him the possibilities of detachment. The context of his childhood was one into which he fitted naturally and happily, that of the next part of his life one in which he was to feel himself at more and more painful odds with his environment.

> Kishorganj, Banagram, and Kalikutch are interwoven with my being; so is the England of my imagination; they formed and shaped me; but when once torn up from my natural habitat I became liberated from the habitat altogether; my environment and I began to fall apart; and in the end the environment became wholly external, a thing to feel, observe, and measure, and a thing to act and react on, but never to absorb or be absorbed in.[1]

His treatment of Calcutta, where he was to spend thirty years, although *The Autobiography* takes him only to the beginning of his career, is as full, as positively thick with information, as ever. His inquisitive, analytic eye turns upon everything from architecture to social relationships, from the method of garbage disposal to nationalist politics, from his own intellectual history to the current taste in furniture. But the tone is increasingly less cordial, the attitude more antagonistic. Place in his early life focussed the paradisal Indian light; Calcutta was a prism breaking it into its component and colder parts. He was of course a failure in a worldly sense. He was a brilliant undergraduate but he collapsed during his graduate studies, and the academic life which would surely have been his natural habitat was shut off from him. Perhaps it needed a near lifetime of failure and poverty to prepare him for writing this book

---

[1] *The Autobiography of an Unknown Indian*, pp. 257-8

C

because behind it burn not simply events but a life and character. He shows himself bitterly forging a will capable of resisting an overwhelming environment. The powerful intellect is the servant of the will and the theoretical speculation is the necessary instrument for making the action of the will rational and defensible. Sometimes he suggests—not altogether mischievously—that the troubles of India are caused by an exclusive diet of carbohydrate sprinkled with chilli, or by a belief, as he puts it, in a pantheon of gods as corrupt as the Indian administration. But at the centre of his work is an attempt to account for the destruction of a spirit originally strong by an appalling external world. He fiercely cherishes what most people would find intolerable, the identity of the alien, but that again he makes coherent—at least for himself— by a theory which involves making half the population of India foreigners in their own country.

If I say that in the end the theories do not count, this is not to dismiss an intellectual framework raised on the basis of great learning and experience; nor is it to reject the force and relevance of Chaudhuri's criticism of Indian society—although I believe that one would really need to be an Indian to be able, and to have the right, to judge this question. But it is to claim for *The Autobiography of an Unknown Indian* a different existence and significance—literary rather than philosophical or sociological. Its achievement rests less on the correspondence of its theory with actuality and much more on an inward life and coherence. It is not the doctrine propounded but the presence evoked which justifies and supports the book. *The Autobiography* depends on a fully realised rendering of the growth of a character of genuine and singular individuality, by turns arrogant, despairing, nervy, complacent, melancholy, but always faithfully Indian and saltily himself. Through the lucid agency of this convincing portrait we see an age-old society, with a powerful disposition towards inertness, in the state of being penetrated by Western concepts of God, nature, personality, nationalism and freedom. The formation of Chaudhuri's character is the means by which we are enabled to observe the transformation of Bengal society, and to watch the fundamental categories of thought and the modes of sensibility altering before a silent onslaught more significant and lasting than the public action of governments or any change imposed on the physical scene of India by the work of administrators and engineers.

The development so exhaustively detailed in *The Autobiography of an Unknown Indian* is not just an evolutionary one in which a Western protestant astringency displaces the warm appeal of an Indian past—although it certainly *is* that. It is also a more personal and strenuous achievement which involves, on the one hand, hacking out an area of freedom and manœuvre from a choked jungle of inheritance; and on the other, constructing a fresh identity which would join a questioning Western mind to a temperament laced with Bengali fury. The instruments of demolition and of building, and the elements out of which the new self was to be made, were concepts and principles, usages and styles, which Chaudhuri found, not in the imaginatively cramped local British population, or the restricted Anglo-Indian tradition, but in the immensely more inclusive source of the English language and its literature. It was an undertaking which required on the part of Chaudhuri not only intellectual energy and analytical skill, but also courage, will, stamina and a quite unabashed interest in himself. The psychological composition or structure which results is a triumph of self-education and a model of the formative power of language, of its capacity to disturb and rearrange at the depths of the personality. It is also—like *The Autobiography of an Unknown Indian* itself—a monument to the creative clash of two civilisations.

CHAPTER II

I OLIVE SCHREINER

THE *Story of an African Farm*, published in 1883 when the author was 28, was written by a small, plump, asthmatic South African, an ex-governess of missionary stock. It is the only thing of note Olive Schreiner produced. It seems that it should belong to that ruck of works which though they may affect the reader at one time, usually when he is young, are happily and rapidly discarded. It is structurally a jumble and emotionally a chaos. It is in many ways thoroughly provincial. It is disfigured by some of the most unpleasant qualities of Victorian sentimentality and self-delusion about motives. It is weighed down with explicit argumentation and debate and littered with the material of youthful essays and solemn parables. But while each of these comments is just, the effect the book makes on the reader is not at all what they would lead one to expect. It is a novel which stays with one—not harmoniously and consciously—but embedded in the cells of one's memory. It is the product of a powerful personality, of strongly neurotic tendencies, self-educated and markedly deficient in intellectual discipline, but with a distinctive and ferociously assimilative sensibility. It is the intense, suffering consciousness of the author which gives the book its undoubted unity, penetrating every corner of its universe, and not primarily the African farm (marvellously observed though this is with a child's clear glance) which is the geographical location and the physical image of the cramped, ugly Boer life, nor the story, the events of which compose not so much a plot as a pattern of memories of an individual's painful emotional growth.

The author's essential interests and manner are present from the start. The novel begins with the farmhouse and its sleeping occupants, the house blanched in the moonlight, appearing as a physical object in a mineral landscape. First there is the owner Tant' Sannie, the Boer-woman, who goes to bed in the clothes she has worn all day, rolling heavily in her sleep and dreaming not of her first and

second husbands, the young Boer and the consumptive English-
man, but of the sheep's trotters she had eaten for supper. 'She
dreamed that one stuck fast in her throat, and she rolled her huge
form from side to side, and snorted horribly.' In the room next to
her slept the two children, the homely, freckled Em and the
exquisite Lyndall. In one of the outbuildings jutting from the
waggon house the German overseer lay sleeping soundly, a
Messiah-like figure, his great arms folded and his bushy black
beard rising and falling on his breast. In the box under the window
his small son lay awake listening to his father's great silver hunting
watch and seeing in terror 'a long stream of people, a great dark
multitude, that moved in one direction; then they came to the dark
edge of the world, and went over'. These three classes of people—
with one exception—make up the world of the novel. Tant' Sannie
embodies the uncouth, grossly superstitious, densely physical folk-
life of the Boer farmer. The two children express two elements of
the author's nature, Em the homely and settled and Lyndall the
intelligent and exotic. They act out in the novel a tension which
clearly exists within the author herself. Together they represent
that feminine nature which is misunderstood and persecuted by the
crudity of Boer society, just as its aspirations are betrayed by the
world outside. It draws its strength from the other kind of nature
present in the house, that of the German overseer and his son. In
them we see the gentlest and most innocent goodness, simple and
untroubled in the old man, more conscious and agonised in the son.
It is German rather than Dutch, and shines with a quietist and
mystical quality. It is something that Olive Schreiner is deeply
appreciative of and extraordinarily successful in re-creating, although she finds the religious element in it finally unacceptable.

The other characters—the exception I spoke of just now—who
make up the novel's population (the Kaffirs are hardly individualised at all; only the German overseer seems to have a truly human
relationship with them) are those who come from outside. They
bring to the farm opportunity and a loosening of its tight bonds but
they also carry with them danger and evil. For while the life of the
farm is shut in and primitive, it also encloses a standard of human
goodness, tranquil in the German overseer Otto in the first part of

the novel, more tortured and tentative but just as strong in his son Waldo in the second part, superior to anything the intruders from the outside can offer. They are shown as comic-sinister, Bonaparte Blenkins; silly-snobbish-unstable, the Englishman Gregory Rose, who transfers his affection from his fiancée Em to Lyndall; Byronic-mysterious—the stranger whose mistress Lyndall becomes. The situation therefore is more complex and interesting than a simple opposition between the prison farm and the free world. The sensitive Lyndall, in whom consciousness is most developed, cries for the moral and intellectual freedom she supposes to exist outside the farm. In fact she is disappointed by the education she receives in the world beyond and finally betrayed by the values upheld there. It is the mild, ungifted Em, a Martha-like figure, and not the brilliant Lyndall, who attains a measure of modest serenity and only Waldo, another citizen of the inner world of the farm, 'an uncouth creature with small learning and no prospect in the future but that of making endless tables and stone walls', who finally finds 'life . . . a rare and very rich thing'.

The rareness and richness of life are certainly things substantiated by the novel, although frequently only in ways which are incidental to the author's explicit purpose. High-minded feminist preaching and shrill agnostic propaganda too often muddle and muddy the real strength of the book. Olive Schreiner's gifts are for the evocation of the concrete, both of natural substance and human feeling. She has great skill, used with a fine functional discretion, for conveying the nature of the country, a strange blend of bleakness and warmth. Amid the stoniness, the heat and the brilliance of the light, the farmhouse, the outbuildings, the walls, the carts, the furniture, the food, the personal belongings are all presented with a countryman's respect for things and a sense of the value and interest of the palpable. The novel is heavy with the weight of physical stuff which gives the necessary solid basis for its more aspiring side. And heavy not only with physical material but with the kind of character close to the nature of matter itself. Two fully successful characterisations of this sort are the Boer Widow Tant' Sannie and Bonaparte Blenkins, the visiting confidence man. Tant' Sannie is a gross, stupid, greedy, wallowing creature, immersed in flesh and superstition. The other, Bonaparte Blenkins, like Tant' Sannie has a powerful physical presence, peculiarly ugly where hers was hugely abundant. Each has immense vitality and each is observed by the writer with a harsh sardonic accuracy. They belong to the tradition of humours as revivified by Dickens and they bring to the first half of the novel, where they are most prominent, the supple strength and humanity of this tradition.

Olive Schreiner's habit, when writing in this mode, is to slide in a terse illustrative physical detail but to allow the exposition of character to proceed through the varying run and turn of the language. Personalities and attitudes become apparent through the mobile expressiveness of speech. Here is a passage from early on in the novel, thick with the material quality she is so good at evoking, which brings together Tant' Sannie and Bonaparte Blenkins and irresistibly suggests the clash of cunning and stupid temperaments, and incidentally the contrast of 'cold' and 'hot' humours!

On the door-step stood the Boer-woman, a hand on each hip, her face red and fiery, her head nodding fiercely. At her feet sat the yellow Hottentot maid, her satellite, and around stood the black Kaffir maids, with blankets twisted round their half-naked figures. Two, who stamped mealies in a wooden block, held the great stampers in their hands, and stared stupidly at the object of attraction. . . .

'I'm not a child,' cried the Boer-woman, in low Cape Dutch, 'and I wasn't born yesterday. No, by the Lord, no! You can't take *me* in! My mother didn't wean me on Monday. One wink of my eye and I see the whole thing. I'll have no tramps sleeping on my farm,' cried Tant' Sannie blowing. 'No, by the Devil, no! not though he had sixty-times-six red noses.'

There the German overseer mildly interposed that the man was not a tramp, but a highly respectable individual, whose horse had died by an accident three days before.

'Don't tell me,' cried the Boer-woman; 'the man isn't born that can take *me* in. If he'd had money, wouldn't he have brought a horse? Men who walk are thieves, liars, murderers, Rome's priests, seducers! I see the Devil in his nose!' cried Tant' Sannie, shaking her fist at him; 'and to come walking into the house of this Boer's child, and shaking hands as though he came on horseback! Oh, no, no!'

The stranger took off his hat, a tall battered chimney-pot, and disclosed a bald head, at the back of which was a little fringe of curled white hair; and he bowed to Tant' Sannie.

'What does she remark, my friend?' he inquired, turning his cross-wise looking eyes on the old German.

The German rubbed his old hands, and hesitated.

'Ah—well—ah—the—Dutch—you know—do not like people who walk—in this country—ah!'

'My dear friend,' said the stranger, laying his hand on the German's arm, 'I should have bought myself another horse, but crossing, five days ago, a full river, I lost my purse—a purse with five hundred pounds in it. I spent five days on the bank of the river trying to find it—couldn't. Paid a Kaffir nine pounds to go in and look for it at the risk of his life—couldn't find it.'

The German would have translated this information, but the Boer-woman gave no ear.

'No, no; he goes to-night. See how he looks at me—a poor un-protected female! If he wrongs me, who is to do me right?' cried Tant' Sannie.

'I think,' said the German in an undertone, 'if you didn't look at her quite so much it might be advisable. She—ah—she—might—imagine that you liked her too well,—in fact—ah—'

'Certainly, my dear friend, certainly,' said the stranger, 'I shall not look at her.' . . .

Upon this the new-comer fixed his eyes pensively on the stamp-block, folding his hands on the head of his cane. His boots were broken, but he still had the cane of a gentleman. . . .

'You might not be a Scotchman or anything of that kind, might you?' suggested the German. 'It is the English that she hates.'

'My dear friend,' said the stranger, 'I am Irish every inch of me—father Irish, mother Irish. I've not a drop of English blood in my veins.'

'And you might not be married, might you?' persisted the German. 'If you had a wife and children, now? Dutch people do not like those who are not married.'

'Ah,' said the stranger, looking tenderly at the block, 'I have a dear wife and three sweet little children—two lovely girls and a noble boy.'

This is a scene in which the comedy contains a note of chastise-ment and moral severity—comedy, with an edge as well as a laugh. It is by no means the best of the several comic scenes in which these two figure. Bonaparte Blenkins's rôle as 'predikant' and his sermon on the text, 'All liars shall have their part in the lake which burneth with fire and brimstone, which is the second death', are nearly as good as the performance of the confidence men at the wake in

Huckleberry Finn. It is the richness of Olive Schreiner's comic sense which we see in the passage I have quoted above. There are, however, certain notes in each character omitted in this picture of their first encounter: on the one hand, the slightly more appealing folk-sagacity in Tant' Sannie which comes out in her reflections on her inexpressively glum and unenthusiastic new young husband, 'nineteen, weak eyes, white hair, little round nose' (' "It's a strange thing," she said, "but you can't love a man till you've had a baby by him" '); and on the other there is missing in the sketch of Blenkins the strain of cold cruelty we see in his relationship with the children and particularly with the boy Waldo. This is how he welcomes Waldo back from a journey as the boy rushes in carrying gifts for each member of the family.

> 'Good-morning, my dear boy. Where are you running to so fast with your rosy cheeks?'
> The boy looked up at him, glad even to see Bonaparte.
> 'I am going to the cabin,' he said, out of breath.
> 'You won't find them in just now—not your good old father,' said Bonaparte.
> 'Where is he?' asked the lad.
> 'There beyond the camps,' said Bonaparte, waving his hand oratori-cally towards the stone-walled ostrich-camps.
> 'What is he doing there?' asked the boy.
> Bonaparte patted him on the cheek kindly.
> 'We could not keep him any more, it was too hot. We've buried him, my boy,' said Bonaparte, touching with his finger the boy's cheek. 'We couldn't keep him any more. . . .'

Bonaparte Blenkins and Tant' Sannie are, then, strikingly individual and thoroughly realised in their own right. They also contribute to the design of the novel, filling out and sharpening the pattern of relationships among the half-dozen principal characters of the book. Their thick fleshy quality sets off the intensely intellectual ardour of Lyndall, while the sottishness of Tant' Sannie and the malevolence of Blenkins are balanced by the New Testament sweetness of the old German and the more troubled spirituality of his son. There is also concentrated in them—and with peculiar force in this peasant and almost biblical household—the authority of the adult world which the growing children, even the commonplace, compliant Em, find constantly uncomprehending and indifferent, and on key occasions menacing.

It is in her treatment of Em, Lyndall and Waldo as children that we see most clearly Olive Schreiner's characteristic talents; it is in her treatment of them as adults that we see her deficiencies. I have referred to her gift for establishing solidly the physical presence of the South African countryside. She also places the children in a convincing social context with the deftest assurance. The life of the farm, harsh and narrow but also full, is conveyed with the raciest gusto, its disciplined dreariness pointed up by the rare, glittering festival, like the brilliantly painted Boer wedding. She shows the endless interest and excitement implicit in the commonest things for children growing up in these conditions. The children's behaviour and the adults' reactions to it, the assumptions and expectations of both—these together project a whole manner of living, thin certainly, repellent in many ways, but undeniably positive and confident and backed with all the force of Dutch Calvinism. Each of the children is nicely discriminated from the others, although the Martha-Mary contrast between Em and Lyndall is unduly neat.

Olive Schreiner has in addition a deep intuition of the organic unfolding of the child's nature and she perfectly grasps the transition from the young child's moments of disconnected, startling clarity of perception, standing out from a shadowy background of forgetfulness, to a state in which images and the subtler stabilities of words become continuous and connected. She understands the serious function of play and the significance of a child's questioning as a means by which he tests out, and then explains to himself, the teasing and often bruising complications of reality outside himself. She has a quick feeling for children's suffering, both for its piercing intensity and the healthy way in which it is rapidly thrown into discard. Not that its apparent transience leaves it without influence. 'The troubles of the young are soon over; they leave no external mark. If you wound the tree in its youth the bark will quickly cover the gash; but when the tree is very old, peeling the bark off, and looking carefully, you will see the scar there still. All that is buried is not dead.' She has, too, a delicate perception of the strange metaphysical promptings which in the most familiar surroundings come with complete naturalness to children.

It is through her construction of Waldo's character that Olive Schreiner elucidates the spiritual gropings of the young child. Waldo is a boy tortured by a desire for God which is contradicted by the emptiness he feels in his own nature as well as by the loveless horror of human life surrounding him, both as a child on the African farm and as an adult working in the world outside. In Em the author stresses the passive, imitative element in the psychology of the young, the desire to fit in without friction, and even without notice. But it is Lyndall who is the main focus of consciousness in the novel and Lyndall's, I am sure, the voice which speaks closest to the author's own. Olive Schreiner feels in an acute way the condition of these children which is never to be nourished by an individual and personal affection. When they have anything at all, it is not much more than a gruel of generalised goodwill; more frequently they have to put up with coldness and even calculated cruelty, as when Bonaparte tramples on the small wooden machine the boy invents or whips him unmercifully. Em's reaction to this emotional environment is a self-deprecating, mousy acceptance. The miseries of reality only correspond to her grey expectations. Waldo floats off into a spiritual ambiance, losing touch more and more completely with other human beings. But it is Lyndall's response which is most finely elaborated. In dealing with her Olive Schreiner shows something of that fine faculty, half analytic intelligence, half identifying empathy, which D. H. Lawrence uses so powerfully in revealing the developing nature of Ursula in *The Rainbow*, a child in very different circumstances, too much rather than too little loved, but one with a similar intelligence and blighted capacity for love.

Character in the child, as Coleridge explained and Olive Schreiner so finely understood, is generated by a tension between the child's concern to protect its frail but real individuality and its other concern to enlarge this individuality by entering imaginatively into many other forms and images of existence. Hence the intelligent child's sensitivity to bossiness, that neurotic species of authority; hence too its passion for otherness and for playing at alien experience. In Lyndall's circumstances the concern to protect became a fierce anxiety, almost an abstract passion, for self-preservation against the encroachment of an unfeeling environment. She developed an extreme, violent force of the will, which imposed itself on the other children and which also obscurely frightened even Tant' Sannie and Bonaparte Blenkins. At the same time she suffered a hardening of feeling, a kind of petrifaction of the self, which made the entrance into other forms of life increasingly difficult, and finally impossible. '. . . there is life, there is warmth,' she wailed, 'why am I alone, so hard, so cold. I am weary of myself! It is eating my soul to its core—self, self, self! Will nothing free me from myself?' Education which she was determined to have meant for her above all the possibility of other kinds of life. As she put it when she grew up, '. . . I like to realise forms of life utterly unlike mine. . . . When my own life feels small, and I am oppressed with it, I like to crush together, and see it in a picture, in an instant, a multitude of disconnected unlike phases of human life. . . .' But the force of self-will enclosed her and shut her off from what she most required. 'I will do nothing good for myself, nothing for the world, till someone wakes me. I am asleep, swathed, shut up in self; till I have been delivered, I will deliver no-one.'

Olive Schreiner is a writer in whom the artist is balanced against the egotist. She is as successful as she is with Lyndall, Em and Waldo as children at least partly because childhood is a state in which remoteness and difference make for a measure of detachment even on the part of a novelist as intrusive as she is. The children show themselves to have what Henry James called 'a truth of resistance' capable of standing up to her strongly absorptive faculty. I hope I will not be read as seeming to imply that Lyndall, Em and Waldo are real children distinct from the artist whose creation they are. Obviously not: but in work of art—and *The Story of an African Farm* is a genuine work of art for all its flaws—the intentions of the writer are stayed from overwhelming the material by what one can only describe as its independent, relatively 'objective' life. When the children are adults, which they are fairly summarily presented as in the second part of the novel, they are much more susceptible to the personal domination of the author. Their separate life thins out to become a more attenuated symbolic existence. They are less themselves and proportionately more projections of the author and her time.

As Lyndall, Em and Waldo, grown up, are emptied of intrinsic significance, they tend increasingly to perform a representative function. Waldo, who keeps more of his original vitality than the others, expresses a standard of unqualified, persecuted goodness, based, it appears from her husband's devout memoir of her,[1] on Olive Schreiner's admired father; Em is the simple, domesticated victim-woman, passively putting up with the conditions the braver Lyndall rejects; Lyndall is the intelligent, agnostic, free woman who campaigns against the domination of men, the superstitious tyranny of a debased Calvinism and the philistine ugliness of South African rural life. What Lyndall stands for (one cannot help thinking of it like this) is in many ways admirable, certainly infinitely preferable to what she is fighting against, and it undoubtedly called for reserves of courage and independence even to express such views in Victorian South Africa, which was obviously in these matters even more provincial than Britain. But the communication is so explicit, self-satisfied and sermonising, so uncontrollably tumbled out without regard for structure or the concreteness of the fable, that the merit of the idea is lost in the stridency of the advocate.

The novel often exhibits those defects of taste and that feebleness of artistic control which were common among much greater Victorian writers. Olive Schreiner has a horribly incoherent sense of structure and the narrative line is clumsily entangled in all kinds of theoretical irrelevancies. The two main parts of the book, for example, are separated by a number of set pieces on human growth which, while they are frequently acute in detail, simply do not belong. She shows an unabashed and almost sensuously caressing sentimentality towards the Franciscan Waldo. She has the peculiar Victorian habit, when she is dealing with love, of diminishing the physical size of the woman and faintly etherealising the body, so that Lyndall tends to be both elfin and child-like. The result is to inject a morbidly incestuous note into the relationship. She swerves wildly from too much theory into the sultriest melodrama. Lyndall, deserted by the lover with whom she has been living, is nursed for

---

[1] S. C. Cronwright-Schreiner, *The Life of Olive Schreiner*, London, 1924

a considerable time through her last illness by Gregory Rose, Em's ex-fiancé, closely shaved and powdered and disguised as a woman! (Lyndall's lingering death has for all Olive Schreiner's progressive highmindedness something about it of the doom appropriate to the fallen woman.) Gregory Rose himself, a silly and snobbish English-man, as unreal as Bertie Wooster but decidedly more unpleasant, is less of a cartoon than two other men in the novel, who bear many of the features of the men in women's magazine fiction. There is the mysterious, cosmopolitan stranger who carries in his bag 'a bright French novel and an old brown volume' (the bright French novel is meant to have irresistible implications of a naïvely provincial sort), who unfolds, like some immensely long-winded and humour-less La Fontaine, an interminable parable to comfort Waldo. Or there is the sophisticated, 'wicked' aristocrat who makes Lyndall his mistress when for reasons of principle she refuses to become his wife. He has a tall, slight figure, delicately pencilled drooping eyelids, a heavy flaxen moustache and he fills his glass from a silver flask. Here is how he and Lyndall are seen at the decisive meeting at which Lyndall, who has in the meantime taken over Gregory Rose from the stricken Em, agrees to become his mistress.

> From under their half-closed lids the keen eyes looked down at her. Her shoulders were bent; for a moment the little figure had forgotten its queenly bearing, and drooped wearily; the wide dark eyes watched the fire very softly.
> It certainly was not in her power to resist him, nor any strength in her that made his own at that moment grow soft as he looked at her.
> He touched one little hand that rested on her knee.
> 'Poor little thing!' he said; 'you are only a child.'

And yet I cannot feel the account I have given, fair as I believe it to be, explains the intense, lasting effect this strange novel makes on the reader. Certainly the incoherence of structure and the defects of taste and of overmanipulation are there. Just as certainly they fail to muffle the brooding influence the book exer-cises. Nor do they nullify the considerable reflective intelligence and the remarkable evocative power shown in it, gifts admirably served in the better parts of the book by Olive Schreiner's clear lithe prose. I have pointed out the imperfections of design and the marked intrusiveness of the author's personality, and I might have made a good deal more of both. But while these are inescapable and limiting facts, bound to qualify one's response, they are also evidence of something else one is aware of going on in the depths of the book. I put it neutrally like this because it is by no means wholly under the author's conscious control. It appears cloudily and jerkily under the agitation of the surface and obscurely informing the structure of character and scene, only assuming a precise and realised form at those times when the author is less feverishly under the influence of one or other of several obsessions. When I try to define for myself what it is I am aware of, what other theme is feeling its way into the life of the novel, I find myself associating it with a flow of feeling which is painful and checked and seldom fully articulated. There are two conditions modifying Olive Schreiner's basic experience and her insight into it. One makes it possible for her, the other important for us. One is a knotty, difficult honesty, the positive side of her personal domination of the material. She is wholly faithful to herself, even when that self is pushed and distorted by private neuroticism or Victorian prejudice or crankiness or blindness. The second condition is the belief under which she always works of the unity of human experience.

> What is microscopic in one is largely developed in another; what is a rudimentary in one man is an active organ in another; but all things are in all men and one soul is the model of all. We shall find nothing new in human nature after we have once carefully dissected and analysed the one being we ever shall truly know—ourself.

What gives the book its life—and in a quirky, clumsy way, it *is* alive—is a bitter, forlorn experience of the necessity of human participation, and a desperate sense of its difficulties and its final impossibility. The development of consciousness and the refinement of natural gifts of intelligence and sensibility have placed Lyndall, who most exactly dramatises the personal engagement and predicament of the author, beyond the point at which she could accept the immemorial, unconscious rhythms of the agricultural community and the Boer farm (just as in her personal life these things had raised Olive Schreiner beyond the level at which she was able to accept the simple religious fervour of her father). The rejection of the beliefs of the family and the community forces on Lyndall a strained, angry individuality and the use of her will as a weapon both of defence and attack. Consciousness, which breaches for her the rationality of the communal pattern, works to prevent her entrance into a life of mutuality and hardens her in her solitary fate. 'Perhaps she thought of the narrowness of the limits within which a human soul may speak and be understood by its nearest mental kind, of how soon it reaches that solitary land of the individual experience, in which no fellow-footfall is ever heard.'

Explicit here, the submerged, pervasive presence of this theme in the rest of the book brings the other struggles and tensions into a common system: both the general ones like that of dependent woman against a male world, child against an adult world, agnostic against a religious world (all, be it noted, situations in which the solitary one is opposed to a compacted mass); and again, the particular conflicts in the lives of Em and Waldo. In Em a resolution is possible both because she exists at a lower level of consciousness and because she is willing to put up with a humdrum substitute for a genuine personal life. For Waldo there is no resolution. His passionate attachment to a divine reality, like Lyndall's to the value of consciousness, cannot be reconciled with the life of human mutuality he despairingly desires. The voice of God is also silent in the solitary land of individual experience. The effect of *The Story of an African Farm* comes from the co-existence of an authentic communal life, in all its colour and vivacity, together with a concentrated sense of the terrible remoteness of the individual—from their co-existence and their mutual, clawing destructiveness.

II   CHINUA ACHEBE

To turn from *The Story of an African Farm* to the novels of the Nigerian writer, Chinua Achebe, the author of *Things Fall Apart* (1958), *No Longer at Ease* (1960) and *Arrow of God* (1964), is to move from a world of Victorian and feminine anxiety to one which

is masculine, coherent and in a curious way classical. The sense of
the classic which the novels provoke comes, I think, from two
things. One is that the Ibo life pictured in them is not so much
adapted to, since that implies a kind of servitude, as in perfect
balance with, the natural world. The rhythms of both run together
without jarring or contradiction. The second is that the fiction creates
a society in which life is rounded and intricate and sensitively in
correspondence with a range of human impulse. It admits both the
aristocratic and the democratic principles. It is a life lived by a digni-
fied clan of equals who meet together in an Athenian way (with one
grievous exception) to make critical communal decisions. At the
same time it allows for an exceptional man and for an organisation
based on achievement. Age is respected but achievement revered.
It is a universe which embodies a traditional and living morality and
an order of reference by which the actual is comprehended and
judged. Its religion is both mysterious and homely, answering to
the instinct for the numinous and the need for practical good sense.
Its vitality calls upon the sincerity of its followers and they support
it with the conviction of living action. It produces impressive and
beautiful artefacts in music, dance, decoration and, above all, in
conversation. 'Proverbs are the palm oil with which the words are
eaten.' The limitation of its products, however, is their transience.
They all exist in an essentially fleeting medium. They do not succeed
in recording themselves for the future, and while they may gain in
spontaneity and vitality they fail in permanence. The tragedy of the
civilisation, indeed, which as it appears in these novels is remarkably
inclusive and humane, is that it is unable to achieve a right or
appropriate relationship with time.

So that a satisfying concreteness of existence is accompanied by
a deficiency in power of abstraction. The society of the nineteenth-
century Ibo is one which exists in a kind of trance, perfect in the
present. It could retain only bits of the immediate past, those which
could be encompassed by an individual memory or those which
were embodied in the modes of social intercourse. It had not
within it the resources for assuming new intellectual postures, so
that when the context which supported it began to be altered by the
intrusion of missionaries and the imposition of British law and

D

administration, the nucleus itself was modified and quickly enfeebled. Whether the vision of Ibo society given in the novels is
justified by history is almost irrelevant. What we have in this
work is a conception of civilisation which has a root in reality. It
includes a world and a group with a coherent anatomy of standards
and beliefs and a solid convincing body. This is a universe perfectly
suited to a novelist. It is complete but small. It incorporates a standard and it expresses itself in a characteristic mode of living, which
is yet sufficiently flexible to allow both for the outstanding success
like Okonkwo in *Things Fall Apart* or a wretched failure like his
father Okoye in the same book. Everything in this universe is saturated with significance: not only every act and motive, which can
be related to the inherited system of reference, but also every person
and thing, which have a meaning because what belongs to the
spiritual and moral order of existence flows in and out of the physical. It is not interrupted either by any enclosing sense of private,
separate individuality or by any impermeable material surface.

I said earlier that the tragedy of Ibo society as displayed by
Chinua Achebe lay in its failure to achieve a workable relationship
with time. The personal tragedy of Okonkwo, the protagonist of
Things Fall Apart, has its own intimate temporal dimension. It is
initiated by his total rejection of the immediate past, dramatised
for him in the person of his father (after all parents *are* the past for
their children) in favour of standards established in a more remote,
more heroic time. His motive is negative, his purpose positive. His
father Okoye was cowardly, improvident, idle, womanish, frivolous, a man without title or respect; and Okonkwo, driven by a
deep fear of a similar fate is, consequently, industrious, severe, rich,
brave, honourable, a modern instance of ancient virtues. He is just
about to take the third highest title in the tribe (this taking of titles
in an ascending order of dignity by exposing oneself to increasingly
difficult tests is another example of that classical blend of the aristocratic and the democratic so characteristic of the world of these
novels). Okonkwo's error, the Aristotelian flaw, for this is the kind
of hero he is, is to suppose that the present is wholly susceptible to
his governing, moulding will. He treats the present and life itself as
something wholly subject to arrangement, or as a disposition of

forces which is completely rational. In this he is beginning to desert the central understanding of his tribe. The tribe, in its collective wisdom, allowed in its system of beliefs for the intrusion into the world of wild, irrational freaks of chance. Anyone, for example, could be without reason suddenly named as an outcast and scapegoat, condemned utterly for nothing at all. Okonkwo's reading of life depended on the present's never throwing up the unforeseeable, irrational disaster, whereas the tribe understood that even at its most obedient the present was capable of sliding away from human control. Okonkwo who has shown himself ruthlessly determined to maintain every observance of tribal law because he understood the idealism it expressed—he even hunts down and kills a boy he loves as a son when he is enjoined to do so by the priests—suddenly and absurdly causes an accidental death and is accordingly exiled for seven years by the law, the spirit of which he wishes most passionately to preserve. He is trapped by the cunning of his most treacherous opponent, the present.

Okonkwo completes his exile in his mother's village, and returns home, subdued but unchangingly concentrated on making himself a great man according to the historical criteria of the tribe, and still failing to realise the slippery nature of time and the present. He is faced by a situation which shows that ironic parallelism we are familiar with from classical drama. Okonkwo's son, Nwoye, now rejects his father, and rejects him because of qualities which the young man discerns obscurely as belonging to the future. The sensitive son, always a disappointment to Okonkwo, is converted to Christianity, which it is clear will, with its attendant British administrative structure, and from the best of motives, ruin the collective integrity of the clan. The whole arrangement has a formal classical character, but it is a formality which is implicit in the material, the formality of a set of crystals, or the elegant structure of a leaf, which is determined from within. Nothing could more naturally be the issue of the combination of temperament and event, of individual purpose and historical process, than the converted son's disavowal of all his father stands for. Okonkwo grew up under a stable system, within which the individual person could certainly exert himself for his own good and in doing so might well clash with others; but the supporting system survived and was accepted both by the successful and the defeated. Now Okonkwo finds the conditions of life itself, the context within which decisions are made, beginning to crumble under the influence of what cannot be opposed since it has both the inevitability of fate and the unopposable impalpability of what is to come.

At the climax of the novel, time present and time past do not come together in any point of intersection but define themselves clearly as lines of opposition. One of the District Commissioner's Court Messengers, who have already intolerably affronted the dignity of the leaders of the tribe and now come to forbid their assembly, is killed by Okonkwo. The mass of the people have already insensibly accommodated themselves to an alien domination and they break up into tumult instead of action. Okonkwo, finally realising that the past has been defeated, withdraws, and splendid in his finest warrior's raiment, with a more than Roman dignity, puts himself to death, achieving with this final stroke the heroic status which the treacheries of time had forbidden him even during the most successful phases of his life.

Things Fall Apart is a short novel, not much longer than a *novella,* but it gives a remarkably massive impression. This, I think, is because of the fine balance drawn between a whole society and an impressive individual, and because of the way in which the fundamental predicament of the society is lived through in his life. It also has to do with the equilibrium established by the novelist between the formality of the structure and the accuracy with which he reproduces individual motive and feeling. And it has to do, too, with the author's manner which is plain, calm, confident and vigorous. Achebe's attitudes are quite uncoated with sentimentality, and uncontorted by anything neurotic or morbid or vengeful. His manner, like the life he deals with, has an air of wholesome sanity and a natural human centrality. His narrative method has the character of speech, the deceptively simple and vividly flexible speech of the formally uneducated who live still by some powerful traditional vision. Its plainness and simplicity allow at relevant moments the touch of muted and unassertive poetry, as when he pictures a flicker of thought in a boy's mind:

Gradually the rains became lighter and less frequent, and earth and sky once again became separate. The rain fell in thin, slanting showers through sunshine and quiet breeze. Children no longer stayed indoors but ran about singing:

> 'The rain is falling, the sun is shining,
> Alone Nnadi is cooking and eating.'

Nwoye always wondered who Nnadi was and why he should live all by himself, cooking and eating. In the end he decided that Nnadi must live in that land of Ikemefuna's favourite story where the ant holds his court in splendour and the sands dance for ever.

Or again, when he presents the unsuccessful, musical grandfather, Unoka:

. . . Unoka was never happy when it came to wars. He was in fact a coward and could not bear the sight of blood. And so he changed the subject and talked about music, and his face beamed. He could hear in his mind's ear the blood-stirring and intricate rhythms of the *ekwe* and the *udu* and the *ogene*, and he could hear his own flute weaving in and out of them, decorating them with a colourful and plaintive tune. The total effect was gay and brisk, but if one picked out the flute as it went up and down and then broke up into short snatches, one saw that there was sorrow and grief there.

The effect of *No Longer at Ease,* Achebe's second novel, is quite different from that of *Things Fall Apart.* It has little of the latter's massiveness and tranquility. It is febrile and edgy, and its unsettled, uneasy atmosphere suits the story of a bright young man (eight distinctions in the Cambridge School Certificate) newly returned with an Honours Degree in English from the University of London to take a senior administrative post—a 'European' post—in the Nigerian Civil Service. The young man, Obi Okonkwo, is the grandson of the Okonkwo in the first novel, a fact which keeps the contrast of character and context steadily operating for the informed reader. Obi is an appealing, limited modern creature, a blend of self-confidence and self-ignorance, of sophistication in taste and moral simplicity, whose problems belong to a different category from those of his grandfather. They are those appropriate to a seedy capital, a money economy, an education wrenching him from one set of values to another, a society which still has its root, though a

weakening one, in the villages, and which is now withering into
something deracinated and indifferently suburban.

But while *No Longer at Ease* contains few of the positive, poetic
murmurations which enriched *Things Fall Apart,* the novel is still
a sharp and honest account of the dilemma of an educated, high-
minded young man suddenly put into a respected, well-paid position in the impersonal capital where the tribe still tries spasmodically
to assert its claim for fellowship, and in which venality itself is a kind
of submerged tribal bond. Obi's scholarship to England has been
paid from the funds of the Umofia Progressive Union, whose
members tax themselves mercilessly to find the necessary £800 in
the hope of getting one of their own people into a position of
influence, preferably a legal one (though once in England Obi,
showing an inadmissible independence, had read English, a course
which now qualified him to become secretary to the government's
Overseas Scholarship Committee). Obi is a rich man by the standards of his benefactors, with fine clothes, a grand flat, a car and a
huge salary, and the Union expect him to repay the loan out of his
own huge resources. But he has also to support an ageing father
and a dying mother as well as a young brother in grammar school;
he has to find money to procure an abortion for his fiancée; and all
the time keep up his expensive way of living. But Obi's financial
crisis is only part of his predicament. He is seriously in love with
Clara who is also one of the magic class of 'been to 's', i.e. those who
had been educated abroad. She is an *Osu,* one of those whose
ancestors had been dedicated to a god and who were forever afterwards condemned as outcasts. Each side of the equation trembles at
the sacrilege of the proposed marriage, the horror of which is
acknowledged even by Christopher, Obi's knowing friend from
the London School of Economics. His parents, even his devoted
Christian father, are appalled. It is a tribute to Achebe's wholeness of
grasp of the Ibo world and of the force with which his imagination
penetrates its every corner that the reader too genuinely shares in
this horror.

In two-thirds of Obi's predicament he is an angry victim, mutin-
ously subject to external influences: in the one, affected by a
monstrous piece of the detritus of the primitive past; in the other, by

the imposition of a money economy on a people untrained to manage it. The remaining third affects him more subtly, although, paradoxically, it is related to his professional rather than his personal life. He had returned from Britain convinced that the old gang of Civil Servants who had worked their way up and were almost religiously committed to bribery should be replaced by a new class of university-trained public officials who would show themselves free of the despotism of the past and who, strong in their inward resources, would be able to resist the corrupting persuasions of their society. Obi acted in this belief at the beginning of his career, refusing the bribes of money offered by Mr Mark to help his sister get on to the scholarship list, and the bribes in kind offered by the good-looking Miss Mark herself. Obi's error was to suppose that he could continue to live in a kind of abstract, untethered way in a society in which bribery offered the only recognised way of getting to the top and in which the idea of corruption was supported by the claims of tribal relationships, so that private advantage was consolidated by an admirable warmth of acknowledged obligation. This is the context in which poor Obi's ruin, which is not very dramatic or very tremendous, is prepared for. He goes down, still charmingly young and appealing, keeping his conscience straight by insisting that the candidates he favoured had at least the mini-mum qualifications. He is not perhaps quite so much the victim as the moral by-product of an incoherent system: or of one which has not succeeded in keeping its connection with the past straight or its route forward open.

Things Fall Apart and *No Longer at Ease* show the characteristic pattern of Achebe's novels: a vivid central figure—in *No Longer at Ease* an appealing rather than a strong one; a ground which is cleanly defined and densely occupied; a background from which we hear the confused mutter of social and historic complexities; and a narrative method which is syntactically plain and direct but which also engages the muscular poetry of the commonplace, a common sense and concreteness of feeling generated by traditional experience and crackling in the multitudinous proverbs with which both speech and exposition are strewn. In *Arrow of God* Achebe returns to an earlier period, to the time when the British were pressing the comforting (to them) device of indirect rule; he turns back, too, from the capital to a rural scene, in which six villages constitute a kingdom and the priesthood of Ezeulu, the chief priest of Ulu, the supreme god of the Umuaro people, is comparable to the Papacy. At the same time the key character is now the powerful and richly orchestrated Ezeulu, an altogether more impressive and enigmatic figure than the puppyishly charming Obi. Where Obi was the jelly-like nucleus of his novel, and is sensitive and stricken, Ezeulu has a stony force of endurance and a positive will, as well as greater skill in manipulating people and events. Obi was the victim and recipient of influence but Ezeulu, while he is supple and responsive to what happens, is a forceful director, a man who arranges—or since he is a traditionalist—re-arranges the patterns of life.

When the novel opens we see Ezeulu, an ageing but vital man, solidly seated among his family, friends and clan, intimately a part of and yet above the traditional, almost biblical, life of the people, the feel and texture of which is conveyed with palpable authenticity. Ezeulu's life moves easily between familiar homely things and the mysteries of his priestly vocation. At one moment he is shouting to two quarrelling wives to be quiet as they prepare bitter-leaf tea; at the next he is engaged in an impressively solemn rite in honour of the god, Ulu. Being at home simultaneously with the sacred and the profane in the way Ezeulu is, that is in a conscious, sophisticated way, argues for a certain inclusiveness and scope of personality, and Achebe is remarkably successful in the unforced manner in which he evokes the intelligence, or rather the intellect and maturity of a remote African priest. Ezeulu's grasp of manifold types of experience marks his priestly life too. He is both the possessor of a religious authority, although by no means an unquestioned one (there are protestants among the people), and also possessed by the mysteries of his religion, a religion which itself stretches up from the house and farm to what is numinous and unspeakable. The energy of Ezeulu's nature, and the force it exerts on the reader, come from the tension between the religious authority which he exercises and the spiritual power which he represents. Ezeulu is deeply assured of the reality and validity of this power, but it requires analysis and questioning on his part to be sure of its application in any given set of circumstances, just as it needs undoubted political skill to bring the god's intentions into existence. He has simultaneously to open himself to become the transparent medium of the god's will while employing all his managerial capacity in dealing with the men whom it is to affect. This is the permanent dilemma of spiritual authority and the character created by Achebe beautifully satisfies the artist's appetite for the illustrational, as Henry James called it, in making him the natural vehicle of a fundamental human complexity.

The events which constitute the novel (one thinks of it in this way rather than as something plotted and calculated, the themes being so wholly submerged in the material) slide into one another with that continuity, original but unsurprising, which suggests not so much cause and effect as living and rhythmic process. These events have to do with three spheres of Ezeulu's existence: with his private family life, with his political struggles, and with his function as religious leader and repository of the spirit. In the first we see him presiding over a numerous and complicated family or clan, a man of insistent will, gruffly overbearing, irritable about the *minutiae* of belief and decorum, with disguised preferences and secret antipathies for his own children, and constantly enigmatic in his response to their attitude towards him, which is a blend of awe for his mysterious powers, attachment to the father, shoulder-shrugging tolerance for his irascibility and a dim awareness of being used by a political manipulator. Ezeulu is by nature a reticent man but he is also expert in the devious communication practised to some degree in every family. The given wife or child may seldom be expressly told, but he is never left in doubt as to Ezeulu's intention for him. Ezeulu looks upon the family, particularly the boys, as members of his political organisation, counters to be skilfully deployed in his political game. One son, Oduche, is even bidden to join the new Christian religion, partly to please Ezeulu's friend CaptainWinterbottom, the District Officer, but even more to give Ezeulu an eye and an ear among one division of his potential enemies. The children are also intimately affected in their personal prospects by Ezeulu's sacred office, since the priestly succession must go to one of them, but while the eldest may expect or fear it, and while Ezeulu's hidden partiality is for the youngest, Nwafo, who has the gifts for it and who is strongly drawn to the god's ritual, this is one of the things in which all are helpless, waiting for the god to reveal his choice.

The reality and the richness of the family relationship are established with the confidence of complete intimacy and by a method which is largely conversational, where the speech is laced with the tough, disillusioned apothegms of those living directly in touch with natural rhythms and processes. Not that this society, nor its most expressive art, its speech, gives any hint of primitive clumsiness. The sophisticated application of developed standards based on a wide scope of experience is a cultivated art, and this is what one is aware of in the speech, in the relationships of family life and even in the political management of men to which I turn now, as well as in the profounder religious experience I shall deal with next.

In an old—not a primitive—society braced by a set of received assumptions and expectations and formed into an intricate social organisation, anyone like Ezeulu who inherits a responsible office inherits also strong hostility. A recognised system of opposition is part of the transmitted social order. The possessor's power is checked by that of others, his ambitions impeded or thwarted by other elements in the system he exists to sustain. Add to this the suspicion generated by the conflict of temperaments, and one sees how the possession of power is inescapably relative and how the possessor, moving among obstacles set up by the system or by personalities, rules by combining force with accommodation. Ezeulu's power is not exercised in an abstract emptiness, and not directed simply from the top down. He operates quite as much by sidling sideways, taking into account the palpable world and the blocks and barriers of a traditional society, thick with custom and differentiation. Ezeulu has a sure feeling for this necessary proportion and a mastery of the craft of control through a balance of intervention and retreat. Silence and surprise and the unlooked for appearance are the instruments with which he keeps in place (not just down) his enemies in this complex society, the most prominent of whom are professional antagonists like the priests of other inferior gods, and again the civil leaders jealous about the expansion of ecclesiastical authority, which Ezeulu, by temperament a Gregory, is vigilant for opportunities to extend. He has, too, to be alert for the threat of the swelling British civil government and the more intimate menace of the Christian religion, which unlike the lay authority represented by Captain Winterbottom, seeks to administer men's minds and beliefs. Ezeulu has the gift, the dangerous tact of not acting when he is expected to and of turning back upon others the force of their own expectations. He counsels his own people against a war they are certain he would be in favour of. He recommends an accommodation with the British which astounds them. He deliberately obeys a summons to appear before a British court although his followers are appalled by the sacrilegious affront to his dignity. But his greatest stroke—a negative one— is to refuse in an unprecedented fashion to name the date for the New Yam Feast, which is something reserved to himself alone, and without which by immemorial custom the planting cannot begin; the renegade people are left to face the horror of starvation so that by simply doing nothing Ezeulu brings home to them their absolute dependence on him. He re-establishes his authority, after a period when his star has fallen, by a tactic of passivity and omission which has an immense positive force: the technique of a Machiavelli with religion.

For all Ezeulu's suppleness in manœuvre and his adroitness in retrieving failure, Achebe leaves us in no doubt that political and ecclesiastical management of the obvious kind is subordinate in Ezeulu's mind to the mysterious demands of his vocation. He has an analytic bent which loves to play with alternative courses of action, 'to dissolve his resolution and to form it again'. He often reflects on the nature of his power, questioning its scope and validity. Does he possess it, or is he possessed by it? At what point does the agent become the patient? How is he to define this middle ground between action and suffering to which so much of his spiritual activity belongs? This is a riddle he cannot solve, and his fascination with the enigma makes him strange to his neighbours, unknowable even by his closest friend Akuebe, whom his talk renders 'uneasy and afraid like one who encounters a madman

laughing in a solitary place'. Towards the end of his life in moments
of spiritual crisis he seemed to live enclosed in total silence. 'He was
used to loneliness. As Chief Priest he had always walked alone in
front of Umuaro. But without looking back he had always been
able to hear the flute and song which shook the earth because it came
from a multitude of voices and the stamping of countless feet. . . .
But never until now had he known the voices to die away altogether.' The remoteness of this side of his life ('. . . one half of you
is man and the other half spirit', his friend tells him) and his
prophetic, preparatory office has in it something of the dried-up
integrity of John the Baptist, and even his appearance as he sets out
on a journey recalls the striding image of the precursor in the
wilderness.

But neither Ezeulu's powerful self-discipline nor his restless
intelligence helps him to unravel the small knot of self-ignorance
at the centre of his nature and to recognise the source of his personal
tragedy. (He sees very clearly the imminent dissolution of his
people's mode of life under the impact of an alien civilisation.)
That is the product of his very force of character. His strong intellect
and will push him on into an area which should be wholly free of
personality and emptied of everything but the god. The sudden
inexplicable death of his son, as the young man performs in a most
sacred rite, shakes his reason because it takes place just at the time
when Ezeulu had deceived himself into seeing his dispute with his
people as something else. 'It was a fight of the gods. He was no more
than an arrow in the bow of his god.' But Ezeulu's identification
of his will with the god's was to prove presumptuous. He was not
the arrow but the victim.

At any other time Ezeulu would have been more than equal to his
grief. He would have been equal to any grief not compounded with
humiliation. Why, he asked himself again and again, why had Ulu
chosen to deal thus with him, to strike him down and cover him with
mud? What was his offence? Had he not divined the god's will and
obeyed it? When was it ever heard that a child was scalded by a piece
of yam its own mother put in its palm? What man would send his son
with a potsherd to bring fire from a neighbour's hut and then unleash
rain on him? Who ever sent his son up the palm to gather nuts and
then took an axe and felled the tree. But today such a thing had

happened before the eyes of all. What could it point to but the collapse
and ruin of all things? Then a god, finding himself powerless might
take to his heels and in one final, backward glance at his abandoned
worshippers cry:

> If the rat cannot flee fast enough
> Let him make way for the tortoise.

In *Arrow of God*, his most mature novel, Chinua Achebe has
produced something which is strong, sure, telling. He has created
an African world, the conditions of which are absolutely foreign
to us, but he has done so with such intelligence and fullness of
sympathy, and with such a lively grasp of what is humanly significant that we are easy with it and unstrained by it, and at the same
time seized of its essential sensibility and values. The vulnerable
virtues of the minutely elaborated Ibo society are lucidly displayed
in a variety of characters, and most thoroughly in the splendidly
realised figure of Ezeulu, who is both an authentic priest and a
stubborn, nimble-minded, cross-grained, haughty old man, continually lacerated by his people and by his time, and formidably
willing to wound them both in return. Chinua Achebe's is the
natural imagination of the novelist which works through particular
events and personalities and discriminated shades of being and
feeling. It is not surprising, therefore, that the general event is
involved in the particular, and that the reader takes without any
feeling that he or the structure of the novel is being manipulated,
the sense in which the collapse of the whole society is implied in the
priest's fall. Towards priest and people, the figure and the ground,
Achebe shows—to use his own figure—'the senstivenesss of a
snail's horns', joining a fine exploratory skill to an unsentimental,
accurate tenderness. This attitude, evidence of a capacity for wholeness of experience, lifts him from the ruck of novelists in whom
analysis proceeds from negative emotions, which are themselves
very often the inverted from of sentimentality. Achebe's emotional
maturity, his masculine force in narration, his calm objective out-
look, his fastidious sense of genuine tradition, the deeply particular-
ising, palpable quality of his imagination, make his a talent of a
rare and significant sort.

CHAPTER III

V. S. NAIPAUL

V S. NAIPAUL is the author of six novels, two volumes of short stories and two other books which can be variously described as—what?—travel books or documentary or autobiography or exploration. He has not had to wait long for recognition. His travel books have been described extravagantly as being on the same level as D. H. Lawrence's, his novels as Caribbean masterpieces. After a career stretched over not more than half a dozen years, he received the distinction of a uniform edition, which is more usually a monument to someone dead and gone. He has been awarded a whole clutch of literary prizes, which might well have sunk a less buoyant talent.

Naipaul was born in Trinidad of a Hindu family, educated at Queen's Royal College, Port of Spain, and University College, Oxford, and has for a long time now lived and worked in Britain. At one time this might have been thought an unusual and distinctive background; in fact it now is decidedly a more representative one and Naipaul himself strikes the reader as being in a significant way a combination of a scrupulously private soul and a public and social rôle. He is not simply *a* but *the* writer, all his private nature absorbed in his function as artist. He is not only a natural writer but a natural novelist. Themes for him assume the forms of action and ideas appeal to him only in so far as they satisfy, for him as for Henry James, 'the appetite for the illustrational'. He never, as some other West Indian writers do, gives the impression that he is writing from the will or that he is preaching a party line or some ethical imperative. His vision is his own, unenervated by contemporary social clichés or political routines. He is independent but also relevant. He is engaged with the stresses and strains we recognise as crucial in our experience now. His writing is nervous and present. This, together with the mixture in him of creeds, cultures and continents, with his expatriate career, his being able to practise an art in and

of totally dissimilar worlds, all gives him a peculiarly contemporary quality.

I should like to begin, then, in what is rather an unconventional
way of dealing with a novelist, by commenting for a moment on
one of the books which isn't a novel, *An Area of Darkness*, where
we see written out pretty explicitly at least one clue to the nature of
Naipaul's sensibility. If that gentle liberal genius E. M. Forster had
to give advice to travellers today, it ought to be, I think, 'Only dis-
connect!' Cut yourself off from your own past. Unbolt your fierce
identity. Dismantle your driving national force, and become something altogether quieter and more passive, a faithful recording instrument. Good but impossible advice as *An Area of Darkness* makes
only too clear. The relationship between a travel writer and the
country he writes about is generally clear enough. Here he is, bold
and assured, nationally and personally organised and quite often
in arms, and there, before him and at some distance, is the observed,
sometimes detested object, the country he is visiting. But the India
of *An Area of Darkness* is within Naipaul. His Trinidadian grandfather was from Uttar Pradesh, and though two generations became
saturated in West Indian life, the secret premises of family action
were in word and image profoundly Indian. So that Naipaul's
return to India is as much a research into himself as into another
country. He is crawling on sensitive naked feet up through the
tunnels of his own self. Or perhaps one could say this book is a
detailed investigation of one side of Naipaul's nature by another,
the Indian supplying the data, the Western the microscope. Naipaul
is a very significant writer indeed and *An Area of Darkness* has the
richness and point of any disturbed experience suffered by a writer
with so genuine, so pure a talent. Naipaul's grandfather went
West, Naipaul came East, and a cold coming he had of it. He
endures within himself Indian agonies. The friction of the two sides
of his nature produces not warmth but despair. He is aware that in
savaging India he is savaging himself. Although this book shows on
every page the novelist's double discernment, which is able to fix
the subtlest nuance of individuality, and with an equal assurance, an
equal skill, to establish it solidly in a social world, it is valuable very
much more as a report, inward and tremblingly exact, of the nature

of Naipaul than as an undistorted chronicle of India. It is the subject, not the object, which counts here.

Naipaul's revulsion at so many aspects of Indian life, his almost Swiftian horror of dirt, his novelist's fierce rejection of the Indian sense of non-reality, his suspicion, even his fear, of the way in which the brutality of fact in India can slide away into formless diction—all these things quiver on every page. But they never qualify or muffle his astonishing sense of detail. The book is lightened and sharpened by this extreme clarity of vision. Even his disgust with the functionalism of caste, which keeps a man gaoled in his private gaol of duty, doesn't stop him from describing with singular precision four men washing down the steps of an unpalatable Bombay hotel.

> The first pours water from a bucket, the second scratches the tiles with a twig broom, the third uses a rag to slop the dirty water down the steps into another bucket, which is held by the fourth. After they have passed, the steps are as dirty as before; but now above the blackened skirting-tiles the walls are freshly and dirtily splashed. The bathrooms and lavatories are foul; the slimy woodwork has rotted away as a result of this daily drenching; the concrete walls are green and black with slime. You cannot complain that the hotel is dirty. No Indian will agree with you. Four sweepers are in daily attendance, and it is enough in India that the sweepers attend. They are not required to *clean*. That is a subsidiary part of their function, which is to *be* sweepers, degraded beings, to go through the motions of degradation.

Perhaps it is this dissolving of action into being which most appals him. But perhaps there is also something Indian in his fascinated horror with such detail. He is, it seems, rejecting not only India but trying to bleach out part of his own nature. His book is a kind of metaphysical diary of the effort to shine a Western novelist's light into an interior area of darkness. It reconstructs, it doesn't simply record, this experience, and it is deeply disturbing.

In his other travel book *The Middle Passage*, an acute but less personally engaged study of a return to a post-colonial West Indies, Naipaul uses as an epigraph a passage from John Anthony Froude's *The English in the West Indies* (1887).

> They were valued only for the wealth which they yielded, and society there has never assumed any particularly noble aspect. There

has been splendour and luxurious living, and there have been crimes and horrors, and revolts and massacres. There has been romance, but it has been the romance of pirates and outlaws. The natural graces of life do not show themselves under such conditions. There has been no saint in the West Indies since Las Casas, no hero unless philonegro enthusiasm can make one out of Toussaint. There are no people there in the true sense of the word, with a character and purpose of their own.

This is the life without natural graces, heroes, saints, without a national identity or a social purpose, inherited by the people of *Miguel Street*, Naipaul's first book. It is a society based upon 'the degrading fact of the Colonial society; it never required efficiency, it never required quality, and these things, because unrequired, became undesirable'. This is the world without 'scientists, engineers, explorers, soldiers or poets', without tradition or standards which shapes the people of *Miguel Street*, Bogart, B. Wordsworth, Eddoes, Man-man, Errol, Titus Hoyt I. A. London (External), and Popo who called himself a carpenter but never built anything except a little galvanised iron workshop under a mango tree at the back of his yard, and who occupies himself incessantly making 'the thing without a name'. Miguel Street is a place where the past also is blank, a thing without a name. All the impersonal elements in civilisation are missing or they are supplied in the tawdriest form by films, radio stars, pop singers, and in their most exalted form by cricketers and the game of cricket, which is itself a kind of history, poetry and art. But there is one great exception. These are people of immense vitality, of great nimbleness of wit, of a vast and disillusioned tolerance, given to the life of feeling, responsive to rhythm, riddled by uncertainty—it is true—but also quick and shrewd, and they have one splendid instrument for ordering their sad, comic, muddled universe, their language.

Naipaul himself writes a prose that is limpidly anonymous and quite free of any personal quirks or distortions. It is decent and direct, syntactically simple and clear, and as it combines curiously an air of civilised restraint with a mischievously deadpan quality, it makes a very elegant instrument for ironic dissection. In this transparent medium the speech of the inhabitants of *Miguel Street* stands out with peculiar colour and density. It is a folk-speech, and

E

intimate therefore, sly and allusive. It also carries with it a curious suggestion of 'objectivity' and passivity. Impersonal verbs abound. Turns of speech deviously suggest the limitations of the agent. Each man carries within him a kind of secret impotence and his life and conduct are made up of his simultaneous acceptance and mockery of it. Because the myths are so thin, the social code so derivative, the people pour their energy into individuality. Each one is a formed identity, without a past, maybe, but with an astonishingly vivid present. These people are not derivations of some rich history of which they are part the inheritance and part the function. They are wholly here and now and there is in each of them an extraordinary concentration of life.

In *Miguel Street* it is the place, public, graceless, huddled, but brilliant with human oddity which is both the ground and the background of the people. The street is also the one permanent relationship uniting them. Their other relationships are intense and transient. They appear and disappear like fish or birds. Suddenly they are here, suddenly gone. People come and go, they are dramatically present, but there are long intervals of silence and absence. In *The Mystic Masseur* the place is enlarged, the protagonist Ganesh Ramsumair more centrally positioned, the other characters Leela the wife, Ramlogan the father-in-law, Beharry the friend, Basdeo the printer, are disposed in relation to him. The story is a decidedly Indian one in feeling, the translation of a masseur into a mystic. It recalls R. K. Narayan's *The Guide*, one of the most distinguished of Indian novels in English, in which Raju the railway guide and near confidence man is transformed into Raju the man deserving of confidence, and in the end the holy man and martyr.

In *The Guide* the organised theme is the complex association of sincerity and self-deception: how these conditions grow out of one another, how they co-exist, disagree, supplant, and in the long run re-attract one another. In *The Mystic Masseur* the theme is less serious than this. It is Ganesh's failure as a teacher that turns him into a masseur, his lack of success with rubbing away ordinary pains that nudges him towards mysticism. Raju in *The Guide* starts out self-conscious and embarrassed by his journey towards sainthood;

he is in fact pushed into the rôle because he cannot disappoint the expectations of the pious Indian villagers. He is one of those whose character is composed by the expectations of others. Ganesh in *The Mystic Masseur* starts from nothing but a clear consciousness of his own potential greatness, and his career is made up of his efforts, dutiful, devious, unscrupulous—each where it is necessary—to give this greatness a chance to shine out. He imposes himself upon his family and neighbours in the honest service of himself. Not that Ganesh is simply a straightforward gangster. There remains about him always, even in his final apotheosis as G. Ramsay Muir, M.B.E. a distinguished Colonial statesman, something enigmatic and inexplicable. Even his crookery is the means for realising his *virtus*. Moreover, Naipaul's attitude to his subjects, though it is as modest and self-effacing as Narayan's, is considerably more malicious. He delights in his mild way when his characters act out in their conduct the truth of Coleridge's assertion, 'cunning is circuitous folly'; morality in these lives is much more a style than an ethic. But his malice is not merely negative because of the tenderness with which he regards every expression of human individuality. Even cruelty, even the beating of wives and children becomes acceptable as it is absorbed into the style of behaviour proper to this or that individual.

Perhaps these last comments may suggest that Naipaul is the possessor of a delicate, attractive talent, at once gentle and mischievous, feeling and unsentimental. And Naipaul's gift clearly is all of this. But there are both in *Miguel Street* and *The Mystic Masseur* hints of deeper resonances, insinuations of less tractable disasters. There is a kind of sadness folded into the quick lines of the sketches in Miguel Street. It is unemphatic and never despairing because neither author nor characters take up any indignant stance about what happens to them. They accept it. And they do so because of a conviction, or if that is too explicit and articulate, because of a profound attitude or a posture in the bones and nerves, that one part of being human is simply hopelessness, and another part is practising a ritual to make that tolerable. There is an image of this cool tragic sense even in the tumultuously farcical career of Ganesh the Mystic Masseur in the death of his father.

When he had closed the door behind him the wailing sounded far away. The coffin rested on a table in the centre of the room and he couldn't see the body from where he was. To his left a small oil lamp burned low and threw monstrous shadows on the walls and the galvanised-iron ceiling. When he walked nearer the table his footsteps resounded on the floor-planks and the oil lamp shivered. The old man's moustache still bristled fiercely but the face had fallen and looked weak and tired. The air around the table felt cool and he saw that it came from the casing of ice around the coffin. It was a room of the dead, strange with the smell of camphor balls, and there was nothing alive in it except himself and the squat yellow flame of the oil lamp, and they were both silent. Only, from time to time, the water from the melting ice plopped into the four pans at the feet of the table and punctured the silence. . . . Ganesh didn't sleep that night and everything he did seemed unreal. Afterwards he remembered the solicitude of Ramlogan—and his daughter; remembered returning to the house where no fire could be lit, remembered the sad songs of the women lengthening out the night; then, in the early morning, the preparations for the cremation. He had to do many things, and he did without thought or question everything the pundit, his aunt, and Ramlogan asked him. He remembered having to walk round the body of his father, remembered applying the last caste-marks to the old man's forehead, and doing many more things until it seemed that ritual had replaced grief.

These possibilities, which in any case are no more than shadowy innuendoes in the West Indian sunlight, are kept in suspense throughout *The Suffrage of Elvira*, in which the target is the representative machinery of an abstract democracy without a sanction in tradition or understanding. And target does seem an appropriate word when one thinks of the aimed and focussed intensity of Naipaul's observation. The special flavour of his work indeed comes from blending the high spirits that could be productive of farce with a most delicately exact sense of detail, and not only the detail of objects but the details of conduct, of feeling, motivation and purpose. This means on Naipaul's part a distrust for conceptual abstractions and vague codes, but a sympathetic acceptance of the most outrageous behaviour when this wells up naturally from traditional or personal sources.

Things were crazily mixed up in Elvira. Everybody, Hindus, Muslims and Christians, owned a Bible; the Hindus and Muslims looking on it, if anything, with greater awe. Hindus and Muslims celebrated Christmas and Easter. The Spaniards and some of the negroes celebrated the Hindu festival of lights. Someone had told them that Lakshmi, the goddess of prosperity, was being honoured; they placed small earthen lamps on their money-boxes and waited, as they said, for the money to breed. Everybody celebrated the Muslim festival of Hosein. In fact, when Elvira was done with religious festivals, there were few straight days left.

The faces and colours are various here; what is common is human concern for a symbol which will guarantee one's safety and be the endorsement of one's action by the gods. Or as black Haq the Muslim puts it in his homely way. 'In God we trust, as the saying goes. In man we bust. *As* the saying goes.' As with the Bible so with democracy: 'Democracy had come to Elvira four years before, in 1946, but it had taken nearly everybody by surprise and it wasn't until 1950, a few months before the second general election under universal adult franchise, that people began to see the possibilities'. When the people include a candidate like the timid dyspeptic lacrymose Hindu Harbans, the tiny, dry formidable local boss Chittaranjan, the goldsmith, who wants the candidate's daughter for his son, the hard-drinking philoprogenitive Muslim leader Baksh and his vast wife prophesying universal disaster and beating the children with regretful relish, a campaign manager like their sunglassed, slogan-bawling son Foam—short for Foreman—and his rival Lorkhoor another 'fust-class loudspeaking man' whose eccentricity it is to speak correct English on every occasion, as well as the proprietor of the rum-shop Ramlogan, swinging instantaneously from chilling ferocity to tear-dissolving cowardice; and when the possibilities include sweetening everybody with dollars, lacing them with rum, terrifying them with obeah and magic, not to speak of baffling them with the intervention of two Jehovah's Witnesses, a pair of prim hygienic witches, and all in the service of democracy and the modern world, then the resultant brew is entrancingly strange. And yet there is a kind of wild logic in the tumult of 'the election bacchanal'.

Harbans steadied his hands. 'Is that self I come to talk to you about. The modern world Baksh. In this modern world everybody is one.

Don't make no difference who you is or what you is. You is a Muslim,
I is a Hindu. Tell me, that matter?' He had begun to coo again.
'Depending.'
'Yes, as you say, depending. Who you for Baksh?'

'Depending': There is a nice dependence at every point between
action and character and between character and community. Crazy
as the behaviour of the characters may be by any soberer standards,
each acts according to the coherence of identity, something which
is established by the clash or mating of his personal stamp with
the style of the society. And this inward control falls in with another,
the instinctive control of a fastidious mind. So that the extravagance
never becomes a mere romp. For a more than Irish eccentricity
in the population—to take an analogy which seems highly suitable
to a multi-racial society—is matched by an almost Latin elegance in
the writer.

The combination of peasant sagacity and cultivated intelligence,
of muscle and nerve, in *Miguel Street*, *The Mystic Masseur* and *The
Suffrage of Elvira* makes the books which are fed from regional
springs and realised in regional detail more than simply regional.
There are murmurations in them all of a more inclusive humanity.
And yet, and yet... These novels communicate an air of capability,
of sinewy resource, which seems more extensive than the matter
being dealt with. Their richness, after all, resides in minute perfections and their force is a limited and contained one. The reader is
aware of considerable powers put to rather too markedly a parochial
purpose. There is perhaps a shade too much emphasis on charm.
One begins to long for something more severe and more testing.
One wants to feel not just powers in the author but power in the
work. And here in *A House for Mr Biswas* it is. If one wanted to
specify one's uneasiness about the first three novels it would have
to do, I think, with one's sense of a certain discrepancy between
the perfection of the surface and the inclusiveness of the theme.
The surface connects, it seems, only with a vague depth whereas
one feels it requires to be supported with something more powerful
and profound: 'requires', that is, if the significance of the work is
to be level with the capacity of the author.

In the three early novels there is an idea floating about, though impalpably and without assuming definition (I do not mean abstract definition),which hints at a more significant and inclusive organising theme. It is the idea of slavery. The members of this community, even those parts of it like the Indian which were exempt from historical slavery, carry about with them the mark, in their attitudes and sensibilities and convictions, of the slave, the unnecessary man. The urgency of the characters comes from their efforts, desperate or ridiculous, to get others to acknowledge, so as to have it validated for themselves, their human necessity. In the comic books this may only amount to doing one's best to leave a dent in an indifferent universe, which often results in a hurt foot and an untouched world. But slavery is one of those ingathering, creative metaphors which have in them both strength and universality. It is this metaphor which initiates and sustains *A House for Mr Biswas.* 'How terrible it would have been,' Mr Biswas reflects as he lies dying in his mortgaged house. 'How terrible it would have been, at this time, to be without it: to have died among the Tulsis, amid the squalor of that large, disintegrating and indifferent family; to have left Shama and the children among them, in one room; worse, to have lived without even attempting to lay claim to one's portion of the earth; to have lived and died as one had been born, unnecessary and unaccommodated.'

Dying in a mortgaged house is just what is happening to poor Mr Biswas, a journalist of Sikkim Street, St James, Port of Spain, aged 46, with a wife and four children. But it is happening too, the novel makes us realise, to his healthy family, to his next-door neighbour, to the community and to all of us. And not simply because of a general metaphor which can be unfastened from its loose attachment to a particular context, but because all of us in Trinidad and everywhere else are indeed dying in mortgaged houses, mortgaged bodies, mortgaged minds and feelings. We are all, all our lives, 'stiffening in a rented mansion'. Mr Biswas—this is his name throughout the novel even when he is a small child, and how can one call anyone with a name like that a hero?—Mr Biswas, the protagonist, is not a bad model of man, the anonymous ordinary man that is. He was born to a family of sugar-estate workers, a scrawny, pot-bellied baby who had six fingers and was born the wrong way at an inauspicious hour. The midwife prophesied 'whatever you do, this boy will eat up his own mother and father'. And his horoscope appalled the pundit.

He undid his red bundle and took out his astrological almanac, a sheaf of loose thick leaves, long and narrow, between boards. The leaves were brown with age and their musty smell was mixed with that of the red and ochre sandalwood paste that had been spattered on them. The pundit lifted a leaf, read a little, wet his forefinger on his tongue and lifted another leaf.

'What about the six fingers, pundit?'

'That's a shocking sign, of course. The only thing I can advise is to keep him away from trees and water. Particularly water.'

'Never bath him?'

'I don't mean exactly that.' He raised his right hand, bunched the fingers and, with his head on one side, said slowly. 'One has to interpret what the book says.' He tapped the wobbly almanac with his left hand. 'And when the book says water, I think it means water in its natural form.'

'Natural form.'

'Natural form,' the pundit repeated, but uncertainly. 'I mean,' he said quickly, and with some annoyance, 'keep him away from rivers and ponds. And of course the sea. And another thing,' he added with satisfaction. 'He will have an unlucky sneeze.'

When Mr Biswas was nine days old the sixth finger fell off and it had to be buried secretly behind the cow-pen at the back of the house. A little unnecessary bit of him died almost before he was under way. The events of Mr Biswas's life might have been arranged to make the structure of his slavery explicit. But he began, of course, as a baby with that warm half-conscious certitude that the way things were was the absolute and perfect way. Life for a child is always brilliantly present and not conceivably other than it is. As an infant he was treated with attention and respect. His limbs were oiled and exercised. He caught cold easily and he had to be watched because his sinister sneeze brought disaster: threepence would be lost, a bottle would be broken, a dish upset. But he grew in spite of malnutrition, though he was always breaking out in eczema and sores. He was never allowed to go near water and to look after the buffaloes as the other children did. But he was given the responsibility for a calf belonging to Dhari the next-door neighbour. Mr Biswas loved the calf and he took it for walks. It was on one of these that he discovered the stream which he visited secretly to play. One day he lost the calf. He couldn't find it although he mooed for it, quietly of course so as not to attract the attention of adults. He decided that it was gone for good. He slunk home, crept into the house, and hid under the bed, where 'the smell of old cloth, dust and old thatch combined into one overpoweringly musty smell'. While Mr Biswas lay, passive but alert, events outside which were remote and dramatic were under way. He was found to be lost and assumed to be at the bottom of the pond. His father dived again and again for him, refusing help partly out of pique, because after all it was his son that was down there. But Raghu, Mr Biswas's father, still steadfastly diving and refusing help went down again and again.

Lakhan said, 'Something has happened.'
A woman said, 'No stupid talk now, Lakhan, Raghu is a great diver.'
'I know, I know,' Lakhan said. 'But he's been diving too long.'
Then they were all still. Someone had sneezed.
They turned to see Mr Biswas standing some distance away in the gloom, the toe of one foot scratching the ankle of the other.
Lakhan was in the pond. Pratap and Prasad rushed to hustle Mr Biswas away.
'That boy!' Dhari said. 'He has murdered my calf and now he has eaten up his own father.'
Lakhan brought up Raghu unconscious. They rolled him on the damp grass and pumped water out of his mouth and through his nostrils. But it was too late.

Mr Biswas had indeed eaten up his own mother and father. The rapacious peasant neighbours closed in, harassing the widow and children and searching the garden at night for money Raghu was supposed to have hidden. The family was broken up among relatives, and the small sum of Mr Biswas's hugged certainties and tiny stabilities crumbled away. From now on life was to point out to Mr Biswas with increasing degrees of ferocity how less and less necessary he was. He was always peripheral. He belonged nowhere. He got in people's way, at his aunt's, at the pundit's where he was sent as a novice, partly, no doubt, because of the curious air of disaster he carried about with him, and where he was bullied in a high-minded way and finally expelled in disgrace because he couldn't control his bowels. He worked in a rumshop where the manager distrusted him as a spy of the owner. He became a sign-writer and lovingly decorated palings and walls in honour of Pluko, a hair tonic, Anchor cigarettes and the candidates for the local Road Board elections. It was while painting signs in the Tulsis' shop on the High Street at Arwacas that he was enlisted into the household—though medieval words like retinue or meinie might be more suitable—of the Tulsis, who had some reputation among Hindus as a pious, conservative landowning family. Their house was dedicated to Hanuman, the benevolent monkey-god, but he was the only benevolent one there. The family combined seediness and ruthlessness. It was governed by Mrs Tulsi, who worked through oriental mystery and passivity, and her brother-in-law Seth, a large, moustached, overpowering man, who used more active methods.

Mr Biswas made a gawky advance to a pretty girl in the shop. Immediately the smooth Tulsi organisation purred into action. Before he knew where he was he was accepted as the girl's official suitor, and before he could understand what that meant he found himself married to her. Mr Biswas was now not only naturally a slave but officially one. The Tulsi menage worked on simple principles. There was one servant, a Negress called Miss Blackie; but the real and many servants were the daughters and their children who swept and washed and cooked and served in the store, while their husbands under Seth's supervision worked on the Tulsi land and looked after the Tulsi animals for which they received food, shelter, and little money, and had their children looked after. But Mr Biswas, though he was a weak man and indeed a victim, was not the suave classical kind of victim who accepts his fate in courage and silence. He had a weak man's capacity for spurts of revolt and querulous malice. He was an irritable, jerking victim, a bit of grit in the oiled machine of the Tulsis. When it was necessary to be solemn he was a clown, when pious he was blasphemous, when appreciative he was ungrateful.

The Tulsis could stand just so much and it wasn't long before they put Mr Biswas out to service. He was put to keep a village shop where he showed himself both incompetent and uncaring. It was true it was not much of a shop, a short narrow room with a rusty galvanised iron roof, with concrete floors and sagging walls which shook and staggered but somehow stood up, and a house attached to it smelling of kerosene and bedbugs. Mr Biswas was cheated and despised by his customers, and frequently deserted by his wife who took off every so often and returned to Hanuman House. He had innumerable bad debts.He was swindled by the lawyer he employed to recover them. Clearly the Tulsis had to rescue what they could.

Seth sighed. 'So what we going to do with the shop?'
Mr Biswas shrugged.
'Insure and burn?' Seth said, making it one word: *Insuranburn.*

Insuranburning took care of the shop, and Mr Biswas, now at once more actively frantic and more passively a utensil than ever, was sent as a sub-overseer at the sugar estate at Green Vale at twenty-five dollars a month. The labourers, sensing the victim in him, mocked and swindled him, and Mr Biswas, who began by wondering how they lived on three dollars a month, soon wondered why they got so much. At Green Vale two things happened to him. He was a man whose salvation depended upon his becoming something, or someone. He might, with his nervous plastic nature and his love of reading Marcus Aurelius, have been saved by developing a style. He might have been held together by a kind of modest elegance. But what style or elegance could he develop in a society where a fine meal meant a tin of sardines and a bottle of soda-water? And what was open to him (for his emptiness might have been supported by the rôle a profession gave) in a community where all he could hope for would be to be a barber or a bus conductor? He decided to become a house-owner. He poured his hope and passion into the queer square structure raised for him by Mr McLean, the carpenter. A house-owner is a man with an identity and a place, a character and a context. But while the miserable little house assumed its one-room solidity, the residue of Mr Biswas's self and sanity began to dribble away. Slavery, a total lack of necessity, being simply a function and a thing turned Mr Biswas from a subject into an object. Human reality crumpled. He became

afraid, then terrified of the labourers, and finally every man and
woman he saw, even at a distance, gave him a twist of panic. And
then every object became sullied by his fear. Objects, as real as he
who was simply another object, stared at him menacingly.

> . . . he thought of the power of the rockers to grind and crush and
> inflict pain, in his hands and toes and the tenderer parts of his body.
> He rose at once in agony, covering his groin with his hands, sucking
> hard on his teeth, listening to the chair, as, rocking, it moved sideways
> on the cambered plank. The chair fell silent and stopped. He looked
> away from it. On the wall he saw a nail that could puncture his eye.
> The window could drop and mangle. So could the doors. And the
> castors of the dressing-table. The drawers.

The only strength in his life seemed to be his past which now
became 'a miracle of calm and courage'. He felt the darkness lapping
about this. The place itself was losing definition as each day the
lucidity of his mind lessened. He had been a mere nobody and now
he was threatened absolutely with being no body. His inward
emptiness no longer had the reassurance of the external world.

> When he got to Green Vale it was dark. Under the trees it was
> night. The sounds from the barracks were asserted and isolated one
> from the other: snatches of talk, the sound of frying, a shout, the cry
> of a child: sounds thrown up at the starlit sky from a place that was
> nowhere, a dot on the map of the island, which was a dot on the map
> of the world. The dead trees ringed the barracks, a wall of flawless
> black.

The rest of Mr Biswas's life was spent striving to keep at least
that much lucidity in his head and that amount of coherence in
his life which would save him from being buried under 'a wall of
flawless black'.

The account of Mr Biswas's dissolution, which is both evocation
and analysis and each shading into the other, is, although but half-
way through, the climax of the novel and perhaps the high point
of Naipaul's art. The shape of the novel is like a great V with Mr
Biswas's collapse at the point of the V and with the lines alive and
shifting, like rivers. The analysis is clinically exact, the evocation
tenderly human. The insight has grace and the grace acumen. The
balancing part of the novel details with a more positive presence

of the comic but with an equally exquisite touch the stumbling and
bumbling progress of Mr Biswas upwards from insanity and despair. The second part of his life, some fifteen years, is spent mostly
in the city, in Port of Spain. He charms his way into a job as a
journalist, where his fantasy and facetiousness appeal to a harum-
scarum editor, though they rub rather awkwardly against a
soberer, more professional successor. He specialised in stories that
combined shape and scandal. His job gave Mr Biswas some small
measure of independence and his purpose—to achieve the dignity
of a house-owner—gave his life form. There were of course hectic
periods, moments when he appeared to be sliding helplessly back
into disaster. He never separated completely from the squalor and
disintegration of the Tulsi family: he was always liable to be involved in their intense intimacies and incomprehensible hostilities.
But he had his measure of good fortune: he was never out of work,
his children turned out to be intelligent, and he finally got his
house—although naturally he was swindled by the seller. But this
being cheated is in keeping with the bias of Mr Biswas's nature.
He could never cease to be a victim (any more than the rest of us).
But at least he was an irritable and suspicious one, and in his turn he
succeeded if not in swindling fate at least in cheating it a little. He
became to some degree, which is perhaps the most that any of us
can hope for, an unaccommodating victim and an accommodated
man.

Naipaul's next novel, *Mr Stone and the Knights Companion,* sustains the theme of slavery but in a delicately subdued, fantastic
manner. The English setting is solid and palpable, genuine in feeling
and authentic in detail, but the vision brought to bear on it is so
idiosyncratic, so wry and curious, that the reader feels he is moving
in a dream where objects and events have an unnatural prominence
and clarity but the universe enclosing them is cloudy and magical.
Mr Stone himself has dreamlike fantasies: he sees himself gliding
up and down on his private moving strip of pavement or flying
along the corridors at work, indifferent to the stupefaction of the
onlookers. Mr Stone's slavery is an individual and intrinsic condition. He is the slave of his past, of his habits, of a fixed identity and
its ritualistic priorities. 'Life was something to be moved through.

Experiences were not to be enjoyed at the actual moment: pleasure in them came only when they had been, as it were, docketed and put away in the file of the past, when they had become part of his "life", his "experience", his career.' This is the problem, the form 'slavery' takes, in a society unravaged by the savagery of extremes, and within that society the peculiar problem of the most settled, the middle aged, who inhabit a world which hardens on the one side into routine and falls on the other into despair. And it is this area of sensibility which is plotted with a kind of tender accuracy in *Mr Stone and the Knights Companion*. The wild folk-gaiety of the earliest novels is muted into an urban, and urbane, comedy, the turbulent Caribbean nonsense into metropolitan and pointed wit. But under the elegant surface there is an edge of grimness in place in a work which for all the slightness of its proportions has great thematic richness. 'And he had a realisation', it is said of Mr Stone, 'too upsetting to be more than momentarily examined, that all that was solid and immutable and enduring about the world, all to which man linked himself . . . flattered only to deceive. For all that was not flesh was irrelevant to man, and all that was important was man's own flesh, his weakness and corruptibility.'

The Mimic Men was published in 1967 and confirms the impression given by *A House for Mr Biswas* that Naipaul is an artist whose work contains within itself large possibilities of growth and development. *The Mimic Men* bends away in several new directions. It brings together West Indian and British themes and sets alongside one another the landscapes of London and Trinidad, of Isabella as the island is called in the story. It is a much more personal work than *Mr Stone and the Knights Companion* in which there is a hint not of the academic but of a rather deliberate 'study'. It is like *A House for Mr Biswas* in its complexity and inclusiveness but the temperament of this novel is more pinched and melancholy. *A House for Mr Biswas* celebrates the fineness of humanity implicit in the feeblest of us. The more clinical eye of *The Mimic Men* discovers the failure in the best, like the worn little pornographic booklet discovered in the desk of the hero's father, and while there are splendid comic touches they are dispersed and rare. The hilarity of the early novels has been turned into something bordering on despair and all that quality of wild high spirits is quite bleached away. Certainly there is no occasion to worry here, as there was in those novels, about too much emphasis on charm. *The Mimic Men* begins with Ralph Singh, an exiled politician—fatigued by disillusion rather than failure—writing his memoirs in an aseptic, *placeless* suburban London hotel. The novel dramatises his reminiscences. The framing effect of the reminiscences, the distancing of exile and the sieve of memory give form to the novel and enable us to grasp the quality of detachment in the protagonist (just as they also remind us of that contemplative constituent in Naipaul's own sensibility which begins to assume a more important place in his fiction).

The nature of Naipaul's hero, an ex-public unsmiling forty-year-old man, Hindu by birth, with a schoolteacher father and rich connections on his mother's side, is marked by a certain icy remoteness unmelting since childhood. An acute intelligence and minute sensitivity to what he sees make him a magnificent observer—but of the kind Coleridge called *spectator ab extra*. His consciousness of self is always kept at a certain critical point, his feelings never blend wholly with those of another. An intellectual and moral distance always persists. He is an aristocrat lacking an order he can submit to. His dreams are cold and distant. '. . . I had visions of Central Asian horsemen, among whom I am one, riding below a sky threatening snow to the very end of an empty world.' He speaks with hauteur of the English politicians he found when he came to England at a time of reform. '. . . Politicians proclaim the meanness of their birth and the poverty of their upbringing and describe themselves with virtuous rage as barefoot boys. On Isabella, where we had the genuine article in abundance, this was a common term of schoolboy abuse; and I was embarrassed on behalf of these great men.' During his seedy, promiscuous London student's life at a college off the Aldwych he plays 'the dandy, the extravagant colonial, indifferent to scholarship', a part in keeping with his schoolboy rôle of brilliant idler at Isabella Imperial. Even on his return to Isabella, now married to a gritty North London undergraduate from the college, where he makes a fortune out of land deals, he does so with an indifferent detachment. 'I did not feel

responsible for what had befallen me; I always felt separate from
what I did.' Nor was he separate only from what he *did*. The society
of Isabella was quickened by one organic and binding relationship,
a relationship which was also an appalling violation. It was that—or
rather the modern version and relic of it—between masters and
slaves. From the mutual and complete comprehension of these
Singh was by origin and nature excluded. So that at the very centre
of this world he feels himself to be no more than a picturesque
Asiatic born for other landscapes.

But which? Ideal landscapes like other ideals glimmer in his
imagination, though when approached they pall and disappoint.

> How right our Aryan ancestors were to create gods. We seek sex,
> and are left with two private bodies on a stained bed. The larger erotic
> dream, the god, has eluded us. It is so whenever, moving out of our-
> selves, we look for extensions of ourselves. It is with cities as it is with
> sex. We seek the physical city and find only a conglomeration of
> private cells. In the city as nowhere else we are reminded that we are
> individuals, units. Yet the idea of the city remains; it is the god of the
> city that we pursue, in vain.

The god of the city is the image of an order which this classically
minded man—Brahmin by inheritance, Greek in sympathy and
Roman in his scholarly interests—is desperately conscious he lacks.
'To be born on an island like Isabella, an obscure New World
transplantation, second-hand and barbarous, was to be born to
disorder.' His family offered no locus for the god, split as it was in
his early years between his father's weakness and failure and his
mother's vaguely wealthy vulgar connections; and in later years
between the grossness of great wealth—of possessions, women,
drink, swimming-pools—and the hysteria represented by his
father's sudden assumption of a crazed Messianic rôle as the leader
of the deprived, a movement which was no more than 'a gesture of
mere protest, a statement of despair without a philosophy or a
cause'.

The achievement of order through the pursuit of political power
is the theme of the middle or active part of his life which he later
calls a parenthesis. This part of the novel communicates with great
strength and depth a sense of outward participation and inward

absence; or to put it as it appears to Singh, a sense of personal reality and public illusion. On the face of it Singh is perfectly prepared for a political career. Elegant, wealthy and cultivated, he is an admirable partner for his schoolboy friend Browne, the Negro folk-leader. But he lacks 'the frenzy, the necessary hurt' which alone makes politics real. They become for him a set of dream-like motions performed by an intruder into a society in which people were linked by no internal connection, except the one, slavery, from which he is excluded. His account of the growth of Browne's political movement is both aromatic and analytical, a genuine novelist's blend of diagnosis and evocation. There is the insensible, almost innocent transformation from the sincere artificiality of the politician on the make to the artificial sincerity of the minister in power. What was happening in Isabella was happening tumultu- ously in twenty different colonies and territories. Singh sees it not as the pace of post-war political change, neither the pace of creation nor destruction, but the pace of chaos on which strict limits had been imposed. Their movement was left-wing, socialist. It stood for the dignity of the working man and of the island. But it was a matter of feeling rather than doctrine, of borrowed phrases and escape from thought. And what it offered above all was drama—a sense of an explosion of life and the composition of a pattern of justice. The marks of success increased: the public meetings, the tours of dusty country roads, the lengthening reports of speeches, the policemen in heavy serge shorts becoming less aggressive and more protecting, the atmosphere of dedication and mutual loyalty. There was also the vanity of those who believed they had the power to regulate what they had created, together with wonder at the suddenly realised concept of the people who responded and could be manipulated. The speeches became more brilliant and more dishonest, the success more dazzling, the sense of inevitable histori- cal process more certain and finally, election night—the sobering moment of triumph, when play-acting turns out to be serious. And then the anxious concern with legality and ritual to consecrate power, and the realisation that power needed a more solid base than applause and the smell of the people's sweat. Finally there was the manœuvring, corrupt or passionate, to hang on to this airy

F

gift which might at any moment be withdrawn. But in Singh, underneath the public dandy, underneath the political mover and organiser there was only a negation. The one prize of politics for him was that he had helped to bring drama to the island. 'Drama, however much we fear it, sharpens our perception of the world, gives us some sense of ourselves, makes us actors, gives point and sometimes glory to each day. It alters a drab landscape.' When the drama failed the landscape returned to its drabness and the images of disorder to his imagination.

> My sense of drama failed. This to me was the true loss. For four years drama had supported me; now, abruptly, drama failed. It was a private loss; thoughts of irresponsibility or duty dwindled, became absurd. I struggled to keep drama alive, for its replacement was despair: the vision of a boy walking on an endless, desolate beach, between vegetation living, rotting, collapsed, and a mindless, living sea.

The final phase of Singh's career is one of withdrawal into privacy and anonymity. This freeing oneself from events and attachments is surely part of that classical Indian tradition one can't help harking back to in thinking about Naipaul himself. In spite of his explicit and wholesale rejection of India, his work, like Joyce's, is saturated by what he, as a person, revolts from. Singh's detachment gives him the satisfaction, he says, of fulfilling 'the fourfold division of life prescribed by our Aryan ancestors. I have been student, householder, and man of affairs, recluse.' It gives him too a negative peace: 'I no longer yearn for ideal landscapes and no longer wish to know the god of the city'. Singh's life had been spent in an attempt to bring under the gods the different areas of his experience. Politics had been the effort to impose order upon a society in disarray, just as his marriage had been an effort to bring discipline to his shabby, promiscuous, emotional life, and the Roman house he built in Isabella, with a swimming-pool instead of an *impluvium*, an attempt to impose a pattern upon the physical chaos of the place. In every case the material had been impatient of, and finally made fraudulent by, the discipline put upon it. The essential struggle of Singh—and isn't it also the central human endeavour?—had been one in which he had attempted to discover instruments of mediation between his private self and the world outside, or in which he had attempted to make the enlargement of himself which was his experience more truly coherent with his nature. He had always failed.

On every occasion, that is, but one: the bleak aftermath of Singh's public life, in the empty context of a suburban hotel, provides him, in the composition of his memoirs, with the chance to discover an instrument of mediation between self and experience which is both appropriate and effective. The contemplation of memory ceases to be merely passive or lapsing and becomes an active management of experience. '. . . this became my aim: from the central fact of this setting, my presence in this city which I have known as student, politician and now as refugee-immigrant, to impose order on my own history. . .' It is explicitly his *own* history now, it should be noted; no longer that of the external world. The recording of his life becomes an extension of his life. Here, as in the Indian ambivalence I have mentioned, we seem to find again the touch of Naipaul the writer as well as the presence of Singh the character. 'So writing for all its initial distortion, clarifies, and even becomes a process of life.' Not that the discovery of the discipline of art disturbs the logic—no, that is too harsh a word—the coherence of the wavering, complex character which is in the end offered to us by the novel. I say 'offered to us', but I mean, painfully, honestly, submitted to us. More than once in the book Singh is struck by the way that personality is created by the vision of others: it seems to be no more than the answer in action to questions and clues proffered by others. But at the conclusion of his career he sees character as having a kind of intrinsic coherence—not the kind he expected, certainly, but a sort of pattern flowing from an inner initiative—which makes him question whether personality *is* merely manufactured by the vision of others. 'I begin to question this, I doubt whether any action, above a certain level, is ever wholly arbitrary or whimsical or dishonest . . . personality hangs together. It is one and indivisible.' This statement applies, I believe, to the character of Singh himself that we finally grasp in the work.

Singh's character becomes one and organic because of the strict honesty, painfully achieved and continually renovated, which controls the relationship between his self and his experience, or because self in him is gradually educated to be accessible to what is authentically his own experience. And this is also true, I believe, of the literary character of Naipaul himself, which has matured to the point where it hangs together and is one and indivisible, where it manifests, as it were, one soul in every part of the body. The narrative technique of *The Mimic Men* is dissolving and non-linear, in correspondence with the starts and swerves of the recovering memory itself. As the reader traces the folded themes of this intricate novel, he is conscious of a constellation of capacities, serious, witty, analytical, evocative and creatively intelligent, unified by the intention to bring into definition, or rather into that degree of it which is possible and appropriate, exact, unmisted actuality together with its trail of vaguer, deeper implication. Not, naturally, that even this considerable equipment, employed with disciplined honesty and rigorous clarity, is equally effective throughout the novel. Sometimes the clarity thickens, the discipline flags. There remains, for example, in Ralph Singh himself a certain acquiescence or passivity at key junctures in his personal or political life which leaves him just a shade too enigmatically impermeable. And the analysis of the character of Browne, the political leader, gives insufficient warrant for the force attributed to him in action. The women in the book, with the exception of the wife, though they are not perfunctory, are seldom treated with Naipaul's characteristic tense energy.

But in so many things in *The Mimic Men* we see an independent and fastidious talent fully engaged and brilliantly successful: in the treatment of the second-hand violated colonial and post-colonial society; in the understanding of the psychology of the sensitive young, appalled by the sight others have of their secret life; in the rendering of political and social ideas, not as untethered formulations but living activities; in the evocation of place and physical context—the London light, the cocoa valleys, houses, weather, hotels—all, we often feel, so much more constant, so much more faithful to themselves than devious, impotently treacherous man; in the general composition and suppleness of tone and the scope of concretely realised experience; and above all in the penetration and vitality with which he develops the novel's central, constitutive theme—one of profound human meaning—an exploration of the ways in which the conscious individual in a given society establishes modes of mediation between himself and his experience.

The Mimic Men reveals the features of a talent of great scope and perhaps of even more promise since it is endowed with what is perhaps the most significant artistic quality of all, the gift of growth.

I PATRICK WHITE

PATRICK WHITE is so different a writer, or so much himself as a writer, that he requires of any reader, and perhaps particularly of the British reader, an unusual steadiness of application. Genuine and stubborn difficulties have to be faced before the reader is at home in a fiction in which the idiom is often opaque and the narrative conducted through choking thickets of imagery. As well as the perplexities provoked by the manner there are those provided by the character of the time and space in which most of Patrick White's work is located. It is not the more extended past, the nineteenth century as in *Voss* which is hard for the reader to grasp but, oddly, the nearer past—say from 1914 to 1939—the period from which so many of White's characters take their habits and assumptions. The sensibility of that time, possibly because of its relative nearness, because it is something we ourselves have shed, seems almost totally gone and bafflingly hard for a contemporary British reader to grasp with spontaneous understanding. Then there is the mystery of Australian space, that beautiful and positive emptiness, which envelops the community and overwhelms the individual. Difficulties of access, however, in the long run diminish, even if they never disappear; and certainly they come to seem less important against the reader's increasing conviction that he is in the presence of a true creative power. It is a power which derives its strength from inner resources. It is free of 'cleverness' and remarkably unaffected by fashion. It has great ease and flow—not facility—of conception, a kind of creative insouciance, which finds subjects and themes both urgent and permanent, lying waiting to be exposed in situations of the seediest simplicity and among characters of quite humdrum mediocrity.

A miniature of that power is displayed in *Down at the Dump*, one of eleven short stories published in *The Burnt Ones* in 1964. The scope of these stories is naturally more confined than in the novels,

but the shape and proportions are the same. There is a similar
sense of the depth of human nature and the same strikingly
individual sensibility, giving off a mixed odour of sweat and
spirituality. The people in *Down at the Dump* are drab, the events
few and ordinary, the context sleazy and down-at-heel, the whole
air wretched and deprived, and yet from these unpromising constituents Patrick White constructs a celebration of human possibility which is at once lyrical and quite unsentimental. White has an
eye which is gluttonous for detail. Each passage is firm from the
presence of discriminated actuality. But all the solid objective
existence, convincing in surface, sure in implication, is submissive
to the initiative of the writer. It is as much the result of reflection as
observation, and it is composed of detail which is both authentic
in its own right and quick at every point with the highly individual
quality of the author's mind. This is particularly evident in the
pace with which details follow one another. They tumble out with
unforced vivacity, products of an endless energy. And they exhibit
the peculiar violence of White's imagination which is capable of
informing the mildest symptom of character or the most delicate
indication of place with a strange intensity. Perhaps this intensity
is the effect of a Manichaean habit of sensibility which throws
everything, moral situations, place, character, age, the whole of
his subject-matter into a powerful system of polarities and anti-
nomies.

Growth from a cell or centre, an organic 'biographical' line of
movement—rather than plot or a more formal arrangement—is
the favoured kind of progression in White's fiction. Discipline as
a self-created order, and love, even when it manifests itself as sexual
feeling, as a form of charity and tenderness, are the positives offered
—embodied rather—and the grounds of hope in White's most
achieved work. It shows a powerful self-confidence in a novelist of
this age to take so unabashed a stand on a morality as traditional as
this. White's is a profoundly moral art but its vitality comes from
an attitude to morality different from that prevalent in most contemporary novelists. The modern writer, when he does not wish
to reject, wants to advance and refine accepted morality. He is in a
strict sense progressive. But Patrick White's disposition and method

are to go back, to investigate, or rather since he is not at all a lucid
analyst, to uncover the sources of morality. He is drawn to the
depths and wells of human nature. This is an aim at once simpler
and more difficult than most writers now propose to themselves.
White's fascination with the sources—or at least always with the
level of significance below the level that appears—makes him, in
this respect, a decidedly traditional, almost a classical, writer.

The classical effect, or the sense the reader has of an art conducted
according to traditional categories, is confirmed by the universal
and humane forms morality assumes in Patrick White's work. He
adds to this effect, however, a peculiarly intense and personal vision
of a morality which has at its heart a religious quality, religious in
the sense of something accepted not constructed, something present
not invented. Morality exists on the plane of action. It is a matter of
things done or undone, of intentions realised or thwarted or for-
gotten, of act and realisation. But it depends on, and it is only alive
when it issues from, a quality of being, or something comparable to
what a religious person might call a state of grace.

At least this observation will bring home to the reader the range
of Patrick White's sensibility. It springs from a pure sense of
existence, which—in the short story I have referred to—stretches
in its sympathy from the dense and dirty embodiments of existence
in the haphazard gear of the rubbish dump through every kind and
modulation of life up to a level of experience which is spiritual in its
candour and fineness. I have called Patrick White a traditional artist.
But this is not to declare that in discriminating grades of existence
he freezes them into any falsely static posture. He is not in that
sense a hierarchical writer. On the contrary there is a constant
touching of different worlds. a Lawrentian sort of mobility and
flow. A point of contrast becomes a point of connection. The
rubbish dump in *Down at the Dump* runs into the cemetery. The
voice of goodness from the grave calls out to the devious town
councillor. It is among the heaving rubbish of the dump that the
young lovers make their first tender enquiries of one another. The
mystery of existence, the mystery of self, the mutuality of experience and self—this 'metaphysical' theme, no more than hinted at
here—rolls like a profound current all through Patrick White's

work. This depth of preoccupation is the animating presence which quickens the multiplying details and orders the vast range of material (but also, and not infrequently, which clouds the clues the artist offers to what he is about with too large and unmanageable a significance).

Just as *Down at the Dump*, simple and brief as it is, involves in undertone and suggestion Patrick White's preoccupation with being, so too it is constantly in touch, at least in hint and intimation, with the other sustaining theme of his fiction—the exploration of self. His precise interest in this short story is one that a distinction of Coleridge lights up: '. . . self—i.e. the image or complex cycle of imagination . . . which is the perpetual representative of our Individuum . . .'.[1] Patrick White is concerned in miniature here, *in extenso* in the novels, with the relations between individuality and the self.

I turn at once to the novels since neither White's poetry (a juvenile volume *The Ploughman and other Poems*, 1935) nor his play (*Return to Abyssinia*, 1946) is at all comparable with his fiction. And among the novels I shall begin with *The Aunt's Story*, 1948—the history of 'this thing a spinster which, at best, becomes that institution an aunt'. His two early novels *The Living and the Dead*, 1941, and *Happy Valley*, 1939, seem to me to be decidedly apprentice work. If they have any interest now it is historical not intrinsic. *The Aunt's Story* begins with the inescapable air of authority and assurance of a writer who has arrived. He has a distinctive manner, a personal idiom, a sense of purpose and pattern, confidence in his theme. Even the first page will, I believe, be found to justify these claims, and perhaps I could quote it here.

But old Mrs Goodman did die at last.

Theodora went into the room where the coffin lay. She moved one hairbrush three inches to the left, and smoothed the antimacassar on a little Empire prie-dieu that her mother had brought from Europe. She did all this with some surprise, as if divorced from her own hands, as if they were related to the objects beneath them only in the way that two flies, blowing and blundering in space, are related to a china and mahogany world. It was all very surprising, the accomplished as opposed to the contemplated fact. It had altered the silence of the

[1] *Inquiring Spirit*, ed. K. Coburn, p. 68

house. It had altered the room. This was no longer the bedroom of her mother. It was a waiting room, which housed the shiny box that contained a waxwork.

Theodora had told them to close the box before the arrival of Fanny and Frank, who were not expected till the afternoon. So the box was closed, even at the expense of what Fanny would say. She would talk about Last Glimpses, and cry. She had not lived with Mrs Goodman in her latter years. From her own house she wrote and spoke of Dear Mother, making her an idea, just as people will talk of Democracy or Religion, at a moral distance. But Theodora was the spinster. She had lived with her mother, and helped her into her clothes. She came when the voice called.

At moments she still heard this in the relinquished room. Her own name spilt stiff and hollow out of the dusty horn of an old phonograph, into the breathless house. So that her mouth trembled, and her hand, rigid as protesting wood, on the coffin's yellow lid.

Here in a single page as in a moment of conception, the nature of the novel is predestined, its frame set up, its area mapped, its *personae* admitted, its development projected, even its method hinted at. The first word, that wrong-footed 'But' (one of Patrick White's more successful uses of an imaginatively dislocated syntax), is a pivot with all the weight on one side. It establishes something of the awkward tension which preceded Mrs Goodman's death. Theodora, moving the hairbrush, smoothing the antimacassar, is shown at the moment of her entrance with the significant symptom of dissociation—'with some surprise, as if divorced from her own hands'. At once too, the imagery which is to be the sustained mode of narration appears. Her hands 'are related to the objects beneath them only in the way that two flies, blowing and blundering in space, are related to a china and mahogany world'. The flies meaninglessly crashing into the china and mahogany world, the mind wildly careering into the cool order of sanity: this is the kind of balance proposed at the very beginning. The ritual of Theodora waiting for her sister Fanny and her family to join in the mourning, the Empire prie-dieu, the mother from Europe, and all that is involved in 'the china and mahogany', point back precisely to her well-bred—well-bred but somehow nervously attenuated—background. Fanny, extrovert, weeping, selfish and so clearly different from the inwardly focussing Theodora makes Theodora seem all the more remote, just as Fanny who is able to soften any painful experience into a vague abstraction, turning the diseased woman into her Dear Mother, makes us feel how utterly exposed Theodora is to what is concretely there—what is there being almost certainly an occasion for suffering.

In a few lines then, a situation is presented, a character conceived, possibilities of development are foreshadowed, a method of exploration held up: and all done with an art which is generous and full but not—at least not here—extravagant. More than this. *The Aunt's Story* is not the history but the rendering in terms of art of the process of mental collapse, and one is conscious from the first, in the tone, in the nuance of word and image, of some disturbing irregularity in the substance of Theodora's experience. Its sound rustles in the 'surprising' friction she finds between the accomplished and the contemplated fact, in her excessively heightened sensitivity to the objects around, in the strange distancing of subject and object, in the sense of menace and trap offered by the physical things—in the room, in the shiny box, in the imagined summoning voice from the dusty phonograph. In the last sentence there is almost a complete reversal of normality in which feeling and subjectivity are attributed to the thing, the protesting wood of the coffin itself, and passivity and the status of object to Theodora, the person.

But the story of mental decay, the fiction which constitutes the material of the novel, is itself a means in the development of a profound and powerful theme, which will be an ordering and clarifying force in the novel and the current managing the drift of event and detail. Fundamentally it is a theme of the same sort as that in *Down at the Dump* which is why I began with that story. It has to do with the nature of the self and more particularly with the release from the self and even indeed with the obliteration of the self. In the story release was achieved I pointed out by giving or accepting; in the novel release, or rather a total obliteration of the self, is achieved through *becoming*. It is this complication, this further resonance, which turns what might have been a clinically exact account of mental disintegration into a richer and more humanly significant composition.

Before I attempt to elucidate the notion of *becoming* which works through this novel, perhaps I could say a word about the shape of it. *The Aunt's Story* falls into three divisions which are temporarily successive as phases in a development but markedly distinct in nature and treatment. The first, which begins and ends formally with the death of Mrs Goodman, is a reconstruction of Theodora's life up to middle age: 'A woman of fifty, or not yet, whose eyes burn still, under the black hair, which is still frizzed above the forehead in little puffs'. The second pictures a mind burning fiercely and melting away the restraints and disciplines of distinction, and particularly the distinction of I and otherness. The third is a concluding phase of contemplation and detachment in which Patrick White allows himself a degree of explicitness not permitted elsewhere in the novel.

Each of us has that in his nature which is incommunicably unique, some small knot which is obscurely impervious and resistant. In Theodora this element is diffused much more generally throughout her nature. She was brought up at Meroë, an old plain 'honest' house, surrounded by ancient trees and hills of black rock which had for all its beauty something marred and unpromising about it. Things were always tumbling down; it was called 'Rack-an'-Ruin Hollow' by the neighbours. The prevailing note of her childhood was awkwardness. She was awkward in her relations with the family, particularly with her self-centred mother and with the pretty 'normal' sister, Fanny. To her mother she was odd and difficult. She could not stitch a sampler neatly or play the piano brightly like Fanny. She had a kind of inarticulate intimacy with her father, in which there were moments of exaltation. But she was puzzled and hurt by his moody incomprehension. 'She was oppressed by a weight of sadness, that nobody would lift, because nobody would ever know that she was shouldering it. Least of all Father, who was thick, and mysterious as a tree, but also hollow. . . .' She was thin and sallow as a little girl, strange to her confident family, peculiar to the strong and wholesome servants. Away at school she began to get used to contempt and to distance. 'The long dark slommacky thing in the striped dress? That is Theodora Goodman.' There was no natural flow of communication between her and others. People seemed to her to group themselves into the arbitrary positions of statues. 'But sometimes a silence or a presence seemed to emanate a will of its own, and this was what she resented. The militant will in an intake of breath. Then she could hate the cut of a nostril, the droop of an eyelid above an eye.'

Negation in Theodora's life was almost a routine. But there were in it moments, if not of illumination, at least of escape from the prison of self. Even to call them moments of release may be too strong. Perhaps they were moments trembling on the brink of release. They occurred in her relationships with the very young, with Lou her niece at the beginning of the novel, with the boy Zack at the end of her life, with certain persons whom she met only glancingly and whose contact with her seemed exempt from the painful, spiny conditions of ordinary life, like an odd, casual tramp who was given his dinner on the verandah, or the enigmatic Syrian pedlar.

> Once when the Syrian left, Theodora went with him some of the way. In the white-lit winter evening her legs grew longer with the strides she took. Her hair flew. She had increased. She walked outside a distinct world, on which the grass quivered with a clear moisture, and the earth rang. In this state, in which rocks might at any moment open, or words convey meaning, she stood and watched the Syrian go. His silence slipped past. The hills settled into shapelessness. She was left with the trembling of her knees.

Sometimes the moments occurred in an activity, when she shot with her father, listened to music, or when she touched the children. 'Since her mother's death she could not say with conviction: I am I. But the touch of hands restores the lost identity. The children would ratify her freedom.'

But mostly humanity failed either as the occasion or the means of release, even those who seemed most apt, like her friend Violet Adams at school, or the rich, urbane Huntly Clarkson with whom she almost had a kind of muted love-affair in later life. Things helped more: things like the filigree ball which filled with subtle fire when the children rolled its distorted hollow sphere across the drawing-room carpet. Or other things, for example the rose. 'Because she felt her own awkwardness. After she had hidden in the garden, she looked at her hands, that were never moved to do the things that Fanny did. But her hands touched, her hands became the shape of rose, she knew it in its utmost intimacy.' Throughout this phase of the novel the reader is conscious of how vividly present things are to Theodora—or perhaps better how vividly present she feels herself to be to them; and simultaneously aware of the powerful poetic sense of concrete existence with which the novelist conveys not only the outline but the bulk and grain and energy of things. Patrick White in this part of the work is the poet of the physics of things. But the intrinsic energy of the things which he communicates is a physical energy. Things do not, like persons, protect themselves by keeping others at 'a moral distance'. They are open. They lie there, full of a secret life and ready to be entered into. 'I shall never overcome the distances, felt Theodora, and because she was like this, she felt consolation in the deal mirror in the room for four.' But with things she could overcome the distances. She could become the stick drifting in the water or the hawk tearing its prey.

Once the hawk flew down, straight and sure, out of the skeleton forest. He was a little hawk, with a reddish-golden eye, that looked at her as he stood on the sheep's carcass, and coldly tore through the dead wool. The little hawk tore and paused, tore and paused. Soon he would tear through the wool and the maggots and reach the offal in the belly of the sheep. Theodora looked at the hawk. She could not judge his act, because her eye had contracted, it was reddish-gold, and her curved face cut the wind. Death, said Father, lasts for a long time. Like the bones of the sheep that would lie, and dry, and whiten, and clatter under horses. But the act of the hawk, which she watched, hawk-like, was a moment of shrill beauty that rose above the endlessness of bones. The red eye spoke of worlds that were brief and fierce.

What we see in such episodes is *becoming*, that kind of knowledge which Coleridge described as 'the coincidence of an object and subject'. The human mind craves to know, and the closer its knowledge is to being, the better. Knowledge in this sense for Theodora was impossible in respect of other people, even those in her own family and household. But the possibility of union with things was endless and neither she nor they ever stood back from it. This view of Theodora is fixed in the snapshot—a curiously static moment between the mobility of the first and the tumult of the second part of the novel. Theodora is sitting with her niece Lou 'her own arm round the child . . . a formal gesture of protection, scarcely flesh', and the child speaks to her:

> 'I wish . . .,' said Lou.
> 'What do you wish?'
> 'I wish I was you, Aunt Theo.'
> And now Theodora asked why.
> 'Because you know things,' said Lou.
> 'Such as?'
> 'Oh,' she said, 'things.'

'Things' continue to figure in the second part of the novel, *Jardin Exotique*, still pressing on the reader their dense and positive existence. But they are solid splinters in a melting universe. They are objects which do not carry with them any strong suggestion of an objective world. Here is a passage in which objects, sharply individualised and palpably present float in a vaguely moving medium. The system of relations which might connect them to a world that includes more than Theodora is abolished.

> It was perhaps *plus modeste*, but recognisable, from the objects she had put there in the morning as a safeguard, the darning egg, the dictionary, and the superfluous leather writing case. Hearing the fainter slippers of Henriette, listening to her own silence form in the small room, Theodora loved her sponge. There are moments, she admitted, when it is necessary to return to the boxes for which we were made. And now the small room was a box with paper roses pasted on the sides. Theodora walked across the carpet, frayed by similar feet in modest circumstances, with arches that have a tendency to fall, in shoes that soon must be mended. She took off a garnet ring which had been her mother's but which had changed its expression, like most inherited things. She put it on the dressing table, inside the handker-chief sachet, which was the garnet's place. I am preparing for bed, she saw. But in performing this act for the first time, she knew she did not really control her bones, and that the curtain of her flesh must blow, like walls which are no longer walls. She took off one shoe, with its steel buckle and its rather long vamp. Standing with it in her hand, her identity became uncertain. She looked with sadness at the little hitherto safe microcosm of the darning egg and waited for the rose wall to fall.

Although the narrative is packed with things and persons (but persons who have become a kind of thing, a projection of Theodora's past, of her reading, of her fantasy and of her desperation), the action retreats more and more into a subjective, and finally a solipsistic world. Everything is consumed in Theodora's private passion to know, or rather to become, since that is the only kind of knowledge she is now capable of, knowing in any other sense implying an inadmissible detachment in Theodora and an intolerable independence of existence on the part of another. I may have suggested that this is the result of a concentrated activity on Theodora's part, but in fact, just as the content is more like a dream, so the state is more like a sleep, a letting go.

> 'You must relax, Theodora Goodman,' said Mrs Rapallo. 'You must relax and float. You will find that figures will evolve, squares, chains, and galops. Sometimes you will place one hand on your hip, sometimes you will feel the hand of your partner in the small of the back. But believe me, the essential is to relax.'

At the end of this delirium sequence Theodora has lost even the minimum grip on the outside world. There is an absolute coherence in the whole and in the parts, but it is the logic of the utter loneliness of madness. Theodora herself at the end has become only one more object among a mass of other objects. She has at last escaped from the prison of self which is now simply an empty cell.

At the start of the concluding phase of the novel, Theodora is discovered drifting passively across the Middle West of the United States. The tone is quiet and withdrawn and a welcome change after the frantic and sometimes strident agitation of the too long and rather repetitive scenes of Theodora's mental disintegration. This part of the novel serves three purposes. First, it completes the simple narrative line which had made her leave Australia to travel after her mother's death and which now sends her on her way home after her breakdown in Europe. This final part links up in sobriety of manner with the first part of the novel and offers a realistic setting for the hallucinatory experiences of the middle section. Secondly, it completes the reconstruction of mental collapse which is the psychological material or theme of the novel. Theodora is now simply something prolonged by various external bits of circumstantial evidence like sheaves of railroad and steamship tickets. Her relationships with others are flat and external except, perhaps, for a fleeting moment of 'rare alliance' with someone constitutionally like herself, her father in childhood and the little boy Zak when she is forty-five. There is a continuity between her child's awkwardness with others and her adult's immeasurable remoteness.

Thirdly, the novel's conclusion suggests not a solution but a partial resolution of the spiritual experience which is central to it. Suffering or the acceptance of suffering pares away everything gratuitous and merely selfish and leaves the sufferer with a special quality of wholeness and unity, like the fundamental unity of bone. Such lucid and simple wholeness is necessary for those who will come to possess a sense of the purity of being. Theodora has now become capable even of hearing 'the difference between doing and being. The corn could not help itself. It was. The man scrabbled on the surface of life. . . .' Theodora, disordered and insane, is utterly herself. Through the abolition of her personal identity, or perhaps of her personality as it is understood by others, she has come 'a little closer to humility, to anonymity, to pureness of being'. Or to use the Coleridgean terminology with which I began, every image which the personality might assume has been cancelled and she is left simply with her totally unalloyed individuality which is something deeper and more valuable even than reason itself. 'In the house above the disintegrating world, light and silence ate into the hard, resisting barriers of reason, hinting at some ultimate moment of clear vision.'

This last quotation is perhaps a clue to an explanation of one's final feeling of dissatisfaction with the novel. Because *The Aunt's Story* is a novel, not a spiritual treatise, and one cannot but suspect that the author himself is looking for some 'ultimate moment of clear vision'. It is a novel, I think, which is a failure when judged as a novel and by the highest standards—standards which Patrick White's own work make appropriate. It is certainly a serious and powerful production, it takes in a great span of experience, it has the most perceptive insight into neurotic psychology, and it at no

G

point backs away from a difficult, important theme. Its deficiency lies in the too prominent presence of the author and in the excessively positive interference by him with the natural significance of his material. He himself is too personally engaged in racking his fiction into the shape of spiritual truth. His hand is too clearly evident on too many occasions forcefully conferring upon character and scenery the status of symbolism. These weaknesses are more serious I think than an occasional clumsiness of diction or an uncontrolled rioting of imagery or unimaginative and ugly uses of syntax. *The Aunt's Story* is a brilliant and daring novel but one in which the art is too submissive to the author's will.

The sense the reader has—the intermittent sense I hasten to emphasise—of the author manipulating the material from the outside in the interest of an idea—is wholly absent from the novel I turn to now, *The Tree of Man*. Here the intention is sunk in the art, the will quite submerged in the fiction. The author's design is gradually composed by what is latent in the situation, and it appears in the end with the flawed clarity and stumbling incoherence which belong to the pattern of a living art, and which are ultimately much more powerfully convincing than any application of an *a priori* design. There is a biblical simplicity and universality about the situation in which a man establishes not simply a home but a place, and constructs it out of the wilderness; in the way in which he first appears as the unnamed man, an anonymous representative of a future race; in the way he takes a wife and founds a family; in the way in which what is wrong in the original pair works itself out in the corruption of the children. What is wrong lies, generally, in the connection of husband and wife; it is the product—must we not say the inevitable product?—of any real relationship. But if it is to be located more precisely, it lies in the wife. The husband is a good man, with the special dignity of those whose life and work are part of a more inclusive natural rhythm. He is a man in whom sturdy, ordinary decency is raised to the level of virtue. He is a peasant, but a peasant in a land which had never known, never been subjected to, an aristocracy. The wife, on the other hand, is a sharper, neater intelligence and has a much higher degree of self-limited interest. She is the wiry, nervy cockney Eve, quick, strong and narrow. The man's is a concrete goodness, the expression of a style of character and life. His whole being is manifest in every action and relationship. The wife is more reflectively self-conscious; there is a greater discrepancy between herself and her conduct, and that, given her upbringing and background, implies, when she is not pressed by the urgencies of life, a disposition towards dreamy romanticism, a characteristic which brings about her lapse into sensuality and infidelity. Concupiscence in her case is as much a matter of discontent as of passion. It is provoked by the romanticism which is part of her nature and which contrasts with the strong and humble realism of her husband. *Her* romanticism becomes enfeebled in her daughter into the exquisitely ugly cult of Australian gentility. *His* realism becomes in his son, where it is uninformed by the kind of sanity which puts one into one's place in a larger, more permanent scheme, the realism of power, which in the boy's situation means petty crime and the more sordid kinds of delinquency.

There is a certain thickness of texture in the manner and idiom of *The Tree of Man* which contrasts with the intensity and neurotic fineness of *The Aunt's Story* but which is in keeping with the centrality and solidity of the common human experience it deals with. It comes out in the feeling for the land which is the sustaining support for everything that takes place throughout. It is a double feeling both for the creative force in the earth and for the homely forms and shapes that man can make it assume. Here is a passage from the beginning of the novel in which Stan Parker, faced with the power of the bush, turns upon it in a kind of loving war to make it expressive of human nature.

So they reached their destination, and ate, and slept, and in the morning of frost, beside the ashes of a fire, were faced with the prospect of leading some kind of life. Of making that life purposeful. Of opposing silence and rock and tree. It does not seem possible in a world of frost.

That world was still imprisoned, just as the intentions were, coldly, sulkily. Grass that is sometimes flesh beneath the teeth would have splintered now, sharp as glass. Rocks that might have contracted physically had grown in hostility during the night. The air drank at the warm bodies of birds to swallow them in flight.

But no bird fell.

Instead, they continued to chafe the silence. And the young man, after sighing a good deal, and turning in his bags, in which the crumbs of chaff still tickled and a flea or two kept him company, flung himself into the morning. There was no other way.

But to scrape the ash, but to hew with the whole body as well as axe the gray hunks of fallen wood, but to stamp the blood to life, and the ground thawing took life too, the long ribbons of grass bending and moving as the sun released, the rocks settling into peace of recovered sun, the glug and tumble of water slowly at first, heard again somewhere, the sun climbing ever, with towards it smoke thin but certain that the man made.

The wife too has a feeling for the natural force of the land, but in her it is shown in a preference for its products, for the cows and cabbages and the house. Her husband submitted himself wholly to the land. He accepted the omnipotence of the Australian distance but she hated the wind and the distance and the road and had for them a sort of jealousy as things she could never possess. The husband responded always to presence and actuality, but the wife could sympathise only with forms she could understand and control. She was also conscious of and frayed by what was absent. The love of the two was from the beginning flawed by this tension between them, an imperfection which makes it all the more convincingly human. In a way the wife longs for the kind of expression the man is incapable of.

So instead of telling her smooth things, that were not his anyway, he took her hand over the remnants of their sorry meal. The bones of his hand were his, and could better express the poem that was locked inside him and that would never otherwise be released. His hand knew stone and iron, and was familiar with the least shudder of wood. It trembled a little, however, learning the language of flesh.

The two passages I have quoted—especially perhaps the second, and in that particularly the phrase, 'the language of flesh'—confirm the suggestion I made before that *The Tree of Man* displays a palpable thickness of texture. It is evident primarily in the physical, substantial quality of a language which is highly appropriate in a novel intent on exploring the intimations of ordinary life, and of life, in particular, which sucks its vitality from the soil. ('Intima-

tions', of course, include not only the steady staple, not only the
corporeal, the grubby and the wretched in life, but also the poetic
and mysterious which the novel testifies at every point is deeply
involved in the tritest human existence.) This thickness of texture,
then, shows itself at the centre of the novel in the solidity with which
the characters and experience of Stan and Amy are constructed—a
sculpting of resistant material—not only in their growth from
ignorance to experience but also, and very beautifully, in their
ageing: in the stiffening of a knee; in the way Stan's mouth becomes
tight and a bit ironic when he recognises that uprooting a stone,
which he could once have done with a single delighted effort, now
leaves him shattered and gasping; in the transformation of motion
from silky smoothness to something brittle and chalky. But it also
shows itself in the densely peopled context, and in the almost
Dickensian prodigality with which subordinate characters and
minor movements in the novel are presented with depth and body.
A swarm of characters crowds round the protagonists, each offering
his own modification of a general human stuff or force, and together
composing a world positively writhing with reality. There is a
careless, spilling power in Patrick White's habit of putting into a
corner of his novel characters which would sustain another novelist
through several chapters: people, for example, like the innocent,
sinuous Con the Greek; or the goitred spinster Dol Quigley and
her imbecile brother Bub; or the dry solicitor Dudley Forsdyke,
Thelma's husband, who was 'so used to examining reports on
living that he had been made drunk suddenly by the smell of life
[which] came up at him down the ploughed field and down the wet
hill'; or Mrs O'Dowd, all flabby flesh and mustard-sharp speech,
whose death-scene is a superb comic achievement, sardonic,
accurate, immensely funny and quite unmocking. Here is one of
those intensely living transients, Horrie Bourke, who had be-
friended and been swindled by Stan's son Ray:

> He was a fat old man with veins in his face, brimming over with the
> injustice that had been done him, and afraid that someday, if not soon,
> even tomorrow perhaps, he would have a stroke. So that mixed up
> with the tears that he shed for the son who was not his but might have
> been, a recipient of presents as well as a giver of them, was hate for the

healthy young man, whose muscles were impressive in his singlet, who stood laughing by the dung heap in a sheen of horses, and threatened him callously with a seizure.

These characters carry the strong stamp of a tradition, the tradition, in fact, of humours as modified by Dickens, to which the acute observation of the author adds the crackle and tang of Australia. But since Patrick White's observation is enlivened by what one must call a religious respect for the quality of pure being, all his characters, even the minor ones, manifest also a nature in which there is always latent the possibility of spiritual experience, so that a dimension of life seldom present in the humours tradition itself, increases and complicates the stature of his people. The exception to these remarks is the character of Madeleine, a Christabel or rather Lady of Shalott-like figure, who becomes the focus of Amy's romanticism as she rides enigmatically round the country on a splendid horse, who when she is rescued from the great fire by Stan stirs his lust (in some way, I must confess, inexplicable to me), and who finally becomes the companion of the daughter Thelma in her well-bred round. She is the one failure in realisation in the novel, the one gratuitous and unconvincing gesture.

I have referred to one literary tradition. Another and relevant one, again influencing the shape of the novel, is the tradition of the four elements of nature. The novel begins with an assertion, reminiscent of Genesis, of the power of the land; it concludes with an affirmation of the continuity of the earth's life: 'So that in the end there were the trees. The boy walking through them with his head drooping as he increased in stature. Putting out shoots of green thought. So that, in the end, there was no end.' In between there are great set pieces (although it does an injustice to what are constituents of a living organism to think of them as tableaux or extractable scenes) on the wind, on the fire and the flood. This combination of ancient cosmology and biblical drama cannot be accidental. It concentrates in a metaphor, which of course is what it is, the author's sense of the intimacy of life and land. The scope of the whole novel is enlarged and deepened by this cosmic sense, and it is something which the reader feels wholly right in that it offers a context, both a ground and background, for the author's vision of human nature. I can best describe that vision by saying that it sees life as a redemption. The presence of human life on the land itself, so nakedly exposed at the beginning of the novel, imposes on man the limitations and imperfection which constitute a kind of unwilled fall. Suffering is a function of that fall, of that existence in time and place. Stan's life dramatises both the actuality of the fall *and* the possibilities contained in human nature itself for healing and redemption. It shows the redemptive initiative coming from within human nature itself and being set in train, not by an act of the will, but by a condition, the condition of simplicity which is the unfretful working out, within some larger but mysterious pattern, of what the individual nature is, of what the individual person signifies.

Just as *The Aunt's Story* showed how neurosis could be the means to an apprehension fuller than the conventionally 'normal' one, so *The Tree of Man* shows the capacity of decent ordinariness to be transformed into a higher order of existence altogether. It requires of course a kind of genius, the genius for *becoming* in Theodora, the genius for *staying* in Stan. There was always an intrinsic fidelity between Stan's inmost nature and each manifestation of it. This loyalty, or stubbornness, when it is complete, produces a special human perfection, intensely 'natural' and in harmony with the natural rhythm of the land and the weather and the bases of physical existence which had so much to do with producing and ripening it. Natural, certainly, in this sense, and thoroughly human but also fine and capable of development into a maturity that is truly spiritual. We see the result of this faculty for persistence at a point in the novel just before Stan's death when he sits in his old man's chair on the grass in the winter afternoon. He was shrinking all the time. He no longer wanted to speak to people. He was possessed by what he saw, or was. 'His eyes had been reduced to a rudimentary shape, through which they observed, you felt, a version of objects that was possibly true.' A young evangelist, foaming with self-indulgent revivalist fervour, wants to convert the old man from his supposed indifference to salvation, although what he sees as indifference is more truly what Henry James called 'the almost helpless detachment of the short-sighted individual soul'.[1] He tells Stan melodramatic stories of the dissolute life of drinking and womanising—even coloured womanising!—he himself had been rescued from. And if he, why not the old man?

The old man was intensely unhappy.

When the young one had finished his orgasm, he presented the open palms of his hands and told how he had knelt upon his knees, and grace descended on him.

'This can happen to you too,' he said, kneeling on one knee, and sweating at every pore.

The old man cleared his throat. 'I'm not sure whether I am intended to be saved,' he said.

The evangelist smiled with youthful incredulity. No subtleties would escape the steam roller of faith. 'You don't understand,' he said smilingly.

If you can understand, at your age, what I have been struggling with all my life, then it is a miracle, thought the old man.

He spat on the ground in front of him. He had been sitting for some time in one position, and had on his chest a heaviness of phlegm.

'I am too old,' he said colourlessly.

He was tired really. He wanted to be left alone.

'But the glories of salvation,' persisted the evangelist, whose hair went up in even waves, 'these great glories are everybody's for the asking, just by a putting out of the hand.'

The old man fidgeted. He was not saying anything. Great glories were glittering in the afternoon. He had already been a little dazzled.

'You are not stubborn, friend?'

'I would not be here if I was not stubborn,' said the old man.

'Don't you believe in God, perhaps?' asked the evangelist, who had begun to look around him and to feel the necessity for some further stimulus of confession. 'I can show you books,' he yawned.

Then the old man, who had been cornered long enough, saw, through perversity perhaps, but with his own eyes. He was illuminated.

He pointed with his stick at the gob of spittle.

'That is God,' he said.

As it lay glittering intensely and personally on the ground.

The young man frowned rather. You met all kinds.

The old man's astounding remark is not an isolated statement which could be checked or corrected or rebutted. It is an utterance

[1] *Turgenev and Tolstoy*, 1897

which includes and is the climax of a life, a life lived with stubborn integrity. What the old man sees—'a version of objects that was possibly true'—is a function of what he is, and what he is enables him to see in the great glories glittering in the afternoon, and in the gob glittering intensely and personally on the ground, that quality which they and it share with God—an incandescent quality of pure being.

This is a tremendous note to finish on. Striking a tremendous note is something Patrick White has a strong predilection for. And perhaps this is not simply a personal bias but the consequence of the position of an Australian writer, or at least of one with gifts like his. He has the use of a medium, the English language, of such resource that no reach of imagination or any conceivable theme is beyond it. Patrick White has the medium, but he also has the courage of his creative power (and this is the peculiarly Australian addition) undiminished and unthinned by any failure of nerve caused by consideration of the oppressive excellence of what others in his immediate tradition have done. He joins together the advantages of the medium and the relative absence of masters or competitors. We accept 'the tremendous note', because, as I have suggested before, the ideal has been totally enclosed in a stubby, grainy actuality. Or to adapt an idiom of Henry James,[1] Stan can be 'the striking figured symbol' he is just because he is 'a thoroughly pictured creature'. And we must add to this enclosure of the symbol within the roughness of reality, the skill and patience with which the continuity of Stan's nature is elucidated. There is a ratio of proportion between the wholly transformed old man with his vision of the glittering miracles of existence from gob to God, and the wiry stripling who with an unblemished and wholly unwarranted faith sets himself to humanise the wilderness.

Mention of the wilderness leads me naturally to *Voss* which was published in 1957. *The Tree of Man* and *Voss* represent Patrick White's different reactions to what he spoke of as his panic at the exaltation of the average.

In all directions stretched the Great Australian Emptiness, in which the mind is the least of possessions, in which the rich man is the

---

[1] *Preface* to *What Maisie Knew*

important man, in which the schoolmaster and the journalist rule what
intellectual roost there is, in which beautiful youths and girls stare at
life through blind blue eyes, in which human teeth fall like autumn
leaves, the buttocks of cars grow hourly glassier, food means cake and
steak, muscles prevail, and the march of material ugliness does not
raise a quiver from the average nerve.[1]

The Tree of Man burrows into the commonplace; *Voss* reconstructs
the extreme. Patrick White describes its origins himself:

> Afterwards I wrote *Voss*, possibly conceived during the early days
> of the Blitz, when I sat reading Eyre's *Journal* in a London bed-sitting
> room. Nourished by months spent trapesing backwards and forwards
> across the Egyptian and Cyrenaican deserts, influenced by the arch-
> megalomaniac of the day, the idea finally matured after reading con-
> temporary accounts of Leichardt's expeditions and A. H. Chisholm's
> *Strange New World* on returning to Australia.[2]

The wilderness which was to be domesticated in *The Tree of Man*
in *Voss* is to school the hero. If we use a biblical analogy, which
seems distinctly appropriate to the character of Patrick White's
work, we can say that *The Tree of Man* is his version of Genesis and
Redemption, and *Voss* his John the Baptist. (But leading to what
Christ, the reader may wonder. The answer, if there is an answer,
suggested by the novel, seems to be some intrinsic or buried Christ
in Voss himself.)

Voss is simply organised into three parts: the preparation for the
expedition, the journey in 1845 across the continent itself, and the
aftermath which consists largely of a second minor expedition to
investigate the calamity of the original exploration. The first part
is a remarkable 'composition' in its own right, which gives me the
opportunity to notice a gift of Patrick White's I have not referred
to yet, namely his sensitive historical imagination. Nineteenth-
century Sydney, an English provincial city set down on the Pacific
shore, with its cathedral, barracks and public gardens (a significant
collocation), presses its identity upon one. White is engaged with
the mercantile part of this society which lives in solid stone houses
filled with mahogany furniture, books of sermons, gazeteers and
almanacs, desks covered with red tooled leather, pieces of engraved

[1] *Australian Letters*, I, 3, 1958   [2] *Ibid*

silver, and tightly buttoned, slippery chairs. These merchants are used to fine clothes and rich food, have an almost mystical—certainly a more than economic—absorption in money, are deferential to the local gentry, and both consciously above, and genuinely under an obligation towards, their inferiors. They observe a cramped but genuine moral code and they are especially sensitive about the respectability it earns. Patrick White catches exactly the whiff of this plum-cake world of colonial gentility, strangely surrounded by mysterious gardens full of feathery bamboos, camellia bushes and scurfy native paperbarks. The people are as convincing as the setting. Massed in the middle is the strongly physical presence of the Bonner family, the complacent husband, his comfortable wife, their creamy daughter and her rubicund young officer.

> Wealthy by colonial standards, the merchant had made money in a solid business, out of Irish linens and Swiss muslins, damask, and huckaback, and flannel, green baize, and India twills. The best-quality gold leaf was used to celebrate the name of EDMUND BONNER—ENGLISH DRAPER, and ladies driving down George Street, the wives of officers and graziers, in barouche and brougham, would bow to that respectable man. Why, on several occasions, he had even been consulted in confidence, he told, by Lady G—, who was so kind as to accept a tablecloth and several pair of linen sheets.

At each end of the scale of intelligence of which the Bonners are, as it were, the norm, are murmurous reminders of different possibilities. At one end is the squat pregnant maid Rose, whose baby Laura Trevelyan will eventually adopt as her own, an elemental being, close to the animals and the instinctive organic world. At the other is Laura Trevelyan, isolated in her small circle by her cool, 'Cambridge' intelligence and taste for the things of the mind. She meets Voss at a time when she is tortured by the possibility of losing her religious faith. Voss is a totally new experience for her, alien both to her conventional connections and to her own preference for moderate rationality. He was like lightning or inspiration, and inspiration, the uncalled for, the unearned experience, is important in a novel which is to be devoted in a major way to exploring the pure and abstract will: important, that is, as another possibility or dimension in human experience. The will causes its consequences but 'inspiration descends only in flashes, to clothe circumstances; it is not stored up in a barrel, like salt herrings, to be doled out'. Voss, the extraordinary German, affects her like poetry so that she deserted when she was with him 'that rational level to which she was determined to adhere' and her thoughts became natural and passionate. The passivity of her existence flares into intensity in his presence. She appreciates him in a way that no others in her circle can but she is also still sufficiently 'rational' to understand his nature.

> 'You are so vast and ugly,' Laura Trevelyan was repeating the words; 'I can imagine some desert, with rocks, rocks of prejudice, and, yes, even hatred. You are so isolated. That is why you are fascinated by the prospect of desert places, in which you will find your own situation taken for granted, or more than that, exalted. You sometimes scatter kind words or bits of poetry to people, who soon realise the extent of their illusion. Everything is for yourself. Human emotions, when you have them, are quite flattering to you. If those emotions strike sparks from others, that also is flattering. But most flattering, I think, when you experience it, is the hatred, or even the mere irritation of weaker characters.'

Patrick White is seldom able to keep within the limit of what is strictly necessary to his design. He loves the pure creative play or flourish. And yet by the end of this first movement—not, I think, an inappropriate term—a considerable amount of the work of the novel has been completed and the rest set in train. The dowdy town and the easy country around it, against which the harshness of the desert will be measured, are clearly in the reader's mind; the decent average of the population against which the ferociously extreme nature of Voss can be tested has been established; the relationship of Voss and Laura has been initiated, a relationship which, since they never meet again, is carried on in the imagination of each and opened up to the reader by their correspondence. The members of the group accompanying Voss have been delineated with just that right degree of definition to mark them off as separate persons and yet to keep them united in a single party. Above all the preliminary work on the gigantic figure of Voss is carried firmly through.

We first see Voss—announced by the puzzled maid as 'a kind of foreign gentleman'—squirming in a social encounter with Laura, but it is rapidly borne in on the reader that his unease is not by any means a mere discomfort at unfamiliar modes of decorum. Voss is one whose powers are concentrated with ferocious intensity upon an inner life. The outer world is either a nuisance or a menace. 'All that was external to himself he mistrusted, and was happiest in silence, which is immeasurable, like distance, and the potentialities of self.' His general seediness and frayed clothes, his contempt of social niceties clothe the arrogance of an unnatural confidence. He was capable of simplicity and sincerity although it was very hard for a stranger to recognise these feelings in him. The approach of others was a threat, much more destructive to his personality than thirst or fever or physical exhaustion. The impulse of Voss's actions was not any general belief or idea but the pure shape of the will which has no content—no describable content—only force and direction. The compulsion he felt to cross the continent came from the desire to fulfil his own nature or, more correctly and more narrowly, came from the force of his will. He was placed in a situation in which the conquering of the desert might seem natural to others for reasons of economics or geography or knowledge itself, and Voss is willing to make an outward accommodation to such notions. In reality for Voss the expedition was a personal wrestling with the continent, the only opponent his pride would acknowledge as adequate. 'Deserts prefer to resist history and develop along their own lines'; they have, that is, a natural hostility to submitting to the will of man and they are therefore a proper target for Voss's colossal pride.

> 'Yes,' answered Voss, without hesitation. 'I will cross the continent from one end to the other. I have every intention to know it with my heart. Why I am pursued by this necessity, it is no more possible for me to tell than it is for you, who have made my acquaintance only before yesterday.'

In the second phase of the novel two lines of narrative are sustained. In one the expedition is conducted through more and more difficult, and finally brutal, country towards its disastrous end; in

the other the relationship of Voss and Laura is developed in a series
of meditations and (unreceived) letters. The two worlds of actuality
and possibility are kept in touch and the latter, it is suggested, offers
in the end a possibility of salvation to the former. There is a passage
at one point in the journey in which this touching of two orders of
existence is itself used as an image of the land.

> Over all this scene, which was more a shimmer than the architecture
> of landscape, palpitated extraordinary butterflies. Nothing had been
> seen yet to compare with their colours, opening and closing, opening
> and closing. Indeed, by the addition of this pair of hinges, the world
> of semblance communicated with the world of dream.

Not only in the architecture of landscape but also in the architecture of people the two worlds of semblance and dream communicate with each other.

Each member of the party obeys the logic of his own nature and
responds to the sufferings of the journey in his own way. But all the
physical horrors are subservient to the monstrous, Marlovian figure
of Voss. He is more intent and successful than any harshness of geography or disease in searching out the weaknesses of his companions.
In a situation in which life itself depends upon the naked force of
will, he is seen, terrifyingly, to concentrate in himself an essential
part of everyone else's humanity. Everyone's will is fused into
Voss's. The question posed is whether any human situation can be
just the realisation of a pure abstraction like the will. Each member
of the party clings to something else, to some other standard
supplied by a different life—the young man Frank le Mesurier to
his poetry, Judd the ex-convict to the common kindness of a
family man, Palfreyman to his science and his religion, Turner
and Angus to a protective selfishness. But all in the end are consumed by the violence of Voss's burning will. 'By some process of
chemical choice, the cavalcade had resolved itself into immutable
component parts. No one denied that Mr Voss was the first, the
burning element, that consumed obstacles, as well as indifference
in others.' The aborigines are the one form of humanity which
evades the absoluteness of Voss's control. Their existence is purely
a passage from moment to moment, hardly directed at all by the
conscious will. They drift as easily as smoke and are as responsive

to the play of the physical life about them. They cannot in fact be positively separated from it, they never take on sufficient antagonist force for Voss to meet and overcome. It is 'right', in keeping with the nature of the fiction itself, that it should be these, surviving as they do by the negation of active will, who in the horrifying end, when the party has split into two fragments, destroy Voss.

If the first narrative line has to do with the world of 'semblance' or reality, the physical progress of the expedition itself, the second has to do with the world of 'dream' and the life of the spirit; and this as it is focussed in the relationship of Voss and Laura. (Not that the Voss-Laura relationship is the sole subject-matter: there is also much sharp—and comic—social observation of the colonial scene.) The only physical substratum for the relationship is the few brief meetings of Voss and Laura before the expedition leaves. On this the imagination of each, moved by deep emotional hunger, constructs a pattern of feeling of great richness, delicacy and conviction. The fact that the relationship evolves by means of an intense and reciprocal empathy causes the reader no incredulity or discomfort because he senses an essential propriety between the nature of the experience and its poetic treatment. If a writer has the creative strength, the sincerity and the tact in realisation which Patrick White shows himself abundantly to possess, he can, and the reader accepts that he can, allow himself a considerable degree of freedom from the logic of a straight-forward representational method. The relationship of Voss and Laura, then, progresses from its simple beginning by means of a sympathetic parallelism into a 'fearful symmetry'. I use the famous phrase advisedly to suggest that blend of love, terror and harmony which the relationship achieves in the moments before Voss and Laura are finally destroyed, he by the journey, she, in resonance, by a total collapse of mind and body.

The novel concludes quietly in the third section in a muted repetition and reminiscence of the positive vision—never too firmly or abstractly formulated—generated by the substance of the novel. (Having said which I must immediately correct myself: never, except at one place, where a melodramatic analogy between Christ and Voss—the spear hanging out of his side, washing the feet of his companions, kissing their sores—is clumsily elaborated. Even the fact that this is a memory of the simple-minded Judd, the only survivor of the expedition, doesn't back it with the weight and density of realised experience.) Patrick White uses the psychology of the explorer as a metaphor of man. The explorer lives at extremes, on borders and edges; he is always pushing back the frontiers of suffering, and suffering is the universal experience of extremity uniting man. Voss is the purest example of the explorer's psychology but he is saved from unconvincing super-humanity by a grubby stain of backsliding man. There is a touch of malignancy, the cruelty of vanity, in the way he treats his companions; it was very rarely that he washed their feet. This, paradoxically, makes his—conversion is too revivalist a word—illumination, which is religious in its source and derived from the acceptance which is part of his love for Laura, possible, and when it takes place, convincing. Only the sinful man can become the redeemed man. *Voss* embodies the belief or rather perception of the novelist that simplicity and suffering are the conditions for the re-making of man. The suffering is sustained and terrible; the simplicity only barely and painfully achieved at the point of dissolution.

Voss is a powerful and humane work coloured with the light and soaked with the sweat and personality of Australia. There is a Wordsworthian strength in the novel's sense of the mineral structure and the uniquely luminous quality of the landscape, which is— strangely—heightened by being made available to the reader through the sensibility of the Teutonically alien protagonist, Voss himself. The presence of the discrepant and blundering Voss makes the occasional, wilful perversities of syntax and expression never wholly absent from White's writing less exasperating than usual. In any case they are never so gross as to detract from the novel's essential humanity and the maturity of its art.

In the third section of *Voss* there occur some lines which would make an apt epigraph for *Riders in the Chariot*, published in 1961. 'It was his niece, Laura Trevelyan, who had caused Mr Bonner's world of substance to quake.' Causing the world of substance to quake is the great shaping activity working through *Riders in the Chariot*. The novel follows the favoured White pattern, a strong central conception, a broad and fairly loose design, development by means of a biographical method, and an endless multiplication of palpable detail. The world of substance exposed in the novel includes not only the hard, thick, resistant one of common life and convention but other and odder worlds too: the world of a crazy specimen of the decayed Australian gentry, the world of an unpretentious working woman, the world of a persecuted German Jew, the world of an uprooted aboriginal. In addition each of the characters in which these worlds are defined and examined gives access to one species of a fourfold variety of experience, experience of the natural world, of plants and animals through Miss Hare's nearly non-human instinct for otherness, of integral, simple goodness in Mrs Godbold, the East Anglian immigrant, of the profoundest religious experience in Himmelfarb, the saintly survivor of the Nazi camps, and of art through the painting of Dubbo, the tubercular half-caste. The four lives, their separate worlds and different orders of experience connect, or are violently knotted together, in the small, dry, dusty town of Sarsaparilla. The range, the imaginative scope is extraordinary, and the control of the varied material has that unstressed ease which comes from a total inward familiarity.

What causes the world of substance to quake is the possession by each of the quartet of a special direct, non-discursive apprehension, the apprehension of realities which the world of substance either does not recognise at all or recognises as dangerous and deserving of destruction. This faculty or organ of consciousness is independent of experience in that it is in some sense a quality of genius, a gift, but it is not at all freakish, not attached to the character like an extra limb or head. It makes its presence felt gradually like any other function of the personality and it speaks through the articulation of the characters' lives and in the idiom of action. The consciousness—of which the chariot is the symbol—resides in each of the four, Miss Hare, Mrs Godbold, Dubbo, and Himmelfarb in a form appropriate to the experience of each. But it has, too, qualities in common. This gift of insight is secret, kept and nourished in privacy, and it is recognised only by those who themselves possess it. Suffering is a necessary condition of its development. Only

H

suffering can reduce the person to that state of painfully earned simplicity which is the essential preparation for a clarified consciousness. And again it invariably provokes persecution, whether it is persecution in the home by a companion or in the factory by workmates or more monstrously in Hitler's Germany by the whole of a society.

The four lives through which the author's vision is transmitted—and vision is a strictly appropriate term for Patrick White's religious reading of life—are shown with that marvellous authenticity which comes when minute fidelity of observation is enlivened by imaginative power. The most remarkable in this respect is that of Himmelfarb. Perhaps one would expect a sensitive and sympathetic Australian to have a special feeling for the life of an aboriginal half-caste, a kind of man in which some part of the essential flavour of Australia must lurk, and one would certainly expect Patrick White with *his* background—solid, Victorian, gentlemanly—to be at home with the character and life of poor Miss Hare, who belongs to the same attenuated, genteel blood-group as Theodora Goodman in *The Aunt's Story* (just as Mrs Godbold is obviously related to Stan Parker in *The Tree of Man*). But Himmelfarb, the central figure of the book, is a wholly new creation, European, Jewish, learned, saintly, wholly new, wholly certain and wholly successful. He embodies that special combination of humanity and spirituality, that grounded and aspiring quality, which is a peculiar mark of the Jewish tradition. The ritual and the discipline of Hebrew practice convey a strong tribal and family quality, but there shines through both the remote, utterly pure spirit of the Jewish religion, and more of religion itself.

Patrick White, like Lawrence, believes that direct, intuitional consciousness at its height is religious.[1] Himmelfarb's consciousness or religious imagination, which in the last resort is shown to be

---

[1] *Selected Literary Criticism* (1955), ed. Anthony Beale, p. 105.'... the imagination is a kindled state of consciousness in which intuitional awareness predominates ... imagery is the body of our imaginative life, and our imagination is a great joy and fulfilment to us, for the imagination is a more powerful and more comprehensive flow of consciousness than our ordinary flow. In the flow of the imagination we know in full, mentally and physically at once, in a greater, enkindled awareness. At the maximum of our imagination we are religious.'

something bestowed, not earned, as the wages of effort, is nevertheless not the simple progression of a religious inheritance. It has
survived, it has been dented and bruised by, the inertness and prejudice both of himself and his co-religionists, by boredom, doubt,
sensuality, actual infidelity, betrayal and persecution. The living
residue is a total clarity of understanding of persons and motives,
relations and values which exist now for Himmelfarb (as it appears
to the reader) absolutely as they are, their pure objectivity unaffected by any disturbing intrusion of self and unblurred by any
mist of unconsciousness.

Himmelfarb's blemished growth to this lucidity of perception is
seen by the reader, through Patrick White's strength of insight and
skill in realisation, as spontaneous in prospect and inevitable in
retrospect, a product of the clash of inward condition and outward
influence. Sensitivity to the supernatural is shown to be the natural
crown of Himmelfarb's persecuted life. Himmelfarb is himself
so concretely convincing as a human being that the reader—rightly,
I think—supposes Patrick White to be maintaining that openness
to the supernatural is the natural conclusion to every man's
development. Here, no doubt, a distinction needs to be drawn.
The naturalness of the supernatural does not indeed follow from
Patrick White's vision of human life, if one concentrates on the
human person as an individual. Perhaps the naturalness of the supernatural really means to Patrick White the sacredness of the individual. But the human person also belongs to a community and the
community in *Riders in the Chariot* reveals itself as savage and
dangerous. Society, in fact, is the natural enemy of the spiritual
life. The antagonism may be gross and violent as in Nazi Germany
where the Jews were thought of as an abstraction to be cancelled
out without a quaver of personal guilt; or it may be rough and
mocking, as in the climax of this novel, where Himmelfarb, a
surrogate Christ, is hung up by his workmates in a parody of the
Crucifixion. The tone of this episode, which could have been an
artistic outrage, is carefully calculated to make it acceptable as a
realistic piece of action. The note of hearty Australian matiness is
sustained throughout in tittering burlesque, in the claimed lack of
personal spite, in cruelty maintained at the level of a joke. 'It was

possible to practise all manner of cruelties provided the majority
might laugh them off as practical jokes. And there was almost no
tragedy which could not be given a red nose.' Mr Theobalds, the
fat foreman who at the end, in his indolent comfortable way, helps
Himmelfarb down from his cross, all the time reducing the tem-
perature of tragedy to that of farce, explains the Australian theory
of social cruelty.

> 'Remember,' Ernie Theobalds continued, 'we have a sense of
> humour, and when the boys start to horse around, it is that that is
> gettin' the better of 'em. They can't resist a joke. Even when a man
> is full of beer, you will find the old sense of humour hard at work
> underneath. It has to play a joke. See? No offence can be taken where
> a joke is intended.'

Jocular heartiness as a coat for destructive ferocity makes the
episode of Himmelfarb's crucifixion tolerable as fact. But this is
only the beginning of the author's intention. Its completion
requires releasing a significance larger than that bounded by the
limits of realistic action, namely to uncover what Henry James
called 'the idea which deeply links in any vision promoted by life'.
Here the idea—or concrete perception—is the conflict, ultimate
in nature, recurrent in time, between the enlightened consciousness and the habitual understanding of sensible men. That the
conflict is ultimate is shown in the total incomprehension of
Himmelfarb shown by his workmates and in their puzzled and
instinctive malice; that it is recurrent by the author's daring use of
the analogy of the Crucifixion. The propriety of this is dependent
on the essentially religious character of Patrick White's vision.
References to the Crucifixion are deliberate and incantatory, in
fact a literary form of the ritual. A ritualistic method is in place
because of the fundamentally religious nature of the experience;
and because the 'spirit' of religion, however much at odds it is with
the 'letter', invariably expresses itself in the 'letter'; and because the
'letter' is hallowed and made effective by ritualistic repetition. Not
that Patrick White has wholly avoided the danger of the explicit
to which a writer of his kind is liable, particularly when he turns,
as he does here, a physical fact into an emblematic rite. There is too
great a degree of completeness in the ceremonial repetitiveness of

the scene. One worker holds up a cloth to the crucified Himmel-farb's lips; Miss Hare sees the marble shudder and crack in her house, Xanadu; Himmelfarb is taken down from the cross into the arms of Mrs Godbold, one of the faithful women; and poor Mr Rosetree, the renegade Jew, an appealing Judas, commits suicide in his bathroom. Nothing is wanting to complete the reflection of Calvary. But the scene is carried forward by the force of the writer's imagination and by the innocent integrity of his vision. So much energy can safely carry a number of errors of tactics.

Patrick White belongs to a line of novelists whose art embodies a concentrated and dazzling vision of man. Such writers are not manipulators of plot or cultivators of a sensibility or critics of manners or chroniclers of a period. Their art is initiated by their vision and its form is determined more by a force from within than by any extrinsic scaffolding. These writers are not lacking in the capacity for the most inclusive and most significant kind of design. And while in some work of this nature minute particulars tend to melt away in the glow of vision, this is certainly not so with Patrick White, in whose novels the multiple detail is perpetually sharp and fresh. It is somewhere between imaginative power and authenticity and crispness of detail that Patrick White's work is imperfect, in the area where architectural capacity and taste are required. The failure is not in the generating concept nor in the worked-out detail—neither in the idea nor the vocabulary, that is—but some-where between in what one might call the syntactical structure. *Voss* and *Riders in the Chariot* certainly answer this account, I believe: impressive in the constructive idea, superb in their palpable concreteness, weaker in the passages of transition and apt on occasion to offer neatness and gratuitous accretion in place of organic design. This is the other, feebler side of what I spoke of before as Patrick White's innocent integrity of vision.

One novel exempt from this weakness is *The Solid Mandala* (1966), the story of the Brown twins, shambling, simple-minded Arthur and brittle, 'gifted' Waldo. The movement between idea and material in the novel is vital and unbroken, and the complex theme is as intimate with the dense material as soul with body. The tension between abstract and concrete understanding, which Patrick White is so conscious of, is sustained throughout although it is not frozen in the neat antithesis which these words suggest, one side to each twin. The twins themselves, divided parts of one whole person, by their essentially complementary relationship draw the conflict into the centre of human nature. They dramatise it as a disturbance within man and within the single man. At the same time they act out that impure mixture of love and hate which is both a condition of the relationship of every human being to another and a condition of the attitude of the individual within himself to himself. The double theme makes the novel a tragedy of human incompleteness, and does so in a decidedly trimmer, sparer way than is usual in the earlier novels.

The Solid Mandala begins at a point in time when the two brothers, now old men and at once appealing and repulsive, stumble hand in hand along the main road from Sarsaparilla to Barranugli. They are made almost unbearably present in their hideous, pitiable humanity. The novel swoops backwards and forwards in time from this moment in a natural rhythm which has all the vitality, arbitrariness, muddle and logic of life. There is a structural tension between the tortured misery of Waldo's impotent fury at human limitation and the personal peace of Arthur's acceptance; and it is a tension which in *The Solid Mandala* is wholly enclosed in the work, and not as some of the other novels suggest, a tension unresolved in the author himself. The result is that the narrative mode of *The Solid Mandala* (which has surely benefited from the discipline of the short stories) is altogether quieter and more collected, although the material it is engaged with is principally the anguish and desperation of Waldo; and Patrick White is seldom to be caught out in this novel indulging in what he calls 'efforts to embrace some recalcitrant vastness', something indeed he is himself habitually inclined to. The clarity of the medium allows effective scope for Patrick White's singular gift for producing a richly orchestrated actuality, an actuality marked not only by accuracy of the surface but by the presence of what exists at varying levels underneath. This complexity of perception is evident not only in the treatment of the physical context but in the presentation of the neighbours and the family life of the Browns, and above all in the delineation of Waldo and Arthur.

Patrick White makes great—and functional—play in this novel with the raw, abrasive elements of Australian provincial life. They serve as a base-line against which the reader can measure the intellectual pretensions of Waldo and the direct simplicity of Arthur's goodness. Those names of people and places! Wally Pugh, Mrs Purves, Mrs Musto, Mr Mutton, Norm Croucher (even the dogs are called Scruffy and Runt); as well as O'Halloran Road, Ada Avenue, Sarsaparilla, Barranugli, Shadbolt Lane, Gibber Gunya, Mungindribble. There is an illuminating contrast between the raw ugliness these names stand for and the beautiful and mysterious space of Australia, hardly more than hinted at, it is true, in this novel but still stretching out illimitably on all sides of the suburban pocket. And there is a further contrast between the common attitude of never completely suppressed truculence on the one side, and the half-aggressive idioms in which it is expressed, the mere sounds of which suggest a jutting jaw, and on the other the openness and freedom of a society unsmothered, incredibly so by European standards, by the oppressive weight of the *a priori* and the inherited. As Mr Brown once said to Waldo and Arthur, 'There's too much you boys, reared in the light in an empty country, will never understand. There aren't any shadows in Australia. Or discipline. Every man jack can do what he likes.'

Patrick White has a strong, not always sympathetic, sense of communal life, and the members of this shadowless, self-determining Australian community appear in the novel with a solid and connected existence; and do so whether they are casual figures merely glimpsed momentarily like Waldo's colleagues in the public library (the old municipal!) or the Allwrights who keep the shop Arthur works in, or the rich local eccentric Mrs Musto; or whether they are more fully developed like the immediate neighbours of the Brown family, the dull, decent Poulters or the Feinstein family who, with their Jewish cultivation and intelligence, bring to the general British surliness a further note of comparative definition. This is even truer of the club-footed father and the willowy mother, both so English in their different ways, the one clogged 'in an impasto of nonconformist guilt', the other, before she takes to the sweet sherry bottle in old age, one of those Tennysonian figures from the English country gentry that Patrick White is so fond of, who seem in the modern urban British scene in fact quite as strange as they were in Sarsaparilla. Nourished by the most anaemic abstractions of high-minded rationalism and genteel socialism the Brown parents live a dumbly desperate life, balancing in the air—just—their hopeless aspirations, their painful memories, their present disappointments, their insoluble problems with the twins.

This is the background against which the obscurities of the twins' relationship, drawn out with a spider-web's delicate, intricate accuracy, become a lucent device for the revelation of human nature. We live in our relationships. Our individuality depends on them. These relationships are always, as they were profoundly with the twins, bedded in flesh and fact. But what they become is not a simple extension of what they were. They are never just the effects of antecedent causes. At some point they are open to the bias of a person's nature or his choice, deliberate or implicit, or his disposition or his intentions or his response to others. The relationship of the twins is genetically determined in the profoundest way but its final form is the product of the purposive will as much as the prophetic genes.

In time indeed the relationship of Waldo and Arthur becomes the opposite of what it promised to be. Waldo is the bright child, the quick boy, the promising young man. Arthur is the soft-headed, slobbery-mouthed, imperfect creature. But it is Waldo's will that becomes destructive and Waldo who ends with the greater incapacity. Arthur, 'a shingle short', defective in intelligence and speech and physically incompetent, by some sweetness of nature or openness to life becomes—still with all his incapacities—a positive and protective influence. Arthur, with all the poverty of his equipment for entering into life, still fastens on enough of life to construct a rich and healing nature—a soul if not an intelligence.

Any abilities Arthur has are practical. He can milk the cow, make butter, prepare the bread and milk, he likes to work in the local grocer's, and oddly enough he had at school an uncomprehending and infallible gift for doing sums. But his slender resources include a childlike simplicity and an instinct for breaking, in however fuddled a way, into the life of others. So that he had friends and was even loved by women, by Dulcie Feinstein and Mrs Poulter, perhaps as a child, perhaps as a person, or perhaps as both. So much of life was beyond the range of his capacity. He could not understand a fraction of what Waldo mastered. But the limitation of range was accompanied during his life by a deepening, intensifying insight into what Lawrence called 'the realities' or 'the other world of pure being'.[1] The image of that limited range and focussed intensity is his 'solid mandala', the most mysterious of the several glass marbles which he fondles in his pocket and peers into entranced. Images of glass occur frequently in the novel: Arthur and his glass taws and Waldo and a mirror in which he constantly examines not only his appearance but himself and the many faceted crystal of his own mind. Waldo carries to extremity the natural bias we are all born with, that of the solipsist. Experience seems to him always a violation of his enclosed perfection, 'an assault on his privacy'. He was an 'almost' man. He almost had an affair with Dulcie, he almost wrote an essay, he almost completed a poem, his sexual experience with Mrs Poulter was that of a *voyeur*, his closest relationship with his mother was a perverse wearing of her dress after she was dead. His tragedy was that his natural solipsism was flawed from the first by the hateful presence of the other half of his self, Arthur. Even his love for and his dependence upon his brother seemed to him a rape of the self. His very existence, clogged by a twin, who is horrifyingly both himself *and* another, is a contradiction of his own crystalline perfection.

The narrative technique of *The Solid Mandala* is not Patrick White's usual steady tracking of the continuity of time. The material is still in one sense 'biographical', but the procedure here is much more one of shading and emphasis, of varying the point of entrance and sweeping backwards and forwards from there, so that *The Solid Mandala* impresses the reader as a 'composition' rather than the linear progress which is more customary with

[1] *Letters of D. H. Lawrence*, ed. Aldous Huxley, p. 405

Patrick White. This method of massing and concentration is apt
for a novel in which the central experience is not drawn out in a
development but given as an immediate revelation. The end is
very emphatically present in the beginning of *The Solid Mandala*,
which starts with the two neglected, aged men, handcuffed by love
and hate, and ends—terribly—with Waldo's pure destructive
malice and Arthur's terrified and unwarranted guilt. There is an
unbroken circular movement connecting the old men, Waldo in
his oilskin, Arthur in the old herringbone, 'sidling brittly down the
path' for their walk out into the dangerous world in which people
lived, and the final horror of Waldo yielding absolutely to the
hatred which he had directed at all living things, destroying both
himself and whatever of Arthur he is capable of destroying.

Indeed, the structure of the novel is composed of a series of
similar movements or concentric circles. The outermost one is
made up of ordinary people like Mrs Poulter and Mrs Dunne and
the whole community of Sarsaparilla. Inside that there is the tighter
circle of the Brown family, and within that again the more intense
circle of the brothers, and within that again the light-imprisoning,
solid mandala itself, Arthur's favourite glass marble, which
becomes by the end of the novel the image, lucid and mysterious,
of the depths and contradictions of human nature in every condition: as it exists in the community, in the family, in a pair of
friends or lovers or brothers, or in the single individual soul that
Waldo and Arthur together compose.

Simultaneity, correspondence, a common centre—these are the
marks of the world seen by Patrick White, a religious, poetic and
profoundly melancholy spirit. The common centre lies in a clouded
paradox, the co-existence of human malice and human goodness
which move in and out of one another like the folds of light and
darkness in Arthur's glass taw. The co-existence is not an equilibrium: malice (not simply evil or disorder) exists as a settled condition of human life but goodness is a flickering and gratuitous
visitation, a pure fluke of genius. Patrick White's writing is not
at all given to the inflections of irony. His prose is too tumultuous,
his thought unqualified by that complex sagacity which is able to
discriminate effortlessly according to a coherent set of standards.

He is not by any means a witty writer. Nevertheless there is a deep irony in the way in which he shows a racy Australian life, physical in its energy and Philistine in its taste, embodying so medieval, or rather so biblical, a vision of man.

Biblical too, Old Testament in fact, is his habit of making the grinding ugliness of the small-town scene and the details of daily life a signal—almost a negative sacrament—of an inward condition rather in the way poverty or disease is used in the Bible. But although there is a distinctly biblical feeling about the tradition of spirituality with which Patrick White's sensibility is saturated, it would be truer to say of the positive part of his attitude towards man that it is religious rather than biblical. It is a concept of goodness which depends upon an unspoilt wholeness of the person and upon what this makes possible, an exact, unsmudged truth of relationship. This is the concrete vision quickening all the best of his work which is focussed with dazzling strength in *The Solid Mandala*. Such goodness, although it may be striven for, cannot be deserved. It is, as I have said already, a stroke of providence or a form of genius, but in any case a gift—and a gift in two senses of the word, both a donation and an endowment—and a gift most likely to be found in the possession of those commonly regarded as blemished or eccentric or disgusting or hateful. With the exception of Stan Parker, who is the saint of ordinariness, all Patrick White's most powerfully realised characters belong to the class he describes in the epigraph to his collection of short stories as 'the burnt ones, the poor unfortunate ones'.

I have been stressing the religious feeling which shines with an almost Franciscan purity and intensity through Patrick White's work. It is the principal constituent of the standard by which he tests the quality of life in individuals and in society, just as it is the main feature in the mind he attempts to project in those who embody most fully what he takes to be a necessary human wisdom. But I should mislead the reader if I seemed to be suggesting that the work exhibits a constant serenity of religious belief. Its religious expression is contorted by more contemporary grimaces and tics. He has much more than his normal share of the current awareness of the nastiness of sex. Apart from *The Tree of Man* where sex for the most part is a tranquil and organic element in the life of Stan and his wife, there is undoubtedly in Patrick White's attitude towards this side of experience a certain flinching distaste which is reminiscent of Eliot. It is a blend of quivering anxiety about the capacity of sex brutally to separate itself from tenderness, and of disgust at its physical, 'excretory' functions. Moreover, the religious quality of his vision is not, as its traditional character leads one to expect, at all sympathetic to the inherited or habitual life of the community. On the contrary he is deeply disturbed by the cruelty of communities and by their inveterate bias in favour of the average, a bias which at the first hint of danger ceases to be a merely comfortable prejudice and turns into a lust for persecution.

The cruelty in Patrick White's reconstruction of human reality is not limited to the bloodshot variety practised by communities against the odd member or the alien intruder. Within the family itself the old, in a rage of incomprehension, torture the young, the young savage the old. Men and women are locked in malice. The individual icily studies the weaknesses of his opponent, calculating where to strike. There is a Manichaean violence in Patrick White's reading of human relationships: on the one side the flow of love so brilliantly exemplified in Daise in *Down at the Dump*, in Stan Parker in *The Tree of Man*, in Himmelfarb in *Riders in the Chariot* and Arthur in *The Solid Mandala*; on the other the conversation of mankind translated as a dialectic of loathing. Rarely do the two come together as mutually confirming elements in an inclusive human order—perhaps only in *The Solid Mandala* do they do so with complete success. Patrick White is a strongly individual, richly gifted, original and highly significant writer. His powers are by any standard remarkable. His achievement is large. His art, which is an essentially poetic discipline, dense and image-ridden and sensitive to the rhythms of Australian speech, is marred by a harking after symbolic symmetry, but it is still a substantial and genuine thing.

We see in his work not only a positive but also a negative revelation. No matter how gifted a writer in Western society, even in so fresh and vital a form of it as the Australian, he cannot, it seems, help reproducing in his sensibility a certain failure of sureness or grasp in the contemporary experience of human nature. A neurotic twist or distortion, the reflection of a defect in our civilisation, forces itself into the work, even when, as with Patrick White, the writer is disposed by temperament and belief to a central and steadily traditional vision of man. An eye so justly accommodated to its object as Patrick White's inevitably brings back an image coloured with the exact stain of the society it scrutinises. Involvement is as much a matter of registration as it is of attitude. The statement of the artist can never be merely a comment; it is always in part the response of a participant. A sensibility so quick and inclusive as Patrick White's, however much it may be spiritually detached from the assumptions ruling contemporary society, is nevertheless bound, as it realises itself in art, to reflect not only the artist's individual vision but the radical disorder of the society it is turned upon.

II   A. D. HOPE

Those who know Australia, particularly certain places like the capital city of Canberra, imperceptible among the trees and overwhelmed by the sky which is so dominant a feature of the *landscape*, will have been struck by the Mediterranean quality of the light. I am reminded of this when I think of the work of the most distinguished of contemporary Australian poets, A. D. Hope. Hope is learned, passionate, sceptical—and in his work there is an insistent, almost fierce sense of a Western Latin tradition. Perhaps one is misled by the analogy of the Latin light. It may be that the creative impulse is discrepancy, an aching consciousness of the dissimilarity between the decorative density of Europe and the emptiness of the arid continent. More probably both impulses work together in the Australian sensibility, work together and work on one another, sharpening into positive existence the Latin elements —not just the linguistic ones—latent in the English language. Certainly, Hope is concerned in a most unusual way for those currently writing in English with order and coherence of feeling and with decorum and regularity in presentation. This preoccupation is a constant presence in the poetry, not always successfully realised, of course, and we have no need to go outside the verse to find a sanction for the claim I have made. But if we did we could find it in several key statements in Hope's critical writings. Hope is in fact a fine practical critic in the Arnoldian tradition. Here is a passage from Hope's remarkable volume—remarkable for assurance, urbanity and point—*The Cave and the Spring*.[1]

> This discriminating taste is the basis of the much misunderstood idea of correctness in poetry, the correctness which Pope in early youth made it his aim to bring to the practice of English verse, and which his *Essay on Criticism* is meant both to explain and to exemplify. Correctness is not primarily a matter of following explicit and ideal rules of versification but of exercising discrimination, of choices that tremble on the very limit of sensibility. Far from being a mechanical skill, it is one that depends on continual acts of judgment so little referable to any rule of thumb that they may look arbitrary to those who do not share the writer's discipline of taste. Correctness is the mastery of all that is implied in Horace's doctrine of the middle way.

This significant set of names and phrases—Pope and Horace, correctness, acts of judgment, discipline of taste, the middle way— not only point to the theme Hope is engaged with but unambiguously project a personal conviction about the artistic necessity for design and control. They also make an appropriate introduction to the poem, *The Lamp and the Jar*, I want to speak of first.

> *You are that vessel full of holy oil:*
> *Wisdom, unstirring in its liquid sleep,*
> *Hoarded and cool, lucid and golden green,*
> *Fills the pure flanks of the containing stone;*
> *Here darkness mellows what the sunlit soil*
> *To purposes unknown, for ends unseen,*
> *Produced, and labour of unnumbered men.*
> *All the unthinking earth with fret or toil*
> *Reared, ripened, buried in the earth again,*
> *Here lives, and living, waits: this source alone*
> *Distils those fruitful tears the Muses weep.*
>
> *And I, the lamp before the sacred ark,*

[1] Adelaide, 1965, p. 57

The root of fire, the burning flower of light,
Draw from your loins this inexhaustible joy.
There the perpetual miracle of grace
Recurs, as, from its agony, the flame
Feeds the blind heart of the adoring dark;
And there the figures of our mystery,
The shapes of terror and inhuman woe,
Emerge and prophesy; there with the mark
Of blood upon his breast and on his brow,
An unknown king, with my transfigured face,
Bends your immortal body to his delight.

The Lamp and the Jar is a remarkably contained poem, each verbal edge firmly finished off and each syntactical contour exactly defined. Two bold images, the female oil-brimmed jar and the burning male lamp are separately drawn out and then drawn together. The tranquil, mellowed richness of the first stanza, 'hoarded and cool', is put into opposition and balance with the agitation, the more personal agitation of the second. Together the stanzas, locked at once in antagonism and passion, produce the strength and scent of sexual encounter. The actual tension and embrace of love are poised above and sustained by the profound processes of organic life.

> *. . . what the sunlit soil*
> *To purposes unknown, for ends unseen,*
> *Produced . . .*

and what

> *. . . the unthinking earth with fret or toil*
> *Reared, ripened, buried in the earth again . . .*

The poem, keeping its varied complexities in place and in connection along a lucid argumentative line, grasps first at the physical basis of life and experience, at the oil and the earth and the calm sagacity it generates, and then touches the quick of human experience at its exquisite crisis in the mysterious meeting of love. The mystery is an essential part of the experience which the poem offers. It includes not only the joyful, physical energy of sexual love, 'the root of fire, the burning flower of light', but also a tissue of social and personal memories and images. These are both serene, 'the perpetual miracle of grace', and terrifying, 'the shapes of terror and inhuman woe'. In the poem the act of love appears as a model of all human experience which has its ancient sources buried in the earth, but which is also immediate and adapted to the light and further transformed by the imagination, itself always a carrier of a more than merely personal cargo, a conductor of both compulsion and aspiration, honour and grace.

Sexual love is a recurrent theme in Hope's work. Occasionally he celebrates it as the beneficent completion of life and personality. More frequently he is concerned with its turbidity and cruelty. He sees it as incestuous, murderous, carnivorous or absurd. Here is a poem *The Gateway* in which love is shown completing the circle and perfecting the broken, and in which Hope's characteristic energy of articulation is given a singing, aspiring quality.

Now the heart sings with all its thousand voices
To hear this city of cells, my body, sing.
The tree through the stiff clay at long last forces
Its thin strong roots and taps the secret spring.

And the sweet waters without intermission
Climb to the tips of its green tenement;
The breasts have borne the grace of their possession,
The lips have felt the pressure of content.

Here I come home: in this expected country
They know my name and speak it with delight.
I am the dream and you my gates of entry,
The means by which I waken into light.

The sense of unalloyed delight in love, spiritual as well as physical, is comparatively rare in Hope's poetry. It is true that whenever he writes of love he conveys in a masterly way the pleasure of the senses and the richness and beauty of the body. But there is always something else breaking in, something sinister or ugly or mean. Monstrous and cogent memories from the Old Testament and the classics, which supply many of the fictions used in Hope's verse, intrude on the enclosed world of lovers: reminiscences of Circe surrounded by snouted beasts, of Lot and his daughters 'crafty

from fear, reckless with joy and greed', of Susannah and the seedy
hatred of the Elders, of Pasiphae, filled with the bull's monstrous
life, of Odysseus and passion punctured by the ridiculous commonplace.

> There at the last, his arms embracing her,
> She found herself, faith wasted, valour lost,
> Raped by a stranger in her sullen bed;
> And he, for all the bloody passion it cost
> To have heard the sirens sing and yet have fled,
> Thought the night tedious, coughed and shook his head,
> An old man sleeping with his housekeeper.

The conclusion of this stanza from *The End of a Journey*, contrasting
sharply and yet following naturally on the formal eloquence pre-
ceding it (the brilliant twist of mood is completely logical) is an
example of Hope's supple virtuosity in modulation, from the
stately and measured to the casual and throwaway. It calls up the
great name of Yeats, and Hope has made no secret of his admiration
for Yeats and

> that noble, candid speech
> In which all things worth saying may be said . . .

as well as his strong preference for Yeats over Eliot. But while
Yeats is clearly a vital (and absorbed) influence on Hope, his idiom
is his own, being at once less gorgeous and Byzantine when full out
and more flatly contemporary in the lower register. Here are two
examples which separate these modes out, the first, the Yeatsian,
from a short poem called *Meditation on a Bone*, about a piece of bone
found at Trondhjem in 1901 with a runic inscription cut on it:

> Words scored upon a bone,
> Scratched in despair or rage—
> Nine hundred years have gone;
> Now, in another age,
> They burn with passion on
> A scholar's tranquil page.

The second is the beginning of *Agony Column*:

> Sir George and Lady Cepheus of Upper Slaughter
> Desire to announce to family and friends

I

That the death has been arranged of their only daughter
Andromeda, aged twenty—Sir George intends

To avoid undesirable pomp and ostentation:
A simple ceremony, a quiet funeral feast
And the usual speeches; a train will leave the station
For the Virgin's Rock at four. No flowers by Request!

An even better example of this calculatedly flat manner and one more thoroughly charged with the macabre, the attraction of which for Hope suggests a certain nauseated disgust with ordinary life as part of his response to experience, is *Conquistador* in which a certain Henry Clay 'a small man in a little way', loves an enormous girl.

And afterwards, it may have been in play,
The enormous girl rolled over and squashed him flat;
And, as she could not send him home that way,
Used him thereafter as a bedside mat. . . .

And when, in winter, getting out of bed,
Her large soft feet pressed warmly on the skin,
The two glass eyes would sparkle in his head,
The jaws extend their papier-mâché grin.

Having said this—that the appeal of the macabre for Hope testifies to some perverse disrelish for common experience—I am immediately conscious of the need to correct or qualify it. There is something nasty, an occasional gratuitous revelling in the garbage-bin and perhaps also the puritan self-hatred to which this is often a clue, in a few of Hope's poems, as for example in *Rawhead and Bloody Bones*:

This Belly too commits
By a strange and self abuse,
Chin-chopper's titbits,
Meat of his own mint, chews.

But more often some quality in the tone, a quaver of amusement, a glint of wit, a touch of self-mockery, even a cry of innocent astonishment, shows that the macabre is being put to a more complicated and controlled use. It becomes an instrument instead of a dead end, another gateway through which the poet's imagination can enter an odd, disturbed but somehow valid world. A poem of this kind is *The Coasts of Cerigo* in which

> . . .
>
> *Strange sister to the polyp and the sponge,*
> *To holothurian and madrepore,*
>
> *The Labra wallows in her bath of time . . .*
> *Her ladylegs gape darkly as a cave,*
>
> *And through the coral clefts a gleam and gloom*
> *Reveal the fronded arch, the pelvic gate;*
> *Spotted and barred, the amorous fish swim in.*
> *But in that hollow, mocking catacomb*
> *Their love-songs echo and reverberate*
> *A senseless clamour and a wordless din.*
>
> *The love-trap closes on its gullible prey*
> *Despite their sobs, despite their ecstasies.*
> *Brilliant with tropic bands and stripes, they dart*
> *Through a delicious juice which eats away*
> *Their scales and soon dissolves their goggle eyes*
> *And melts the milt-sac and the pulsing heart.*

Even this short extract will be sufficient to demonstrate Hope's great technical skill in recreating the cold marvels of the submarine universe. One sees too how the manner, at once Augustan and efficiently direct, and the eye coolly intent on the object makes the biological savagery it discerns glittering and frightening. The gliding rhythm, the glassily clear imagery, the almost scientifically detached attitude themselves make 'a delicious juice which eats away' at our comfortable assumptions about life and tenderness, at once inviting our acquiescence and dissolving it with intimations of the implacable cruelty of a biologically determined life. Hope is said to be a severely traditional poet, which indeed he is in his bias towards accepted patterns and rhythms. But he has also a pointedly contemporary gift—that of conducting the permanent functions of poetry through new categories of experience and through new classes of imagery, imagery particularly drawn from the sciences of biology and psychology. The Labra is one figure drawn from such a source, the Tapeworm another. Who but Hope

would conceive of celebrating this creature as one of the heroic
figures of life, as he has in *The Kings*.

> *The lion in deserts royally takes his prey;*
> *Gaunt crags cast back the hunting eagle's scream.*
> *The King of Parasites, delicate, white and blind,*
> *Ruling his world of fable even as they,*
> *Dreams out his greedy and imperious dream*
> *Immortal in the bellies of mankind.*

> *In a rich bath of pre-digested soup,*
> *Warm in the pulsing bowel, safely shut*
> *From the bright ambient horror of sun and air,*
> *His slender segments ripening loop by loop,*
> *Broods the voluptuous monarch of the gut,*
> *The Tapeworm, the prodigious Solitaire.*

The grotesque depends on discrepancy, on a measured friction
between manner and material or on discordant experiences crushed
together. Both types of contrast contribute to the effect of *The
Coasts of Cerigo* and *The Kings*, as they do in another startling poem
in this *genre*, *The Dinner*. *The Dinner* is of unusual interest in that it
adds a further note to our understanding of Hope's use of the
grotesque. We see in the poem how the imagination of a poet of
the grotesque hurls itself from the given situation to one at the
extreme point of difference. In this violent dialectical swing the
shock of the poem comes from our realising that the second stage
in spite of its immense dissimilarity is really a development of the
first, that it was there all the time grinning under the original elegant
surface. We notice, too, how Hope arrives like a poetic zoologist
at the second fiercely contrasting situation by a kind of compressed
evolutionary method which appears in several poems. The reductive habit of the scientist, his concern with origins and causes,
becomes in Hope's hands an instrument of poetic exploration. In
The Dinner the lovers, risen from bed, prepare to dine:

> *Delicate, young and cradled in delight,*
> *You take your seat and bare your teeth to bite—*
> *What is my courage then to suffer this*

Miracle of your metamorphosis!
For in that instant I behold the jaws
Of the most terrible of carnivores
Tear at its prey; the ravening human packs
Pull down their terrified victim in its tracks;
The wit, the charm, the grace, the pride of life
Adore the bloody edges of a knife!
The nakedness I had my arms about
Was gorged with death—I see the cayman's snout
Snap the deer's nostrils as they touch the flood;
The tiger's hairy muzzle sweet with blood;
The condor, flapping from the rocky peak,
Light on the carrion, plunge his grisly beak
Into the rotting porridge; through the dark
Slides the lithe, cold torpedo of the shark.
The air, the jungle, the salt, cannibal sea
Hold no more ruthless beast of prey than she.
For her the ox falls snoring in his blood;
The lamb is butchered for her daily food;
Her exquisite mouth, that smiles and tastes the wine,
Has killed by proxy a whole herd of swine— . . .

The poem continues its backward evolutionary line and the young woman, delicate and baring her teeth to bite, becomes the world of prehistoric mankind. We see the ancestral giant and giantess,

Talking in deep, soft, grumbling undertones
They gnaw and crack and suck the marrowy bones.

I have called the technique rehearsed in this poem tracing an evolutionary line. But it is also, and perhaps more so, a method of burrowing into the image evoked in the first two lines, to release and elucidate the intimations latent there. The ravening animals, the condor plunging his beak 'into the rotting porridge', and the ancient ancestors in the cave, are the imaginative issue of the first lines of the verse paragraph I quoted earlier:

Delicate, young and cradled in delight
You take your seat and bare your teeth to bite . . .

I have referred, then, to Hope's writings in the formal Yeatsian mode, to his flatter, more markedly contemporary manner, and to work of the kind I call macabre-grotesque, although I recognise the infelicity of a term which misleadingly suggests some Gothic thrill-inducing intention on the part of the poet when the most notable thing about these poems is the control and application with which the *genre* is put to serious, indeed sombre, purposes. Use, management, the employment of a style for purposes beyond what it seems capable of is even more strikingly evident in another set of poems which look immediately to be no more than deliberate imitations. Members of this series are *Man Friday*, *The Elegy*, *An Epistle from Holofernes*, *The Cheek*, *An Epistle*, *Soledades of the Sun and Moon*. This last poem is not, Hope has told us,[1] as its name suggests an attempt to imitate Gongora, but it is strongly reminiscent of certain religious poems of the English seventeenth century.

What in the seventeenth century Hope fastened on was a composite sensibility made up of the passionate subtleties and the intellectual sensuousness of the metaphysical poets and the masculine, ironic force of Dryden. *Why* the seventeenth century should be looked to as the source has to do with the congruence between Hope's own poetic nature and the adult, ardent, almost mathematically reasoning habit of the metaphysicals: a balance further modified by another, the symmetry between Hope and his admired Dryden's gift of sensitive manliness, his way of being at once independent and level with his experience, however intricate; and modified yet again by Hope's sympathetic understanding of Dryden's skill in calling upon a range of poetic resonance within a strictly defining, disciplining pattern. Nor should we overlook that Hope had to make his choice of exemplar at a particular time and from within a certain literary tradition—not only the wider one grounded on the English language and the English literary tradition but within the local Australian one based on the altered language of his own country. It could not be a purely personal choice, although it had to be primarily a personal one, answering to the need felt in the poet's own nerves. The poet as poet is not engaged in any explicit mission to renovate a literary tradition. But of course he is involved in such an undertaking, and the more significant he is as a poet, the more profound is his involvement.

[1] *Selected Poems*, A. D. Hope, Sydney, 1966, p. 55

Hope's 'conservatism' in fact is truly radical. His poetry had to be freed from the influence of home, from a tradition still too much domesticated within the nineteenth century in which British gentility and blandness were curiously reinforced in their parochialism by an unambitious, and suspicious, Australian matiness. The seventeenth century so different, so remote from the nineteenth century in its inclusiveness and in the very assurance of its scepticism, to which poets in Britain earlier directed their attention, could be the same cleansing, tonic influence for Australia: above all if the connection were to be made by an Australian poet.

I called the set of poems which gave rise to these remarks 'imitations', and although I wanted to use the term in an active Aristotelian sense, it still carries an unfairly passive or partial connotation, quite unjust to the controlled energy of the art the poems represent. They might more aptly be called 'translations', in the sense in which Scott-Moncrieff's version is a translation of Proust, a personal and creative reproduction, with the added and powerful difference that Hope is primarily concerned to construct original poems. A technique of translation of this kind when applied by a modern Australian poet to a period as remote in time and sensibility as the English seventeenth century requires the skill to accommodate the curve of contemporary speech to the contours of another age and the ability to sink oneself in its diction and feeling. It also requires with a verse like that of the seventeenth century, depending so much on almost syllogistic structure, mastery of and intense sympathy with an alien syntax of reasoning. At the same time the poet if he is to use and not be used by his literary instruments must preserve a measure of detachment. If not, the sinking turns into a helpless drowning, the sympathy into an impotent identification. Here are two examples of this mode: the failure of the first, the success of the second depends precisely on this point of tactfully insinuated independence. The first is from *The Cheek*:

> *Here's a new Genesis; the year is One;*
> *This bed and we a world, our lamp its sun.*
> *Love to its single dark dimension bound*
> *Rules its volcano Kingdom underground:*

> *The feet at their remote antipodes*
> *Twine their smooth roots; at Capricorn the knees*
> *Nuzzle together; intershafted lies*
> *The amplitude of firm and polished thighs. . . .*

The effort at minute fidelity betrays the poet into merely mirroring shadows. Here now is the first stanza of *Soledades of the Sun and Moon*:

> *Now the year walks among the signs of heaven,*
> *Swinging her large hips, smiling in all her motions,*
> *Crosses with dancing steps the Milky Valley.*
> *Round her the primal energies rejoice;*
> *All the twelve metaphysical creatures and the seven*
> *Swift spheres adore her vigour; the five oceans*
>   *Look up and hear her voice*
> *Ring through the ebony vault, where Ara Celi*
> *Flames, and the choiring stars at their devotions*
>   *With pure and jubilant noise*
> *Praise and proclaim four seasons in her belly.*

This stanza exhibits the fine proportion which the whole poem sustains, between, on the one side, an exactly directed historical imagination highly responsive to the original form and, on the other, the pressure of the poet's personal experience. The rhythm moves with diplomatic ease from the ceremonial stateliness appropriate to 'the choiring stars at their devotions' to the more checked and modern run of

> *the five oceans*
> *Look up and hear her voice*
> *Ring through the ebony vault,*

and to the sliding glide of the star-actress-year. And to make this bold image consort without embarrassment with 'the primal energies' and 'the metaphysical creatures' in as 'metaphysical' a connection as one could conceive of is a conclusive demonstration of an authoritative and achieved art. As fine as *Soledades of the Sun and Moon*, each in its different way, are *Man Friday*, a sardonic extrapolation from *Robinson Crusoe*, and *An Epistle from Holofernes*, a grim, angry evocation of tragic love which is Roman in the strength of its despair. Both these poems are written in vigorous rhymed couplets which have something of Dryden's pace and force: Dryden's because the medium, handled by Hope with remarkable naturalness, is used as the instrument of strength rather than delicacy. Indeed the heroic couplet, employed in an easy, open way is splendidly adapted to communicate the peculiar quality of Hope's poetry which one is aware of even in his earliest, lightest pieces. This is its powerfully—almost physically—energetic character. It is muscular, quick and solid—with the relaxed poise of the gifted athlete who brings all his force to bear rhythmically and without strain. Hope is the least neurotic of poets and even when he is scrutinising the stages of his own childhood, as in one of his best poems *Ascent into Hell*, his regard is gravely objective without the least touch of narcissistic droop or any suspicion of anxious self interest. Right from the start of Hope's poetic career, the reader is aware of the formed personality beneath the finished literary character. It is positive, independent and radical in the Australian manner—in the manner of the Australian *people*, that is; the accepted Australian literary convention lacked precisely this very virtue. It is free of the fog of middle-class pretension and gentility: sharp where that was bland and harsh where that was cosy. At the same time Hope's poetry asserts a profound commitment to the great constitutive works of the Western—not just the British—tradition; and not only in poetry but also in thought and morality—accepts and asserts, namely, the principles of an intellectual aristocracy, and in doing so avoids, or ignores, the clogging dangers of Australian democracy. The result is a powerful and unfashionable maturity which joins a naked freshness of original response to a richly realised conception of an ideal order.

This is a conjunction which appears in the best of the poems I called translations, *An Epistle: Edward Sackville to Venetia Digby*, the fable of which is taken from Aubrey's *Brief Lives*. Sir Kenelm Digby when little more than a boy fell in love with Venetia Stanley, a neighbour's daughter, but the match was disapproved of and his mother had him sent abroad where he stayed for several years and was at length assumed to be dead. During this time Venetia became the lover of Sir Edward Sackville, later Earl of

Dorset, Digby's friend. The despair which is implicit in the situation and the grimness of a passionate and impossible love call to powers deep in Hope's nature and are transformed in his treatment to become the implacable conditions of tragic human life itself. It is written in language which very much obeys the prescription Hope lays down—that the language of poetry should be 'plain, lucid, coherent, logically connected, syntactically exact, and firmly based in current idiom and usage'.[1] It begins with short, stabbing, cleanly effective phrases, in a staccato rhythm and in a voice which has nothing in it but despair.

> First, last and always dearest, closest, best,
>   Source of my travail and my rest,
> The letter which I shall not send, I write
>   To cheer my more than arctic night.

The poem mingling sadness and sensuousness in a strange, dry way manages unfalteringly to convey at once the coldness of present misery and the radiance of remembered passion. Not that the effect is at all romantically intimate or soft. The logical structure, the severe form and the carefully worked out syntax, both of grammar and feeling, generalise the experience into something highly organised and impersonal. So that the love passages, luminous and distant in the memory, have the refinement and the deadliness of expert swordplay, and the hopelessness and regret become positive and tense, abrasive and bleakly affecting. Here is the conclusion in which we see the particular aspiring through the lucidity of form towards a larger, general order:

> Nature, who makes each member to one end,
>   May give it powers which transcend
> Its first and fruitful purpose. When she made
>   The Tongue for taste, who in the shade
> Of summer vines, what speechless manlike brute,
>   Biting sharp rind or sweeter fruit,
> Could have conceived the improbable tales, the long
>   Strange fable of the Speaking Tongue?
> So Love, which Nature's craft at first designed
>   For comfort and increase of kind,

[1] *Selected Poems*, Sydney, 1966, p. ix

> Puts on another nature, grows to be
>   The language of the mystery;
> The heart resolves its chaos then, the soul
>   Lucidly contemplates the whole
> Just order of the random world; and through
>   That dance she moves, and dances too.

An Epistle: Edward Sackville to Venetia Digby is a statement—but more than a mere 'statement'—about the ideal order which is implicit in, and which by means of poetry can be extracted from, the grubbiness and detritus of life. But, of course, the poet could be, and is, as concerned with the other side of the duality, with the disordered elements in their chaos. In another poem, a true translation this time, *The Twenty-Second Sonnet of Louis Labé*, he speaks of this preoccupation.

> *They would break frame and order, and disperse*
> *With random steps through a wrecked universe*
> *Like me to search, and search, like me, in vain.*

The broken frame and the wrecked universe describe very well the form under which society and the modern world appear to this tough-minded, independent poet. The search describes the general, bracing aim which keeps his observations tart, the random steps, the self-confidence of the approach. The tone of these social poems, which include some of Hope's most effective and personal work, is better seen in the beginning of *Letter from the Line*:

> *Island-hopping in the rough, the rumbustious season,*
> *The migratory poet, most solitary of birds,*
> *Having left Los Angeles with a Kyrie eleison,*
> *Repacks his baggage of carefully chosen words.*

> *For lucky Jim has given his last lecture,*
> *From the bogus mission his wits emerge alive,*
> *From a land where, despite de Tocqueville's shrewd conjecture,*
> *The liberal arts, like living fossils, survive.*

The tone here, untensed and self-mocking, is a recognition that we are all, not excluding the poet himself, 'most solitary of birds', in the same boat, or plane, and an almost amused confession of innocence—in that whatever is wrong—and so much is, both in the observed and the observer—derives from a common impersonal fault. It is the classical Western awareness—but light, wry and quite without guilt—that everything issues from a single, tainted source, an original flaw or sin. But at other times the poet collects himself into a more feline and separate contempt. *A Comminution* spits at the mass-communicating world, *Lambkin* at the malevolently stupid mob, *The Martyrdom of St Theresa* at the formal cruelties of religion, and *The Age of Innocence* straight into 'the grey eye of science'. Sometimes the tone is harsh and disgusted. *Heldensagen* savagely rejects those with all the answers,

> *Admirals with power to organise my search*
> *For Ithaca through this ten years monstrous dream:—*
> *To all Messiahs the same reply, I am*
> *Sinbad and on this Roc you build no church!*

Phallus ignominiously acknowledges the huge irrelevance of individuality, of thought and will, beside the brutal biological coercion of sex. The power and the beauty of the body roused by sex is a subject of profound importance to Hope. It has for him an absolute, intrinsic value in its natural energy, concentration and sincerity, and as a focus of experience which is completely without pretension or fake. His command of an idiom capable of expressing this reality is extraordinarily firm and clean. His attitude to it may be serious and reverent, as in the first poem I quoted, *The Lamp and the Jar*; or it may be surgically detached as in *The Damnation of Byron*, which lays bare the neurotic emptiness of the professional lover, a performer moved by fear and moving into despair. Or again it may be, as it often is in these social-satirical poems, randy and rollicking. A remarkable example of that mood is *A Blason* in which the phases of the act of love are rehearsed solely by means of an alliterative accumulation of dancing Saxon and Norman exclamations and expletives. Here are the first, preparatory stanzas of this astonishing exercise in pure verbal vitality:

> *My foundling, my fondling, my frolic first-footer,*
> *My circler, my sidler, shy-sayer yes and no,*

Live-levin, light-looker, darter and doubter,
Pause of perhaps in my turvey of touch-and-go;

My music, my mandrake, merry thought to my marrow-bone,
Tropic to my true-pole and ripe to my rich,
Wonderer, wanderer, walker-in-wood alone
Eye-asker, acher, angel-with-an-itch;

My tittup, my tansy, tease-tuft in tumble-toil,
My frisker, my fettler, trickster and trier,
Knick-knacker, knee-knocker, cleaver in kindle-coil,
My handler, my honeysuckler, phoenix-on-fire. . . .

Vastly different from this curiously innocent celebration of bodily joy, in address, tone and intention, is the maliciously analytic *Return from the Freudian Islands* (written, incidentally, as early as 1942), in which an almost impudently insinuating blandness of the deadpan, tongue-in-cheek, irresistibly Australian variety, mocks at Siegfried the Saviour for whose sake the islanders have abandoned the worship of their fathers' ghosts. The saint shocks and delights them as he brings into their consciousness 'the unacknowledged body' and forces them to see

How it bred night-sweats, the disease of shame,
Corns, fluxions, baldness and the sense of sin,
How clothes to the Analytic Eye became
Fantasies, furtive symbols of the skin.

The poem makes solemn, wicked fun of the reductive habit of the contemporary mind, of its technique at getting beneath the delusive surface in the interests of uttering some pure abstract truth. Hope combines a gravely ironic parody of psychiatric investigation with a medievally gruesome pondering on the horrors of the body, including 'a common skin disease they had called love'. Successively, clothes, skin, flesh are peeled off until the saint-sage lays bare 'the ultimate visceral reality'.

At the Fertility Festival that year
The skinned men blushed to see the skeleton,
A bone-cage filled with female guts appear
Tottering before them in the midday sun.

Its slats and lowering rods they saw, the full
Cogged horseshoe grin of two and thirty teeth,
The frantic eyeballs swivelling in the skull,
The swagging human umbles underneath,

The soft wet mottled granite of the lung
Bulge and collapse, the liver worn askew
Jauntily quiver, the plump intestines hung
In glistening loops and bolsters in their view. . . .

The Swift-like gravity of procedure, simultaneously recommend-
ing and undermining the modest monstrous proposal, and the
hideous exposure of the skinned body are devices used in the
service of a serious intention but one which can express itself in a
less ferocious, more bantering species of ridicule than the master of
devastation would ever allow himself. The touch of tolerant light-
heartedness is confirmed by the crisply humorous conclusion. It
holds out a small hope that a sense of reality is perhaps recoverable
—but only as the issue of total absurdity.

Pimples and cramps now shed with pelt and thews,
No dreams to fright, no visions to trouble them,
For, where the death-wish and self-knowledge fuse,
They had at last The Human L.C.M. . . .

Here the saint paused, looked modestly at the ground
And waited for their plaudits to begin.
And waited. . . . There was nothing! A faint, dry sound
As first a poet buttoned on his skin.

I come now to what I see as the peak of Hope's achievement, not
a great one in bulk it may be, but still substantial enough and
unusually even in quality. It is made up of a handful of poems
written at intervals over the period 1942-61, a fact of composition
in keeping with my feeling that Hope already had a fully formed
literary personality when he began to publish. His *Collected Poems*,
'those poems which I would still care to publish',[1] contains one
poem written in 1930, one in 1934, two in 1938, and two in 1939.
The body of the work, and the best, appeared between 1940 and

[1] Hope, A. D., *Collected Poems*, London, 1966, vii

1965. Perhaps there are accidental reasons in addition to those I have suggested for a situation which I take as at least partly significant about the nature of Hope's talent—the adult confident character it had from the beginning. 'I cannot remember an age at which I did not make up verses,' he writes, 'but my childish rhymes perished in an *auto-da-fé* at the age of fourteen when a friend persuaded me to burn them all and start again. Another fire, for which I was not responsible, later destroyed the evidence of prentice work up to the age of twenty-five.' 'If not symbolic, these were, I feel, at least representative fires.' The poems I have in mind are *The Wandering Islands* (1943), *Ascent into Hell* (1943-44), *The Pleasure of Princes* (1947), *Imperial Adam* (1952), *Pseudodoxia Epidemica* (1961). There are others in the cluster but these are the main lights.

The Wandering Islands is a powerful meditative poem on the theme of isolation. It makes the characteristically solid impact of Hope's best poems, seeming to have behind it the weight of personal experience which has been grasped and deeply pondered. It starts with a general statement, an announcement about human feelings which carries with it some of the certainty of a physical law, and which calmly joins the order of emotion to the geographical world of the wandering islands:

> You cannot build bridges between the wandering islands;
> The mind has no neighbours, and the unteachable heart
> Announces its armistice time after time, but spends
> Its love to draw them closer and closer apart.

It goes on in a stiffly effective way, in an idiom which is almost a combination of the language of cartography and law (the work of a dusty official working on maps in a remote office) to define the position of the unfixed islands. 'Position' may be a paradoxical term here, but it sufficiently indicates both place and nature.

> They are not on the chart; they turn indifferent shoulders
> On the island-hunters; they are not afraid
> Of Cook or De Quiros, nor of the empire-builders;
> By missionary bishops and the tourist trade

They are not annexed; they claim no fixed position;
They take no pride in a favoured latitude;
The committee of atolls inspires in them no devotion
And the earthquake belt no special attitude.

A refuge only for the shipwrecked sailor;
He sits on the shore and sullenly masturbates,
Dreaming of rescue, the pubs in the ports of call or
The big-hipped harlots at the dock-yard gates.

But the wandering islands drift on their own business,
Incurious whether the whales swim round or under,
Investing no fear in ultimate forgiveness.
If they clap together, it is only casual thunder....

The *Wandering Islands* by nature, the shipwrecked sailor by fate, cannot share or touch another, except accidentally or momentarily; experience for them is ultimately singular and solitary. As it is, the poet suggests, for us and for the sullen shipwrecked sailor—not an admirable but certainly a real character, whose unappealing wretchedness makes him a fit figure for the common human person in this iron context. Nor is our, or the Islands', incapacity for participation any protection against suffering. The most lacerating and the most human suffering is produced by the actuality of ultimate separation and the hopeless aspiration for union. We suffer because the edge of individuality and the rigour of isolation cannot be softened, or only for an instant and by an illusion, which is itself swept away by 'the huge monotonous voices' of reality.

And yet they are hurt—for the social polyps never
Girdle their bare shores with a moral reef;
When the icebergs grind them they know both beauty and terror;
They are not exempt from ordinary grief;

And the sudden ravages of love surprise
Them like acts of God—its irresistible function
They have never treated with convenient lies
As a part of geography or an institution.

An instant of fury, a bursting mountain of spray,
They rush together, their promontories lock,
An instant the castaway hails the castaway,
But the sounds perish in that earthquake shock.

And then, in the crash of ruined cliffs, the smother
And swirl of foam, the wandering islands part.
But all that one mind ever knows of another,
Or breaks the long isolation of the heart

Was in that instant. The shipwrecked sailor senses
His own despair in a retreating face.
Around him he hears in the huge monotonous voices
Of wave and wind: 'The Rescue will not take place'.

The Wandering Islands is a strongly objective poem, written in
a mood of dry, almost grim composure, in which the settled author,
unfrayed by his own situation and its isolation, stares bleakly at
what is the case, namely the twin realities of the wandering islands
and 'all that one mind ever knows of another'. Much of the
intensity of the poem's effect comes from the simultaneous and
equal treatment of the two themes, not in a way which uses the
geographical figure as a simple analogy or parable but as an exercise
in positive ambiguity.

Australians are sometimes thought to be fustily conformist—it
is a criticism the Australians often make of themselves—but there
is also in the Australian psychology a quality of lissom independence corresponding, perhaps, to the marvellous bodily suppleness
generated by a regimen of sun, protein and sport. Only an Australian, and one of Hope's gifts—onlyHope himself, I suppose—could
use the antiquarian vocabulary at the start of *Pseudodoxia Epidemica*
with such an unembarrassed lack of self-consciousness. There the
words are, his attitude seems to imply, still with a quirky flair of life
not yet quite snuffed out, as well as a degree of dubious charm. Let
me use them, therefore, taking advantage of their antique attractiveness, and consciously manipulating them in a new direction, like a
batsman who makes not simply an unorthodox but an astonishingly
original stroke, staying all the time strictly within the rules.

> *By acupuncture or by moxibustion*
> *The soul repairs its vulnerable sheath;*
> *And beetle paste is love's electuary.*
> *True tales and false alike work by suggestion.*
> *Cure palsy with a poison-ivy wreath*
> *Or squeeze the devil's cherry to vamp an eye.*

K

There is a checked or controlled comic impulse at work here which
enables Hope to use a set of superannuated terms as though they
were colloquialisms, and to employ what could easily be units of
rhetoric as terms of slang. Two modes of discourse, rhetorical and
familiar, run together through the poem. At one point, as in the
third and fifth stanzas, the rhetorical is more strongly present; at
another, as in the second and the fourth, the casually colloquial is
emphasised. The half-amused, shoulder-shrugging tolerance keeps
the rhetorical from becoming fustian while it gives a sardonic edge
to the slang. Here are the third and fourth stanzas in which one can
see the succession and friction of the two manners.

> Let reason ignore the reasons of the heart,
> Pure knowledge is a sow that eats her farrow;
> But wisdom's children may hear mermaids sing
> In latitudes not found on any chart.
> Fledged without feet, to miss the hunter's arrow
> The bird of paradise keeps on the wing.
>
> Taken full-strength, truth is a drug that kills.
> They say that when he rose, the morning after,
> Faith took a tot and felt as right as pie;
> But, having accurately checked his bills,
> Clairvoyance was found dangling from a rafter,
> All the true facts reflected in his eye.

We see too in these lines the opposition between pure reason and
poetic experience which is central to the poem, a conventional
enough dichotomy, it is true, but one given a personal bite in
Hope's treatment since it is shown to be the structural condition of
the poet's own life, which was a movement from a green youth of
'probe and test' to the 'ripe years' writing of love. The clairvoyance
of reason which governed his youth gave way in maturity to poetic
faith with its reviving tot. The poem has a surface inconsequence
but it is supported by a spare and credible logic. Beginning with the
old wives' drugs which work by suggestion, it goes on to the other
side of the equation, our response, which itself exerts its influence
upon what it meets. 'Our questions choose the answers they think
good.' If this offends the accuracy of clairvoyant reason, it is

because that mode of understanding is partial and selective, bent
upon law and coherence, whereas human experience is large and
thick with oddity and absurdity. Poetic power seeks for the unique
and makes its rule discovering the exception. The poem, which
begins with the ancient old wives' remedies, beetle paste, poison-
ivy wreath and devil's cherry, and then slips through reflection,
example, and the poet's own history, comes in the end in an
unbroken curve to a figure taken from medieval logic, and to the
exception with which the poet's (and the human being's) experience corrects the arid concept.

> *A thousand years pen-white was the tradition.*
> *There was the lake: one only had to look*
> *To see truth's emblem paddling in her snow;*
> *The black one was a joke of the logician.*
> *And yet there was a wild swan in my book*
> *Proved him a liar. But how was he to know?*
>
> Cygnus mansuetus *may be just a bird.*
> *With you my fabled swan, I give up trying*
> *To disbelieve what science cannot prove.*
> *Let ornithology find our tale absurd:*
> *The cob that sings at last when close to dying*
> *May prove at last my parable of love.*

The next two poems in this group, *The Pleasure of Princes* and
Imperial Adam recall to me the comment with which I began about
Hope's positive, almost fierce, sense of the Western Latin tradition.
In the first of these poems a Roman severity outlines the Machia-
vellian content; in the second, another species of Latin tempera-
ment appears, mellow and disillusioned and ironically conscious.
Here are the openings of both poems:

THE PLEASURE OF PRINCES

> *What pleasures have great princes? These: to know*
> *Themselves reputed mad with pride or power;*
> *To speak few words—few words and short bring low*
> *This ancient house, that city with flame devour—*

To make old men, their fathers' enemies,
Drunk on the vintage of the former age;
To have great painters show their mistresses
Naked to the succeeding time; engage

The cunning of able, treacherous ministers
To serve, despite themselves, the cause they hate,
And leave a prosperous kingdom to their heirs
Nursed by the caterpillars of the state. . . .

IMPERIAL ADAM

Imperial Adam, naked in the dew,
Felt his brown flanks and found the rib was gone.
Puzzled he turned and saw where, two and two,
The mighty spoor of Jahweh marked the lawn.

Then he remembered through mysterious sleep
The surgeon fingers probing at the bone,
The voice so far away, so rich and deep:
'It is not good for him to live alone'.

Turning once more he found Man's counterpart
In tender parody breathing at his side.
He knew her at first sight, he knew by heart
Her allegory of sense unsatisfied.

The pawpaw drooped its golden breasts above
Less generous than the honey of her flesh;
The innocent sunlight showed the place of love;
The dew on its dark hairs winked crisp and fresh. . . .

In *The Pleasure of Princes*, the stony, stoical quality and the
regular edge of the verse match the author's notation of the unavoidable brutality and loneliness of life, even for one who lives it
in one of its most intense forms as the possessor of power. In
Imperial Adam, a milder but equally unquestioning regard is turned
upon the myth of Genesis. In cool, strict verse the poet accepts and
appreciates the grandeur of imperial Adam and the contrast
between the paradisal innocence of the garden and the splendid
sensuousness brought in by Eve. He registers the real humanity of
the myth, the naturalness of the human experience in its animal

context, and the irony by which evil is brought out of good: and Cain, the first murderer, by the union of imperial Adam and generous Eve.

. . .

It was the beasts now who stood watching by:

The gravid elephant, the calving hind,
The breeding bitch, the she-ape big with young
Were the first gentle midwives of mankind;
The teeming lioness rasped her with her tongue;

The proud vicuna nuzzled her as she slept
Lax on the grass; and Adam watching too,
Saw how her dumb breasts at their ripening wept,
The great pod of her belly swelled and grew,

And saw its water break, and saw, in fear,
Its quaking muscles in the act of birth,
Between her legs a pigmy face appear
And the first murderer lay upon the earth.

Some Australian critics have found metaphysical complexities in this poem, a view of the world and a sense of sin, particularly of the sexual sort; but to me the poem seems most remarkable for its wholeness and simplicity. A tranquil, pagan eye, not by any means without humour, is turned upon the Jewish-Christian story. This itself makes for freshness. And it is the naturalness of the events in the fable which the poet emphasises, the warmth, and goodness and human incongruity of the story; the theological implications are quite suppressed, are not in fact really there at all. If there is a view of life implicit in the poem, it is certainly not a religious or philosophical one; it is not even a psychological one in which the poet's own tensions are involved; it is, I believe, an aesthetic view, which sees the excellence of life as the shaping of experience into an objective and harmonious pattern.

If one wanted as Mediterranean but a more intimately personal and self-involved poem, one would go to *Ascent into Hell*, where the poet travels into his interior life in search of a meaning and an explanation and uses again, in keeping with that scientific habit which was part of his education, the reductive method he employed

in *The Dinner*. But while there the poet was the evolutionary bio-
logist, here he is the genetic psychologist. The difference between
Hope and the psychologist, however, is that Hope brings to bear
upon his enigmatically impalpable subject, the vaguely glimmering
beginnings of his existence, not external measuring instruments but
that most refined and disciplined of faculties, the matured poetic
consciousness. Each glimpse of, each hint about, the beginning of
his life has a poetic definition and actuality of being, and the whole
poem itself has the solidity of an event. He defines first his point of
entry, the conscious intention which is something distilled as much
by his total situation as by what he deliberately means to do.

> *I, too, at the mid-point, in a well-lit wood*
> *of second-rate purpose and mediocre success,*
> *explore in dreams the never-never of childhood,*
> *groping in daylight for the key of darkness;*

The Dantesque reminiscence reminds us not to forget Hope's
characteristic and wholly unaffected daring. But such nerve is
justified by the naturalness with which the poem starts, and the
propriety and evenness with which the body of it flows from the
opening. He next defines the location, Tasmania, where the
marsupial territories and the gum trees together with the twilight
poplars and the church pines combine the genius of Australia and
Britain, that particular blend of sensibility which is the poet's genius
too. This place, the product of two national sources, is not just an
enclosing context but an inward condition of the child's psychology. Implicit in that condition is a powerful sense of distance, of
distance as a positive and creative dimension of imagination.

> . . . .
>
> *revisit, among the morning archipelagoes,*
> *Tasmania, my receding childish island;*
> *unchanged my prehistoric flora grows*
> *within me, marsupial territories extend:*
>
> *there is the land-locked valley and the river,*
> *the Western Tiers make distance an emotion,*
> *the gum trees roar in the gale, the poplars shiver*
> *at twilight, the church pines imitate an ocean.*

He follows the 'dwindling soul' back to where memory, no longer a solid continent, splits into disconnected fragments and images, to a point where the language of thought and feeling falls away into words which are no longer supported by rational syntax. This is the child's universe distorted by violence and terror, existing wholly in its parts, in terrifying bits and pieces, 'the inner world of panic'.

> . . .
> *the bayonets and the pickelhauben gleam*
>
> *among the leaves, as, in the poplar tree,*
> *they find him hiding. With an axe he stands*
> *above the German soldiers, hopelessly*
> *chopping the fingers from the climbing hands.*

The fantasies of the young child strike the adult as deficient above all in reality, since they seem to him to lack the essential content of experience. But they are real in other ways: they have the intensity of lightning and the permanence of scars; and they are real not only as events but as influences, laying down and affecting the very cells of personality and fastening real things and real influences into the foundations of self.

> . . .
> *Dreamlike within the dream real names and places*
>
> *survive. His mother comforts him with her body*
> *against the nightmare of the lions and tigers.*
> *Again he is standing in his father's study*
> *lying about his lie, is whipped, and hears*
>
> *his scream of outrage, valid to this day.*

The substance of the poem is made up of memories of violent moments from infancy to childhood, shot through with guilt and fear, which stand out in the poet's life as passages of naked existence when a mysterious sense of being worked in a pure and powerful way. The poem is, in fact, a footnote in shorthand to *The Prelude*, in a Tasmanian rather than a North British accent. But because it is genuinely personal and totally identified with its own conditions, it is novel and quite underivative. And while it is not religious

or numinous in the Wordsworthian manner, it has a dimension of
the same kind. The poet is aware of the unique in his experience and
the mystery surrounding it. Completely conscious in an altogether
contemporary way—he is after all casual, Australian and post-
Freudian—he is still able to acknowledge the inexplicable in his
life; and there is no absurdity in his calling upon whom he does to
enforce this admission.

> *Beyond is a lost country and in vain*
> *I enter that mysterious territory.*
> *Lit by faint hints of memory lies the plain*
> *where from its Null took shape this conscious I*
>
> *which backward scans the dark—But at my side*
> *the unrecognized Other Voice speaks in my ear,*
> *the voice of my fear, the voice of my unseen guide;*
> *'Who are we, stranger? What are we doing here?'*
>
> *And through the uncertain gloom, sudden I see*
> *beyond remembered time the imagined entry,*
> *the enormous Birth-gate whispering, 'per me,*
> *per me si va tra la perduta gente.'*

   Hope is a remarkable poet, the most distinguished his country
has produced. His very positive literary character is both grainily
individual and strongly in the main Western literary tradition. It
is, it is clear, the central tradition he adheres to: accretions, whether
modish or cliqueish, he has no use, and indeed considerable scorn,
for. The lucidity and correctness which he is at pains to develop in
his work are qualities he admires from artistic conviction, as a
humanist opposed both to romantic haze and conventional trends.
But they also testify to a profound cultivation of spirit, a certain
wholeness and harmony of nature, as they do too to a fine independence of literary fashion.
   Hope comes at a sensitive and influential point in his nation's
history, when a separate national consciousness has become clear
and firm, and when the humanising influence of the arts is more
than ever necessary as wealth, power and material energy increase.
In Hope's poetry we sense not only the presence but also the
pungency of values which are an extension of personal and national

character, namely vitality, order, honesty and the capacity for not being unduly impressed. The future requires that the consciousness of the race be articulated in, and refined by, arts generated on its own soil, above all by the supremely expressive art of language, since nothing has more human reality than the savour of home. Hope has made his own invaluable contribution to this essential purpose.

CHAPTER V

KATHERINE MANSFIELD

KATHERINE MANSFIELD was born in Wellington in 1888 to a prospering business family—her father later became Sir Henry Beauchamp. There were two older sisters and a younger brother in the family, together with unmarried aunts and a grandmother. She was educated at a boarding school in New Zealand and later in London. Her wealthy father made her an allowance which continued throughout her life and she left for London for good at the age of 19. She led a confused and wretched personal life. There was a pregnancy, marriage to a man who wasn't the father of the child, a miscarriage, other love affairs, and finally comparative peace with John Middleton Murry when their life together began in 1912. They were not able to marry until 1918. Almost from the time she came to London her health was poor and she died of tuberculosis at Fontainebleau in 1923. Her writing career was spent in Europe and her reputation made there. Most of the critical attention accorded to her—at one time it was considerable—concentrates upon her as a European writer. Very little, with the exception of the fine essay by Professor Ian Gordon,[1] takes into account what becomes increasingly a significant fact about her, that she was a New Zealand writer. This is not merely a matter of provenance but of substance. The brilliance of her innovating contribution to the short story and her subtle mastery of its technique seems to place her firmly in the European world of the 20's and 30's. But as time has tended to diminish the glitter of this particular part of her reputation, or at least to give it a more purely historical importance, we have to see that it is impossible fully to realise the nature of her sensibility without understanding the nature of the experience she aimed to communicate. It is not an exaggeration to say that in her best work this is experience saturated

[1] Gordon, I. A., *Katherine Mansfield*, Longmans Green & Co., London, 1954

with the quality of the rejected country. She was a writer of a markedly autobiographical sort. She explored and used and organised what had happened to her. And in the best part of her best work she was concerned intensely with the world of childhood, or rather the world of children and adults linked together. She is indeed the poet of a family with young children. And the material of which that poetry was made was New Zealand life.

I am not thinking of muted but audible differences in the description of physical life, the strange birds, the paddocks and creeks, the tussoch grass, purple orchids and the manuka bushes, the red and white camellia trees, or the corrugated iron roof which bangs in the wind; not even locutions—'Night O' or 'Kezia thieved out the back'; but of a certain idiom of vision and style of feeling. It includes perception which is quick, candid and exact; reaction which is open and uncommitted by a cargo of presupposition: an expression which is limpid and fluent; a technique which accumulates finely registered detail with such density as to produce massive, reverberating effects; and an interest which is intimate with the past and thoroughly domestic. Let me illustrate this last point expressly, and the other points incidentally. Here is a passage from *Prelude*, one of the early, important New Zealand stories.

. . . Old Mrs Fairfield's arms were bare to the elbow and stained a bright pink. She wore a grey foulard dress patterned with large purple pansies, a white linen apron and a high cap shaped like a jelly mould of white muslin. At her throat there was a silver crescent moon with five little owls seated on it, and round her neck she wore a watch-guard made of black beads. . . . It was hard to believe that she had not been in that kitchen for years; she was so much a part of it. She put the crocks away with a sure, precise touch, moving leisurely and ample from the stove to the dresser, looking into the pantry and the larder as though there were not an unfamiliar corner. When she had finished, everything in the kitchen had become part of a series of patterns. She stood in the middle of the room wiping her hands on a check cloth; a smile beamed on her lips; she thought it looked very nice, very satisfactory. . . . Linda leaned her cheek on her fingers and watched her mother. She thought her mother looked wonderfully beautiful with her back to the leafy window. There was something comforting in the sight of her that Linda felt she could never do without. She needed the sweet smell of her flesh, and the soft feel of her cheeks and her arms and shoulders still softer. She loved the way her hair curled, silver at the forehead, lighter at her neck, and bright brown still in the big coil under the muslin cap. Exquisite were her mother's hands, and the two rings she wore seemed to melt into her creamy skin. And she was always so fresh, so delicious. The old woman could bear nothing but linen next to her body and she bathed in cold water winter and summer.

We see drawn in this passage the confining line within which Katherine Mansfield is able to act with remarkable spontaneity and freedom. The personal past, the known place, the home, the physical context and the chores of the household, family relationships which combine continuity and intensity and in particular the to and fro, the friction and harmony of young and old—these are the points through which the line goes. The area it encloses is narrow but capable of endless treatment. Katherine Mansfield's exquisite clarity of the eye reveals marvellously unfilmed surfaces, and her decorative sense makes brilliant patterns from the details the eye discovers. ('Discovers' because they are not faded by custom but seen in their original excitement.) Moreover, the fluency with which her vision moves releases the details from any static quality and composes them into a moving process. In these household scenes in the New Zealand stories we see none of that bitchiness and getting back at the world we feel in many of her other stories where the art, or technique, is a kind of therapy for the self used by a clever and dissatisfied personality. It is a strange thing that nostalgia which for so many writers is the occasion for indulgence is for Katherine Mansfield a discipline of remembrance. Her feelings are strong but disinterested, and the fidelity and accuracy of her observation brace and control her attitude.

Prelude, one, and one of the best, of the New Zealand stories, was written in 1916 as *The Aloe* but not published till 1930. There are three generations in it, the grandmother, then Stanley and Linda Burnell, and Linda's unmarried sister Beryl Fairfield, and the children, Isabel, Lottie and Kezia. The co-presence of the several generations was a device which enabled Katherine Mansfield to add a temporal thickness to her feeling for the light texture of immediate life. Two of the generations appear in the piece I have given above, and there is a significant contrast between the grandmother and Linda which recurs in the other stories. Grandmother is 'seen' in vivid particularity from the detail of her ornaments to the quality of her skin. Her movements in the kitchen, precise and rhythmic, her gift of conferring her civilising influence on the new, raw house, and the freshness of the whole impression she makes show a regard on the author's part which is closely attentive and appreciative but also sufficiently detached to be coolly in proportion.

Linda on the other hand, the vaguely dissatisfied, not definitely ill or well wife and mother, is not seen in the same way. She is as invisible as one is to oneself. She is the enigmatic present which is never wholly comprehended. Her feelings are misty, her identity a puzzle. She acts as the author's present consciousness which requires a dimension of distance in time to see its objects with total clarity. The grandmother represents for the daughter, and for the author, a wholesome and experienced wisdom, not passively but grittily resigned to reality. But the daughter is all the time nervously anxious to escape or evade it. Her romantic aspirations float about her, never quite grasped, but never strong enough to submerge her appreciation of the grandmother's richness. The grandmother is both Linda's ideal and her hold on reality. Retired from time, her creamy skin exquisitely fresh, able to bear nothing but linen next to her body, bathing in cold water winter and summer, she represents the value and definition which the misty, unformed Linda so much feels the lack of in her own nature.

The children, also distanced by time, are 'seen' in the same way as the grandmother. The members of Linda's generation, however, the husband Stanley and the sister Beryl as well as Linda herself, are felt rather than seen. Which is not to say that they are not substantially realised. They are, but in a different mode. The grandmother and the children are the objects of a kind of creative observation, whereas Linda, her husband and sister, are projected out of the author's shared nature and common predicament. If there is a patch of incomprehension or an unresolved knot in their nature, this belongs properly to their state of relative formlessness.

And indeed, each of them is marked by a certain arrest of development. Stanley is bustling and muscle-conscious, but flinchingly uncertain within. His peremptory casing conceals the softness of the ungrown rather than the gentleness of the experienced. Beryl's romantic fantasies, which the author reproduces with the exact nuance of self-hypnotised wonder, are punctured by bouts of frantic domestic activity and grim moments of self-recognition. But even these last are turned into passages of drama. If Stanley has failed to mature, Beryl is just (although there are hints that she may remain always so) immature. Linda herself, balancing (perhaps too neatly) the character of Stanley, achieves her purposes —but she is never quite sure what these are—through a kind of ruthless helplessness. Wavering and uncertain in action, she is concentrated and even fierce in desire. She has the selfishness of the beautiful and the spoilt, in spite of her 'three great lumps of children'.

The animating theme of *Prelude*—the theme is an event not an issue or a problem in psychology—is the Burnell family's taking-over of the new house, and their gradual soaking of it with their presence. Each generation does it in its own manner. For the grandmother it meant accommodating the new place to the rhythms she had established during her long life; it meant arranging things symmetrically and relating whatever she saw there to a significant and remoter past. When, for example, she notices the tiny corkscrew tendrils of a knotted vine she remembers the vine on the back verandah of her old Tasmanian home. When she puts the crocks away on the dresser, she does it as part of an habitual and hallowed practice. She touches the new house with her own essence. For the children the move to the new house is altogether natural, since its freshness and novelty match their own open nature with its exciting impulse to discover. The middle generation of Stanley and Linda and Beryl have a less clear-cut relationship with the new house. Just as their own rôle, at this time of their life, is more baffling than the children's or the grandmother's, so their connection with the new house is more ambiguous. Stanley is thrilled with the possibilities of a more solid and better ordered life; at the same time he has sudden terrors about possible disasters.

Beryl adores the new opportunities for fantasy, but is appalled at being shut away to rot in the country.

On Linda, the most complex of the three, the move to the new house hardly registers as such. Profounder experiences than this, like love and birth, have only brushed her in the lightest way. The novelty of a new home is too abstract an experience for her, for whom the fascination of life lies in two things, one, the fine free floating life of her own feelings and two, in her strange empathic faculty for sharing in the secret life of things. The intensity of these experiences is a function of her personality and is unaffected by a change of context. Linda is one of those whose concentration on detail leaves her unaware of the larger shape. But the detail itself has a fierce and passionate life, as well as a kind of sadness, since part of the impression it always leaves is its own limitation and imperfection.

> . . . She turned over to the wall and idly, with one finger, she traced a poppy on the wall-paper with a leaf and a stem and a fat bursting bud. In the quiet, and under her tracing finger, the poppy seemed to come alive. She could feel the sticky, silky petals, the stem, hairy like a gooseberry skin, the rough leaf and the tight glazed bud. Things had a habit of coming alive like that. Not only large substantial things like furniture but curtains and the patterns of stuffs and the fringes of quilts and cushions. . . . But the strangest part of this coming alive of things was what they did. They listened, they seemed to swell out with some mysterious important content, and when they were full she felt that they smiled. But it was not for her, only, their sly secret smile; they were members of a secret society and they smiled among themselves. Sometimes, when she had fallen asleep in the daytime, she woke and could not lift a finger, could not even turn her eyes to left or right because THEY were there; sometimes when she went out of a room and left it empty, she knew as she clicked the door to that THEY were filling it. And there were times in the evenings when she was upstairs, perhaps, and everybody else was down, when she could hardly escape from them. Then she could not hurry, she could not hum a tune; if she tried to say ever so carelessly—'Bother that old thimble'—THEY were not deceived. THEY knew how frightened she was; THEY saw how she turned her head away as she passed the mirror. What Linda always felt was that THEY wanted something of her, and she knew that if she gave herself up and was quiet, more than quiet, silent, motionless, something would really happen.

'It's very quiet now,' she thought. She opened her eyes wide, and she heard the silence spinning its soft endless web. How lightly she breathed; she scarcely had to breathe at all.

Yes, everything had come alive down to the minutest, tiniest particle, and she did not feel her bed, she floated, held up in the air. Only she seemed to be listening with her wide open watchful eyes, waiting for someone to come who just did not come, watching for something to happen that just did not happen.

Katherine Mansfield was a writer who succeeded in her best work, in *Prelude* for example, in raising a whole world on the slim basis of half a dozen members of a provincial New Zealand family. She was able quite unportentously to suggest the human universality implicit in the Wellington household. Taking over a new house is itself an instance of the way in which domestic commonplace becomes more largely significant since it is a natural extension of the human impulse to turn impersonal things in the direction of humanity. The conditions of success required by Katherine Mansfield for making the brilliantly pictured particular expressive of substantial human nature were the creative action of memory working in a setting with which she was intimate without strain, a set of characters in whom lurked all the actualities of her own past and a nest of relationships which were rich and ancient but also thronging with possibilities of development and contrast; and as well as these, a general sense, not by any means present in most of her stories, the sense that Beryl has intermittently in *Prelude*— that 'life is rich and mysterious and good. . . .' The goodness comes from the coherence of value and attitude which supports the life of the family and its society; the richness from the emotionally grounded and significantly interesting and worthwhile life its different members live, in which variety is sustained by the strength of the family union; the mysteriousness from the writer's power to reproduce the radiant and inexplicable in human experience. (Linda's version of this mysteriousness appears in the passage I have just quoted.) In these New Zealand stories Katherine Mansfield's sympathetic imagination is controlled by a gift for allowing freedom to the subject so that an extraordinary sureness of touch goes with a remarkable absence of manipulation or forcing of the material.

And the world represented in the New Zealand stories is almost completely uncramped by inherited rigidities. It is open, aerial, unfoggy, lucent. Not that it is without its blemishes of prejudice, like Beryl's icily superior behaviour to the servant Alice in *Prelude*, or the adults' stiff imperviousness to the feelings of the bereaved working class family in *The Garden Party*. But these are, perhaps, more defects of personal sensibility than the formal coldness of class. The Wellington world may not be class-free but class is not the principle on which it is based. Nor is class anything like so strong in its hold on society as family. The divisions of this society are vertical, from family to family, rather than horizontal, from social layer to layer. Within the family the ideal lies in the combined keeping of the very old and the very young. The old, like the grandmother in *Prelude*, offer a standard of life which combines in a surprising but harmonious way the virtues of the well-bred with the qualities of classlessness. The young, on the other side, show vitality unqualified by the bias of *a priori*. Their innocence is not merely negative but a living capacity for experience. The old represent experience carefully gathered up and modestly preserved; the young the intensity with which we live. Between them are the puzzled adults, much less sure of themselves than the very young, much more puzzled about what they aspire to than the old. It is an open universe full of air and freshness. But there runs through it, too, saving it from becoming a nostalgic paradise, a vein, not so much of personal evil, as of natural harshness and even cruelty. We feel the existence of this in the scene in which the good-hearted servant Pat cuts off the heads of the ducks for the amusement of the children in *Prelude*, or where Linda thinks of her husband as an animal, often a nuisance, on occasion a savage, hunting dog. The image of this unavoidable condition of existence, a kind of grimness of reality, is the aloe.

> ... Nothing grew on the top except one huge plant with thick, grey-green, thorny leaves, and out of the middle there sprang up a tall stout stem. Some of the leaves of the plant were so old that they curled up on the air no longer; they turned back, they were split and broken; some of them lay flat and withered on the ground.
>
> Whatever could it be? She had never seen anything like it before.

L

She stood and stared. And then she saw her mother coming down the path.

'Mother, what is it?' asked Kezia.

Linda looked up at the fat swelling plant with its cruel leaves and fleshy stem. High above them, as though becalmed in the air, and yet holding so fast to the earth it grew from, it might have had claws instead of roots. The curving leaves seemed to be hiding something; the blind stem cut into the air as if no wind could ever shake it.

Not all the stories have the rich, many-levelled seriousness of *Prelude* or *At the Bay*, which I shall turn to shortly. There are some, a few no more than sketches, where the strain of impersonal, harsh reality, figured in the aloe, would in fact be out of place. One such is *Her First Ball*, another *Taking the Veil*. Both register with great rapidity the ecstatic, momentary moods of adolescence, and its gift for arguing itself into, and out of, a theoretical despair. Katherine Mansfield in her best New Zealand stories disciplined the expression of self, subduing it to the composition and content of the fiction. In the stories of adolescence this shows itself in an ironic crispness which sympathy keeps just on this side of cool amusement. But the suspension of self-intrusiveness is most evident in the stories about children, in *Prelude* itself, *Susannah*, *How Pearl Button was Kidnapped*, *The Little Girl*, *Sixpence*, *The Wind Blows* and *The Doll's House*. Childhood at one end of the scale like age at the other offered Katherine Mansfield less temptation than more contemporaneous themes to project her own dissatisfaction and tensions into it.

In these stories an attitude of personal detachment supports a subtly perceptive insight. A stance of objectivity and a gift of empathy combine in her technique of modulating the narrative voice at every point into one exquisitely suited to the character and feeling of the moment. Whether it is the very young, as with Kezia in *Prelude*, or the irritated schoolgirl voice of Matilda in *The Wind Blows,* the tone and idiom are exactly right and the transition from author to character conducted with the tact of perfect control. Here are some lines from *The Wind Blows*:

> She has a music lesson at ten o'clock. At the thought the minor movement of the Beethoven begins to play in her head, the trills long and terrible like little rolling drums. . . . Marie Swainson runs into the

garden next door to pick the 'chrysanths' before they are ruined. Her skirt flies up above her waist; she tries to beat it down, to tuck it between her legs while she stoops, but it is no use—up it flies. All the trees and bushes beat about her. She picks as quickly as she can, but she is quite distracted. She doesn't mind what she does—she pulls the plants up by the roots and bends and twists them, stamping her foot and swearing.

'For heaven's sake keep the front door shut! Go round to the back,' shouts someone. And then she hears Bogey:

'Mother, you're wanted on the telephone. Telephone, Mother. It's the butcher.'

How hideous life is—revolting, simply revolting. . . . And now her hat-elastic's snapped. Of course it would. She'll wear her old tam and slip out the back way. But Mother has seen.

'Matilda. Matilda. Come back im-me-diately! What on earth have you got on your head? It looks like a tea-cosy. And why have you got that mane of hair on your forehead?'

'I can't come back, Mother. I'll be late for my lesson.'

'Come back immediately!'

She won't. She won't. She hates Mother. 'Go to hell,' she shouts, running down the road.

The maddened, and I think calculatedly inaudible, 'Go to hell' suggests in a certain sense the gulf between the generations. But much more the words convey, not the uncrossable gap between youth and maturity, but, rather, their paradoxical connection. Friction is as close, perhaps even more searchingly intimate, and certainly more constant than amiability. If this is the negative testimony to the continuity between the ages, the positive evidence is the unimpeded flow of mutual understanding between very young and very old, as in the attachment between Kezia and her grandmother in *Prelude*.

Alert as Katherine Mansfield was to the continuity of childhood, to the mysterious ongoing rhythm which carries it forward, she was equally sensitive to its uniqueness and autonomy. She understood the absolute world of the child, in which things and feelings are there or not, brilliantly in the foreground or vanished altogether, in which the present is dominant and neutrality intolerable. She felt the bitter sense of injustice which children frequently suffer from, like poor Kezia in *The Little Girl*, whipped for tearing up her father's speech to fill a pin-cushion she was making as a present for him, or the cruelty practised against them by mealy-mouthed or merely foolish adults, like Mrs Spears and Mrs Bendall in *Sixpence*.

> 'Oh, my dear,' said Mrs Spears, and she laid her sewing down. 'I don't wonder Dicky has these little outbreaks. You don't mind my saying so? But I'm sure you make a great mistake in trying to bring up children without whipping them. Nothing really takes its place. And I speak from experience, my dear. I used to try gentler measures'— Mrs Spears drew in her breath with a little hissing sound—'soaping the boys' tongues, for instance, with yellow soap, or making them stand on the table for the whole of Saturday afternoon. But no, believe me,' said Mrs Spears, 'there is nothing, there is nothing like handing them over to their father.'

She had a sense of the tip-tilted and melodramatic universe which children inhabit, and of their need to turn objective events into personal crises. She conveyed quite beautifully the way in which for the very young child life is based on a series of incidents, inexplicably unfolding and changing. She saw, too, more intimate things like the significance of touch in the life of the very young, as the essential means by which they break into the world of otherness, and are reassured of its existence and goodness. Think of the deep, the powerful comfort Kezia finds in the touch of her grandmother in *Prelude*, or from her father in *The Little Girl* after a nightmare—the same father, incidentally, who had appeared a ponderous, uncomprehending enemy earlier in the day. She grasped the part sheer size played in the consciousness of children, the menace of what was too large, the delight in manipulating the tiny. What a relief for Kezia again in *The Little Girl* when the immense figure of her father departed after a perfunctory kiss. 'He was so big—his hands and his neck, especially his mouth when he yawned. Thinking about him alone in the nursery was like thinking about a giant.' Or how clearly we see the pleasure of Kezia, in *Prelude*, in arranging the minute bits and pieces of the surprise she is going to make for her grandmother.

> . . . She looked down at the slope a moment; then she lay down on her back, gave a squeak and rolled over and over into the thick flowery

orchard grass. As she lay waiting for things to stop spinning, she decided to go up to the house and ask the servant girl for an empty matchbox. She wanted to make a surprise for the grandmother. . . . First she would put a leaf inside with a big violet lying on it, then she would put a very small white picotee, perhaps, on each side of the violet, and then she would sprinkle some lavender on the top, but not to cover their heads.

All the perceptions I have abstracted flow together in the elegant, strong story, *The Doll's House*. At the centre of this 'composition' stands the doll's house, making an emphatic and solid impact; its colours are thick and bright, and its sharp definition and bold actuality insist on the importance it has for the children. Its diminished size and the minuteness of its appointments show reality reduced to a controllable size, a model of the way the children would wish existence to be.

There stood the doll's house, a dark, oily, spinach green, picked out with bright yellow. Its two solid little chimneys, glued on to the roof, were painted red and white, and the door, gleaming with yellow varnish, was like a little slab of toffee. Four windows, real windows, were divided into panes by a broad streak of green. There was actually a tiny porch, too, painted yellow, with big lumps of congealed paint hanging along the edge.

But perfect, perfect little house! Who could possibly mind the smell. It was part of the joy, part of the newness.

'Open it quickly, someone!'

The hook at the side was stuck fast. Pat prised it open with his penknife, and the whole house front swung back, and—there you were, gazing at one and the same moment into the drawing-room and dining-room, the kitchen and two bedrooms. That is the way for a house to open! Why don't all houses open like that? How much more exciting than peering through the slit of a door into a mean little hall with a hat-stand and two umbrellas! That is—isn't it?—what you long to know about a house when you put your hand on the knocker. Perhaps it is the way God opens houses at the dead of night when He is taking a quiet turn with an angel. . . .

It becomes a great thing in the children's lives, a dream realised. It is the rage at school, the one subject during dinner-hour when the children sit under the pine trees eating the thick mutton sandwiches and big slabs of johnny cake spread with butter. The Burnells who own it glow in its reflection and all their relations with

the others are modified by their status as owners. Access to it
marks the division in the school between those who belong, like
the Burnell children and their friends, and the others like Lil and
Else Kelvey, who for lunch 'chewed their jam sandwiches out of
a newspaper soaked with large red blobs'.

> ... It was the only school for miles. And the consequence was all the
> children of the neighbourhood, the Judge's little girls, the doctor's
> daughters, the store-keeper's children, the milkman's, were forced to
> mix together. Not to speak of there being an equal number of rude,
> rough little boys as well. But the line had to be drawn somewhere. It
> was drawn at the Kelveys. Many of the children, including the
> Burnells, were not allowed even to speak to them. They walked past
> the Kelveys with their heads in the air, and as they set the fashion in
> all matters of behaviour, the Kelveys were shunned by everybody.
> Even the teacher had a special voice for them, and a special smile for
> the other children when Lil Kelvey came up to her desk with a bunch
> of dreadfully common-looking flowers.

This is one of the most explicit of Katherine Mansfield's comments
about class in New Zealand, although to a British reader it has a
certain gentleness and lightness about it which one would not find
in a society more strenuously committed to class. The judgment that
'the line had to be drawn somewhere' points more to a desire for
differentiation—of dress and behaviour, perhaps—than the plain
recognition of it one would get in a society irremediably involved
with class. But in whatever way class existed in Wellington, the
doll's house was the occasion for its intrusion into school in the
fiercer and less compromising way it takes with the young. The
purity of the children's attitude to the doll's house is muddied as
the toy becomes a piece in the political game of in-and-out.
Fascination becomes hysterical excitement, then impersonal cruelty
as the children turn on the outsiders, Lil and Else. Here is a case
where the children's merciless satisfaction in playing with their
victims is sanctioned by the authority of adults, for whom the
freakishly clothed, near-idiot Lil and Else, standing for everything
'common' and graceless, are the fit objects of respectable distaste.

> Lil ... a stout, plain child, with big freckles, came to school in a
> dress made from a green art-serge tablecloth of the Burnells', with red
> plush sleeves from the Logans' curtains. Her hat, perched on top of

her high forehead, was a grown-up woman's hat, once the property of Miss Lecky, the postmistress. It was turned up at the back and trimmed with a large scarlet quill. What a little guy she looked! It was impossible not to laugh. And her little sister, our Else, wore a long white dress, rather like a nightgown, and a pair of little boy's boots. But whatever our Else wore she would have looked strange. She was a tiny wishbone of a child, with cropped hair and enormous solemn eyes—a little white owl. Nobody had ever seen her smile; she scarcely ever spoke. She went through life holding on to Lil, with a piece of Lil's skirt screwed up in her hand.

Only two children, the single-minded Kezia, the youngest Burnell, and the simple-minded our Else (for her sister Lil with her foolish smile and weird, grown-up hat is a soft, co-operative victim, accepting her subordinate station) escaped the general infection, an image, this, of the wider corruption outside. They are saved by the rapt intensity of their self-forgetting attitude to the doll's house.

. . . The Kelveys came nearer, and beside them walked their shadows, very long, stretching right across the road with their heads in the buttercups. Kezia clambered back on the gate; she had made up her mind; she swung out.

'Hullo,' she said to the passing Kelveys.

They were so astounded that they stopped. Lil gave her silly smile. Our Else stared.

'You can come and see our doll's house if you want to,' said Kezia, and she dragged one toe on the ground. But at that Lil turned red and shook her head quickly.

'Why not?' asked Kezia.

Lil gasped, then she said, 'Your ma told our ma you wasn't to speak to us.'

'Oh, well,' said Kezia. She didn't know what to reply. 'It doesn't matter. You can come and see our doll's house all the same. Come on. Nobody's looking.'

But Lil shook her head still harder.

'Don't you want to?' asked Kezia.

Suddenly there was a twitch, a tug at Lil's skirt. She turned round. Our Else was looking at her with big, imploring eyes; she was frowning; she wanted to go. For a moment Lil looked at our Else very doubtfully. But then our Else twitched her skirt again. She started forward. Kezia led the way. Like two little stray cats they followed across the courtyard to where the doll's house stood.

The children's trance of contemplation in front of the doll's house, and especially before the tiny lamp which sums up all its perfections, is splintered by the cold, proud voice of Aunt Beryl (the shift from child to adult and back to child is managed with silken ease) who represents the adult world they are attempting to deceive. She berates them viciously, brutally shattering their dazed felicity. The ugly and clinically observed thing here is that Beryl's anger is not really genuine, in the sense of being directly provoked by the children's disobedience. She is using them as the means of relieving her own tension. 'The afternoon had been awful. A letter had come from Willie Brent, a terrifying, threatening letter, saying if she did not meet him that evening in Pulman's Bush, he'd come to the front door and ask the reason why! But now that she had frightened those little rats of Kelveys and given Kezia a good scolding, her heart felt lighter. That ghastly pressure was gone. She went back to the house humming.'

In the volume *The Dove's Nest* (1923) in which *The Doll's House* appeared, Middleton Murry quoted from Katherine Mansfield's *Journal* (*Journal*, as he called his arrangement of what was more a rather haphazard Note Book) under the heading *Stories for my New Book: 'N.Z. At Karori: The Little lamp. I seen it. And then they were silent'*. Out of this glimpse of its ending the story shapes itself with buoyant certainty, beautifully exemplifying the wish which appears under another *Journal* entry for July 1921. 'I want to be nearer—far nearer than that. I want to use all my force, even when I am taking a fine line.'

I turn now to a group of stories, published in a number of volumes, which seem to me to go naturally together. These are *The Garden Party*, *An Ideal Family*, *The Voyage*, *Six Years After*, *The Stranger*, and *The Fly*. All but *The Fly* have a New Zealand ambience, and even in this, as Ian Gordon[1] points out, the two protagonists express different aspects of the father-figure, Burnell. These stories have three things in common. They concern themselves with a variety of family relationships spread over a full lifetime. In all of them we are aware of death as a presence or a

---

[1] Gordon, I. A., *Katherine Mansfield*, Longmans Green & Co., London, 1954, p. 16

threat or as the initiator of action. And each of them exhibits the combination spoken of in the *Journal* of force and a fine line. There is no unabsorbed wash of feeling in them. They are defined by a line which is delicately sinuous, tracing each modification of the narrative contour, but also sure and strong. And at key points they come to considerable, almost painful, intensity.

In *The Voyage* the young girl Fenella, whose mother has just died, is seen off by her father (another solid and nervous member of the Burnell species) on a voyage on the Picton boat with her grandmother, with whom it is suggested she is going to live. The dramatic clarity with which Katherine Mansfield evokes the dock-side, the embarkation, and as they arrive, the landfall, brings out the peculiar island-consciousness of the New Zealanders; and the meaning of the ship in the people's lives is felt in its being not another form of transport but a different kind of home, with a saloon for a sitting-room and bunks instead of beds. The little girl is disturbed but not distraught and her grandmother, although agitated at leaving her bereaved son, has learned to sway with the blows of life. The grandmother is beautifully realised, dry and withered but also energetic, efficient and brimming with vitality. She is the natural focus for touches of something I have not spoken of yet, Katherine Mansfield's gift of a serenely mellow good-humour.

> . . . An immense basket of ham sandwiches caught her eye. She went up to them and touched the top one delicately with her finger.
>
> 'How much are the sandwiches?' she asked.
>
> 'Tuppence!' bawled a rude steward, slamming down a knife and fork.
>
> Grandma could hardly believe it.
>
> 'Twopence *each*?' she asked.
>
> 'That's right,' said the steward, and he winked at his companion.
>
> Grandma made a small, astonished face. Then she whispered primly to Fenella, 'What wickedness!'

The domestic scene is given all its fullness and value in grand-mother's undressing in the tiny cabin, in Fenella's washing at the basin.

> The hard square of brown soap would not lather and the water in the bottle was like a kind of blue jelly. How hard it was, too, to turn

down those stiff sheets; you simply had to tear your way in. If everything had been different, Fenella might have got the giggles.

This richness of the domestic interior, a poetic homeliness, meets
them also when they arrive at grandmother's house where 'lying
to one side of an immense bed, lay grandpa. Just his head with a
white tuft and his rosy face and long silver beard showed above the
quilt. He was like a very old, wide-awake bird.' This slim, or rather
wiry, story has complete honesty and real power and it is quick with
implications of the rhythm of life. The desolation surrounding the
child is there—'Oh it had been so sad lately. Was it going to change?'
—but it is seen as part of a more encompassing movement which
includes promise and comfort as well as death. Its fascination lies
in the way in which life here belongs to the aged, the tiny grandmother and the ancient, gay grandfather.

In *The Garden Party*, life is with the young, with the unformed
and generous Laura. The story depends on the gap which exists
between two worlds: Laura's, where the gardener is up since dawn
sweeping the lawns in preparation for the garden party, where
friendly workmen consult her on where the marquee should go,
and where florists bring trays of crimson-stemmed canna lilies, a
world of Godber's cream puffs, cooks, icing and gorgeous hats;
and on the other side, a world of mean cottages where the garden
patches hold nothing but cabbage stalks, sick hens and tomato
cans, swarming children and minute birdcages. 'When the Sheri-
dans were little they were forbidden to set foot there because of the
revolting language and of what they might catch.' These alien
worlds are joined at one point and by one person but through two
opposing forces; life which brims in Laura, and death in the fatal
accident to one of the workmen from the cottages. When this event
breaks into the beautiful morning Laura's reaction is total. She
wants the garden party cancelled. But the family's cool, superior
common sense muffles the force of her response. She is sent in what
is a gesture towards her to the cottages with a basket—a basket!
—of remnants from the party. When she arrives at the stricken
house she finds the mystery of death set about with cheapness and
ugliness and oily neighbours and with just as much convention as
surrounded the garden party at home. There are two absolutes

in this story, life and death, but they are conveyed without the least hint of abstraction in the rapture of Laura's morning and in the remoteness of the young man dead in the cottage. There is not a false or contrived moment in the piece, whether in feeling, character, construction or transition. What the words promise *is* there, even if this is inarticulate or evanescent, like Laura's nearly dumb, deeply felt sense of communication with her brother, Laurie.

In two other stories in the series, *Six Years After*, and *The Stranger*, life is more worn and the faces more ravelled. These too have to do with ships, that constant in New Zealand life. In them both death is the separator—but of the living. In *Six Years After* a mother remembers her son killed in the war as she stares through the rust-spotted railing of the ship at the gulls flying listlessly by: 'they looked cold and lonely. How lonely it will be when we have passed by, she thought. There will be nothing but the waves and those birds and rain falling.' A deeply romantic nature feels even this intolerable grief in a romantic form, as some vague presence calling out to her from the sea. Her nature and its burden had in fact made it impossible for her to grasp the present experience for what it is, and this light impenetrable veil stands between her and her vigorous, but dependent husband. In *The Stranger*, Mr Hammond, again a Burnell type, immensely active and confident but worried, too, and avidly possessive, waits on the dock for his wife's ship to arrive. The harder he tries to get closer to her the more inwardly remote she becomes. And again it is death, not love or life, which is the divisive force. A stranger at sea had died in her arms.

> 'You're not—sorry I told you, John darling? It hasn't made you sad? It hasn't spoilt our evening—our being alone together?'
> But at that he had to hide his face. He put his face into her bosom and his arms enfolded her.
> Spoilt their evening! Spoilt their being alone together! They would never be alone together again.

In both these stories one has the impression of observation rather than participation. The author is looking on and reporting back with disciplined fidelity. Death she sees as a force subtly intruding upon and modifying the nature of the living in accordance with the bias of their being.

Where the mood in *The Stranger* was melancholy and in *Six Years After* plangent, in *An Ideal Family* it is bleak, the cold recognition not so much of the laceration of old age as of the onset of death. Old Mr Neave is not really ill or feeble but he is becoming aware—in bones, nerves and soul rather than mentally—of the mutter of mortality. The irony of the title comes from the division between the family reputation—'You are an ideal family, Sir, an ideal family. It's like something one reads about or sees on the stage'—and the vulgar actuality he meets on returning to his house, the fractious family, the bright social chatter, the suave son, the spoiled daughters, the tennis parties, the dressing for dinner, the smart clothes and the frivolous quarrels. All this was too much for old Mr Neave's thinning blood and diminishing appetite. But it is not so much that he embodies a finer spirit than his coarser family as that their vulgarity speaks of life flooding in them, ebbing in him. Another expression of that difference enlivens the splendid first paragraph describing old Mr Neave's encounter with Spring. It was the swirl of life in the Spring which confused and numbed him.

> He stumped along, lifting his knees high as if he were walking through air that had somehow grown heavy and solid like water. And the homeward-going crowd hurried by, the trams clanked, the light carts clattered, the big swinging cabs bowled along with that reckless, defiant indifference that one knows only in dreams. . . .

In the same way, more profoundly antipathetic than his family's suburban commonplace, is the vitality, the life which is suggested by his wife's 'warm, plum-like cheek' or his daughter Ethel's bright hair, or Lola's violent responses. 'They were too . . . too . . . But all his drowsing brain could think of was—too *rich* for him. And somewhere at the back of everything he was watching a little withered ancient man climbing up endless flights of stairs. Who was he?' Nor is there anything particularly stoic or noble about poor Mr Neave's experience. The quality of his coming death is shaped, like the quality of his life, by his own thin nature. When he sees himself in the detached telescopic way of one slipping away from life, what he sees is 'that little ancient fellow . . . climbing down endless flights that led to a glittering, gay dining-room. What legs he had! They were like a spider's—thin, withered'; and what he hears is 'the wind of evening [shaking] the dark leaves to a thin airy cackle'.

In the scale of grimness made up by the series of stories I have just been considering, *The Fly* is the most savagely mordant. Its setting could be any British city. But the two elderly men meeting in the boss's office are two faces of Katherine Mansfield's New Zealand male, the Burnell father-husband, the one before, the other after the crisis of finally giving up work. Old Woodifield, the retired employee, stares almost greedily at the boss, sitting rosily in his chair, and deriving deep satisfaction from the frailer, muffled figure before him. There is a great business of a glass of whisky given and accepted which conveys not simply pity from the active to the inactive but even a half-submerged fear at what is about to happen to oneself. A visit to Belgium brings up the subject of the boss's son, killed in the war six years ago. (Here again is that echo from Katherine Mansfield's personal life, the beloved brother lost in the war.) The puzzled boss discovers that he now feels no grief, that in fact he feels nothing. At this point he notices a fly in his inkpot, feebly trying to climb out. He rescues the fly out of admiration for its courage, and in a detached, dreamy way he drops a blob of ink on it, giving himself a chance to admire its pluck again; and he does it once more after it has painfully cleaned its legs, and then again.

> He leaned over the fly and said to it tenderly, 'You artful little b . . .' And he actually had the brilliant notion of breathing on it to help the drying process. All the same, there was something timid and weak about its efforts now, and the boss decided that this time should be the last, as he dipped the pen deep into the inkpot.
> It was. The last blot fell on the soaked blotting-paper, and the draggled fly lay in it and did not stir.

The paradox of the story is that the living man, not the dead boy, is the representative of death. The dead boy was alive when he died. The old man with his inky fly is simply embalmed. It is a cold, terrifying story and it speaks for the stony, impersonal quality, the indifferent process of life which is a theme running through many of the stories, and which was present in a more generous context in *Prelude* in the shape of the aloe that held 'so fast to the earth it grew from, it might have had claws instead of roots'.

A Katherine Mansfield story is a complex, subtly woven organism, making its point, or its several points, by a blend of implication, imagery, contrasting half-tones and the manœuvring of distinct but chiming voices, each voice and each viewpoint melting without grating or jar into the next. It is, that is, a poetic technique with the characteristic of such, a capacity to stay transparently faithful to the author's vision and also to take on colour, whether it be subdued or strong, perfectly fitted to the theme at any given moment. That this is the mode natural to Katherine Mansfield's genius is clear if we look at two stories, the one a failure, the other not her finest, where a prosaic is contrasted with a poetic technique. *The Woman at the Store* is violent and clever in an obvious way. There is in it no throb of personal experience or history, and certainly no sanction in the self. It is a plotted, too carefully plotted, sequence of events with a calculated crisis and a neat twist. A gang of sweating muscular workers are riding between jobs on their way to the store, randily in hope of game, and they are met by a scrawny woman, deserted and whining, and her moronic child. This youthful exercise in the wild colonial boy manner labours on its predestined route to a predictable climax: a mean, chemical kind of sex between the woman and one of the men provokes the child's spite at being excluded from its mother's bedroom. It puts its only talent to service by drawing a picture of the forbidden subject, the mother shooting and burying the father. Any value the story has comes from its indignant sense of the female exploited by the rapacious and fundamentally indifferent male, and from the way in which the scene and the weather are made to echo the mood. But the melodramatic seeps in here too. 'There is no twilight in our New Zealand days, but a curious half-hour when everything appears grotesque—it frightens—as though the savage spirit of the country walked abroad and sneered at what it saw.'

The same theme, the used woman, and the same device, making mood resonant in scenery, appear in *A Birthday*, which for all its

German names and its publication in the volume *In a German Pension* is distinctively New Zealand. The theme and the device, however, are very much more sensitively handled. The connection with the physical world is more obliquely made and the feminine theme is realised solely through the consciousness of the husband. One notices particularly, too, how time, which was used in *The Woman at The Store* as a successive medium, in which each event is provoked by and provokes another, is in *A Birthday* much more characteristically simultaneous. Time is a wavering direction and its tenses have no absolute status. They are qualified by feeling and by intention and they waft back and forth as the fiction requires. Andreas Binzer, one more male member of the Burnell species, whose wife is in labour; the doctor, a hearty man protected by certainty and conceit; and the maid dramatically ready to yield her allegiance at the slightest encouragement, are all vividly delineated and marked off from one another, perhaps more sharply than is the case in her subtler stories. Andreas is physically tough but infinitely vulnerable, above all to any pain of his own, even when this is induced in him by the sounds of his wife's labour. He reveals himself in that kind of analysis in which self-deception is more revealing than sincere confession. Monster as he is in some ways, he is monstrous in a genuinely human way. We can all grasp and share in the macabre drama which goes on behind Binzer's set, social face. In this story character shades into place—the neglected street in the small sordid town—and feeling into atmosphere, 'Suddenly he realised that the wind had dropped, that the whole house was still, terribly still. Cold and pale, with a disgusting feeling that spiders were creeping up his spine and across his face, he stood in the centre of the drawing-room, hearing Doctor Erb's footsteps descending the stairs.' His wife's suffering presents itself to Andreas as a form of cruelty, and this inversion of reality is completely acceptable, and, we realise, universal. This perception of the collision, or rather conflation, of the categories of experience, produced by stubborn human self-centredness, is made with telling, ironic economy in the last lines, where death and birth themselves are rolled together.

He saw Doctor Erb come into the room; the room seemed to change into a great glass bowl that spun round, and Doctor Erb seemed to swim through this glass bowl towards him, like a goldfish in a pearl-coloured waistcoat.

'My beloved wife has passed away!' He wanted to shout it out before the doctor spoke. . . .

'Well, she's hooked a boy this time!' said Doctor Erb. Andreas staggered forward.

'Look out. Keep on your pins,' said Doctor Erb, catching Binzer's arm, and murmuring, as he felt it, 'Flabby as butter.'

A glow spread all over Andreas. He was exultant.

'Well, by God! Nobody can accuse *me* of not knowing what suffering is,' he said.

True, and effective, and comic as this is, I still think the man versus woman concern in *A Birthday* is just one degree too generalised, just as the characters, grossly husbandly husband, hearty doctor, foolish maid, seem a shade too firmly defined or outlined. Nobody could have this feeling about the thoroughly penetrated material of *At the Bay*. In this story, as in *Prelude*, Katherine Mansfield possesses perfectly, and uses marvellously, the kind of knowledge Henry James spoke of in his essay on Flaubert, 'the knowledge by which he was subsequently to measure everything, appeal from everything, find everything flat'. This was the ultimate premise of Katherine Mansfield's work, a knowledge which was the assimilated, mastered experience of family, home, New Zealand. The story itself is composed of twelve separate pieces, each one marking a certain phase of the day. There is a faint temporal connection from section to section. The first one begins 'Very early morning', the second 'A few moments later'; and so on. The central impression, however, is not of the successiveness of time but of its presentness, an immediacy in which there is nothing hard or fixed. The moment contains, as it were, an incurving space in which the forms of people and events appear, act and turn away. Each piece combines the mysteriousness of existence with the homeliness of actuality. When her attention is turned to the physical world, a tentative contingent note, and the feeling of the senses concentrated, even strained, in recording it imply, not uncertainty, but a discipline of accuracy. How far? She asks at one point, and a little later, What was it?—Questions which by limiting and defining ratify the fidelity of the recording instrument and establish more

firmly the existence of the place—or rather the event which is
what her response turns place into. The introductory section
evokes the misted, edge-dissolving morning,

> It looked as though the sea had beaten up softly in the darkness, as
> though one immense wave had come rippling, rippling—how far?
> Perhaps if you had waked up in the middle of the night you might
> have seen a big fish flicking in at the window and gone again. . . .

This cloudy context is interrupted by the passage of the sheep—
'their thin, stick-like legs trotted along quickly as if the cold and
the quiet had frightened them', by the sheep-dog, and then by the
shepherd,

> He was a lean, upright old man, in a frieze coat that was covered
> with a web of tiny drops, velvet trousers tied under the knee, and a
> wideawake with a folded blue handkerchief round the brim. One
> hand was crammed into his belt, the other grasped a beautifully
> smooth yellow stick. And as he walked, taking his time, he kept up a
> very soft light whistling, an airy, far-away fluting that sounded
> mournful and tender.

This use of a liquid, lapsing movement together with the presentation of exact, absolutely immediate actuality, the first the medium
in which the second has its brilliant, complete existence, fits both
the sensibility of the author, which works by combining lucidity
and suggestiveness, and also the nature of her purpose, which is to
extract from minor occurrences the essential dimensions of reality.
Memory, in Katherine Mansfield's work, consecrates the commonplace and particularly the routine of family life, not in any muffling
or mystical way, but in a manner which made it capable of revealing
the intricate, amazing richness of the ordinary.

She reveals, for example, the unexpected folds which lie beneath
the simple, straight lines of routine family behaviour, the malice
felt towards the close relative who invades one's privacy by sharing
the ocean with one at eight o'clock in the morning, incidentally
betraying to oneself one's raw susceptibility to his maddening
intrusiveness; or the significance in the family context of *not*
passing the sugar at the breakfast table. 'What did this mean? As
Stanley helped himself his blue eyes widened; they seemed to
quiver'; or the pleasure of the women when the man leaves in the

M

morning. 'Oh, the relief, the difference it made to have the man out of the house. Their very voices would change as they called to one another; they sounded warm and loving and as if they shared a secret.' There are subtler observations of the truth of family relations than these. There is the portrait of Linda Burnell in a romantic posture, dreaming the morning away under the manuka tree while the baby lies beside her on the grass and then the shock of realising while she poses in a setting clearly designed for a more traditional emotion, her indifference to the baby, and to all her children. Half her life is spent in the dread of having children, and the other half in disliking the ones she has had. The relationship of the husband and wife, Stanley and Linda, apparently so calmly conventional, is really agitated and ambiguous. His fury at her unoffered sympathy is balanced by his unrecognised punishment of her.

'Stick, dear? What stick?' Linda's vagueness on these occasions could not be real, Stanley decided. Would nobody sympathise with him? . . .

Stanley waved his arm to Linda. 'No time to say good-bye!' he cried. And he meant that as a punishment to her.

The Stanley Linda had married, 'timid, sensitive, innocent Stanley, who knelt down every night to say his prayers, and who longed to be good', this Stanley is now wrapped in activity and buried in the business man. It was very seldom she saw *her* Stanley.

There were glimpses, moments, breathing spaces of calm, but all the rest of the time it was like living in a house that couldn't be cured of the habit of catching fire, or a ship that got wrecked every day. And it was always Stanley who was in the thick of the danger. Her whole time was spent in rescuing him, and restoring him, and calming him down, and listening to his story.

This relationship is an example of the intimacy which divides; there is another of the remoteness which draws together. The relationship of Kezia and her grandmother is the purest and most disinterested of the many explored in the story—a positive abundance, in fact, in view of the limitation of the form. It is one in which each party is totally concerned with the other and the flow of feeling between them is completely free and undisturbed by any subjective twist or knot. An image of this wholesome simplicity is supplied by the very furniture of the room in which the little girl and the old woman are taking their siesta together.

This room that they shared, like the other rooms of the bungalow, was of light varnished wood and the floor was bare. The furniture was of the shabbiest, the simplest. The dressing-table, for instance, was a packing-case in a sprigged muslin petticoat, and the mirror above was very strange; it was as though a little piece of forked lightning was imprisoned in it. On the table there stood a jar of sea-pinks, pressed so tightly together they looked more like a velvet pin-cushion, and a special shell which Kezia had given her grandma for a pin-tray, and another even more special which she had thought would make a very nice place for a watch to curl up in.

Kezia and her grandmother are talking of Kezia's Australian Uncle William, and it is fascinating to see how the grandmother instinctively pares off every adult accretion and irrelevance from her account, and how this is translated in Kezia's mind.

'Well, what happened to him?' Kezia knew perfectly well, but she wanted to be told again.
'He went to the mines, and he got a sunstroke there and died,' said old Mrs Fairfield.
Kezia blinked and considered the picture again. . . . A little man fallen over like a tin soldier by the side of a big black hole.

This relationship contrasts in its clarity with the obscure one existing between Linda and her own children, and in its candour with the equivocal one between Beryl and Mrs Kember, 'a long, strange-looking woman with narrow hands and feet', who looks at Beryl as they undress to bathe in a bold, pawing way. It contrasts, too, in the perfect satisfaction Kezia and her grandmother get out of it, with the vague bond—no more than a common sense of failure—which unites Linda and her brother-in-law, Jonathan, a character who seems faintly to dissolve in the aura of romanticism surrounding Linda and who is hardly seen as a person in his own right. It contrasts, finally, in what I can only call its reality, with the fantasy of Linda's relationship, uneasily longed-for, violently rejected, with the dissolute Mr Kember.

'Reality', I agree, is an off-putting word. But it is difficult to

avoid it, portentous as it may be, when one attempts to define the
nature of Katherine Mansfield's achievement. Not that she hadn't
her failures. Her art was frequently impure, distracted by cleverness
or softened by sentimentality or clouded by being used as a kind
of personal therapy; and why not in her time at her age with
her disease, troubled with the terror of death? But in the New
Zealand stories where she has a rich subject and a deep personal
engagement, where the best of her capacities are used at the pitch
of their force, and where there is a genuine subordination of self
to the work, she succeeds quite beautifully in communicating the
plural quality of human experience and the several levels on which
our lives are conducted. I have referred to the mingling of generations, natural in the family setting, which makes human experience
in these stories a concert of time and character, merging tenses
and moods. Her mobile conception of experience is realised in the
light, rapid run of the prose. Or, since the athletic figure hardly
fits the smooth continuity of the medium, perhaps I should say,
realised in something more like the flow, the wavy motion, of the
prose—which may also suggest its sensitive obedience to every
current of feeling and every turn and impulse of action.

And the sensitivity of the medium, also, to the forms and flux
of physical life, whether this is the land itself in its own unqualified
existence or the landscape as it is modified by human action. Here
are some lines from the start of *At the Bay* in which we see the shift
from a naked, solitary world to one affected by listening, watching,
human presence.

> Ah-Aah! sounded the sleepy sea. And from the bush there came the
> sound of little streams flowing, quickly, lightly, slipping between the
> smooth stones, gushing into ferny basins and out again; and there was
> the splashing of big drops on large leaves, and something else—what
> was it?—a faint stirring and shaking, the snapping of a twig and then
> such silence that it seemed someone was listening.

Katherine Mansfield had an exquisitely sure sense of the fine
gradations of existence and the passage between them. 'The breeze
of morning lifted in the bush and the smell of leaves and wet black
earth mingled with the sharp smell of the sea'. But one also finds
the beach when it is 'strewn with little heaps of clothes and shoes

[and with] big summer hats, with stones on them to keep them from blowing away . . . it was strange that even the sea seemed to sound different when all those leaping, laughing figures ran into the waves'. Or again she shows the garden as land deeply interfused with human influence, occupied in the morning by Linda Burnell, stared at excitedly by Beryl at night. 'But the beautiful night, the garden, every bush, every leaf, even the white palings, even the stars, were conspirators too.' Then she reconstructs those forms of physical life so thoroughly modified by human action that they become expressive symbols of character, like the furniture in grandma's room or the washhouse in which the children played in the evening.

> It was a small tin shed standing apart from the bungalow. Against the wall there was a deep trough and in the corner a copper with a basket of clothes-pegs on top of it. The little window, spun over with cobwebs, had a piece of candle and a mouse-trap on the dusty sill. There were clothes-lines criss-crossed overhead and, hanging from a peg on the wall, a very big, a huge, rusty horseshoe.

And in certain key passages, like this in section nine, she rehearses the process by which each category of existence supports and shades into the next.

> And now the quick dark came racing over the sea, over the sand-hills, up the paddock. You were frightened to look in the corners of the washhouse, and yet you had to look with all your might. And somewhere, far away, grandma was lighting a lamp. The blinds were being pulled down; the kitchen fire leapt up in the tins on the mantel-piece.

Katherine Mansfield's gift for summoning in her art the manifold differences of being in the physical world has its equivalent in the human one, where it shows itself as the nimblest skill in discriminating the various planes and levels of life. In *At the Bay*, *Prelude*, *The Garden Party*, *The Doll's House* we find the *personae*, each in an appropriate tone and idiom, and without the least sacrifice of an unaffected realism, contributing to a lucid system of contrasts, and composing together a scale of experience differentiated according to the degree of 'spirit' or delicacy of being. It is not an hierarchical array where Katherine Mansfield's admiration, as one might perhaps expect of someone with her nature, is accorded to the characters most closely mirroring her own painful strivings after spirituality. It is very much more an objective recognition of the qualitative variety of human life. Nor should one think of it in a straight-forwardly cognitive way as an arrangement of different kinds of knowing, from the highly intelligent to the lively, from the conventional down to the stupid. This would be to overlook the author's sense of the plurality of being which is actively productive here, and her fascination with the rich oddity of human nature. In *At the Bay* Linda's mysterious aspirations and Jonathan's puzzled gropings speak of one part of our nature. The liveliness of the children, their perfect adaptation to the moment and the marine environment ('On the other side of the beach, close down to the water, two little boys, their knickers rolled up, twinkle like spiders') express a vitality balanced between the refined but somehow impoverished quality of Linda's consciousness of life, and the toughness of Stanley Burnell's, at least of the usually visible Stanley Burnell.

> A few moments later the back door of one of the bungalows opened, and a figure in a broad-striped bathing-suit flung down the paddock, cleared the stile, rushed through the tussock grass into the hollow, staggered up the sandy hillock, and raced for dear life over the big porous stones, over the cold, wet pebbles, on to the hard sand that gleamed like oil.

A position on a different part of the range of human existence is taken by Mrs Stubbs, Alice's shopkeeper friend. She embodies the heavy, corporeal element at the furthest distance from Linda. This episode is narrated with Dickensian gusto and a humorous relish for our thick, commonplace—but how appealing!—flesh.

> 'Draw up your chair, my dear,' said Mrs Stubbs, beginning to pour it. 'Yes,' she said thoughtfully, as she handed the tea, 'but I don't care about the size. I'm having an enlargemint. All very well for Christmas cards, but I never was the one for small photers myself. You get no comfort out of them. To say the truth, I find them dis'eartening.'
> Alice quite saw what she meant.
> 'Size,' said Mrs Stubbs. 'Give me size. That was what my poor dear husband was always saying. He couldn't stand anything small. Gave him the creeps. And, strange as it may seem, my dear'—here Mrs

Stubbs creaked and seemed to expand herself at the memory—'it was dropsy that carried him off at the larst. Many's the time they drawn one and a half pints from 'im at the 'ospital. . . . It seemed like a judgmint.'

Alice burned to know exactly what it was that was drawn from him. She ventured, 'I suppose it was water.'

But Mrs Stubbs fixed Alice with her eyes and replied meaningly, 'It was *liquid*, my dear.'

Liquid! Alice jumped away from the word like a cat and came back to it, nosing and wary.

'That's 'im!' said Mrs Stubbs, and she pointed dramatically to the life-size head and shoulders of a burly man with a dead white rose in the button-hole of his coat that made you think of a curl of cold mutton fat. Just below, in silver letters on a red cardboard ground, were the words, 'Be not afraid, it is I'.

'It's ever such a fine face,' said Alice faintly.

The pale-blue bow on the top of Mrs Stubbs' fair frizzy hair quivered. She arched her plump neck. What a neck she had! It was bright pink where it began and then it changed to warm apricot, and that faded to the colour of a brown egg and then to a deep creamy.

'All the same, my dear,' she said surprisingly, 'freedom's best!' Her soft, fat chuckle sounded like a purr. 'Freedom's best,' said Mrs Stubbs again.

I do not want to suggest that the array of differences I have been pointing out is set in some formal, abstract structure. These distinctions are implied; they run under an unbroken surface. Perhaps the strongest impression one gets from *At the Bay* is of a distinct sensibility fluently bending this way and that, and endlessly capable of assimilating without destroying diversities of experience. The manner in this and other New Zealand stories is neither sweetening nor souring. There are none of those infusions of sentimentality and cynicism common enough in the European stories, particularly the 'clever' ones. Nor does the individuality of the style or the idiosyncrasy of rhythm force or twist the material. There is a kind of sensitive neutrality in the medium and it is notable for what I should like to call its non-interference with the subject. A manner making for accuracy and an attitude allowing for respect: these two things witness to the power of the whole New Zealand theme and to Katherine Mansfield's full and controlled response to it. All the poetry of her nature is enlisted, as well as her observer's unblinking attention to the symptom and the illustrative detail, to the wrinkle on the face, or the vein on the pebble, or the fleeting evidence of even not quite articulated feeling.

The world reconstructed with such fidelity—and warmth—in these stories is physically and morally attractive: beautiful in its blend of the Pacific and Western scene, fundamentally decent in its code, and humane in its aspiration. It sustains a mode of life in which children can live imaginatively and adults freely, in which there is a reasonable openness of communication between the sexes and between the different parts of society, and in which the frictions and imperfections, of which there is a full measure, are inward and universal, the products of a substantial, permanent human nature. The figure in which the virtues of this society are collected is the grandmother, Mrs Fairfield. She stands outside the action, mild, firm, tranquil, weathered, having about her an air of bodily sweetness and sober radiance. She has won through to a point of equilibrium between the unavoidable accommodations and the necessary resistances to the rhythms of life. She is saved from any touch of old lady sentimentality by—not a stiffness or severity—but a certain angularity of temperament; and as her exquisite and luminous relationship with her granddaughter Kezia shows, she has, though worn, kept the capacity for true, spontaneous feeling. This relationship stands for all that her New Zealand life meant to Katherine Mansfield herself. It was the ground, the standard, the subject and the nurse of her best art.

CHAPTER VI

MORLEY CALLAGHAN

IT would be hard to find a writer who contrasts more vigorously with Katherine Mansfield than the Canadian Morley Callaghan, whom I wish to consider now. For one thing he works at a much greater psychic distance from, and with a considerably lower degree of sympathy for, the English literary tradition, in which Katherine Mansfield felt so intimately at home. For another, there is in his work, as in that of other Canadians writing in English, a further strain, an implicit sense of oppression by the powerful tradition of the United States. Moreover, Morley Callaghan is a writer whose intentions are simpler than those of Katherine Mansfield, and whose achievement is more restricted—a difference manifested in the contrast of their prose styles: where hers is poetic and suggestive, his is crabbed; where hers is light and gliding, his is stiff. And how extraordinarily discrepant are the materials they treat and the worlds they construct. The world evoked in Morley Callaghan's work is a bleak, industrial one, and its gritty presence rubs off even on the countryside. It is a shut-in, remorseless place in which the individual person even when he lives in a family is painfully isolated. Morley Callaghan's characters in the short stories, with which I shall begin, are mostly drawn from the middle and lower reaches of society: the bereaved poor, the workman, the forsaken wife, the widow, the hard-up young man, the nervous curate and the elderly parish priest, the part-time pugilist, the small girl with a dying mother, the amateur criminal, the drug-store keeper, the apprentice reporter, the cocky young man, the pianist in the tavern. His style is plain to the point of drabness and often painfully clumsy, and yet, in spite of the raw, northern world, the graceless manner and the dreary ordinariness of the characters, the reader is increasingly conscious of an awkward, stubborn and unfashionable conscience, and of a bluntly honest endeavour to dig out and to hold on to some evasive human truth.

'To dig out': as I use the phrase to convey something of Morley Callaghan's hard, blow-by-blow prose, it comes to me that the words say more about him than I had thought. They carry with them a sense of investigation and reporting, and Callaghan's stories strike one precisely as reports—as reporters' reports, in fact. They give the feeling of pre-1914-18 provincial newspaper chronicles, and sometimes of provincial newspaper prose, too. (In fact, Morley Callaghan began his career as a reporter on the *Toronto Star* when Ernest Hemingway was working on the same newspaper.) The storyteller's function as Morley Callaghan practises it is in keeping with this bias in his work. It is to impose an arrest upon time, and to outline for a moment an interruption in the flow of life, which, it is clear, continues as before once the observer's eye is withdrawn. His is a restrictive, framing technique. He is concerned with events, which are shown as instances and images of experience, while the people involved are planed down to an extreme simplicity. A Morley Callaghan story presents a special combination of realistically rendered happening and of people denuded of complication, who are seen as strangers are seen in the street in a single concentrated glance, as types and illustrations. Realism, and a somehow surprising strain of formality, blend in a drily personal way. Indeed, as the reader begins to find his way about the stories, he becomes gradually aware—the effect is slow and cumulative—of an authentic individuality strong enough to show through the plain prose and the straightforward narrative technique.

The reader's sense of that presence is arrived at by continuous application. The unremarkable medium, which has none of the literary sophistication of Hemingway, one of Callaghan's early heroes, takes time to make its mark. And yet it is exactly suited in its unpretentiously humdrum way to the intention on which all this work is sprung, the effort at scrupulous fidelity to the facts of the case. And the 'case' in these stories is the mysteriousness of the ordinary, the inexplicable sequences of feeling, the bewildering discrepancies of human fact, *and* the logic, 'as severe as it is fleeting' as Coleridge has it, which the imagination can elicit from these frictions and inconsequences.

Short stories by Morley Callaghan appeared in 1929 (*A Native*

Argosy,) 1931 (*No Man's Meat*) and 1936 (*Now that April's Here*), and in the two-volume collection (*Morley Callaghan Stories,* 1959). Most of them are strikingly uniform in quality and even a random choice provides the characteristic Callaghan combination, an undistracted concentration on essentials, a rather grouchy but unquestionable honesty, a grave sobriety of mood and treatment and a naturally discriminating moral imagination. Let me look for a moment at the first story, *All the Years of her Life,* in the 1959 collection. The dim and oddly innocent Alfred Higgins is caught by his employer pilfering from the drugstore in which he works silly little objects which he sells for spending money. From this thin, commonplace situation there springs a movement towards complexity, not through analysis but by the natural growth of the action. Alfred's crime, at first denied, and then admitted, becomes an event, a phenomenon, which is gravely scrutinised by Mr Carr, the employer, Alfred himself, who from now on is the registering instrument rather than an active protagonist, and Mrs Higgins, Alfred's mother. She is large and plump with a little smile on a friendly face and seems an intensely positive person beneath her deference. The employer is dislodged from his position of moral superiority, which he had indeed begun to enjoy. Alfred realised that 'Sam Carr was puzzled by his mother, as if he had expected her to come in and plead with him tearfully, and instead he was being made to feel a bit ashamed by her vast tolerance. While there was only the sound of the mother's soft, assured voice in the store, Mr Carr began to nod his head encouragingly at her. Without being alarmed, while being just large and still and simple and hopeful, she was becoming dominant there in the dimly lit store.' The mother's contained strength deflects the angry proprietor. His expression of regret at what happened is almost an apology to her. When Alfred and his mother return to their home he begins to see that the force she showed in the shop was not what it seemed to be. It was not some intrinsic strength of character but a force which issued out of a passion for protection, and once home, with the crisis over, it collapses. As she drinks her tea her hand is trembling and she looks very old. 'He watched his mother, and he never spoke, but at that moment his youth seemed to be over; he knew all the years of her life by the way her hand trembled as she raised the cup to her lips. It seemed to him that this was the first time he had ever looked upon his mother.'

A moment of consciousness—of true recognition, not the usual routine registration—is necessary to clinch the existence of an event, like Alfred's petty crime, or a state of feeling like the mother's weary anxiety, and as it were, to sanction the disturbance it will produce. Or the point of awareness may be necessary to conclude the existence of something long supposed to have been operative: as in the story *An Old Quarrel* where two old ladies, whose nervous trembling age is established with quiet, unsentimental firmness, meet again after many years, one of them under the impression, the illusion as it turns out, that her friend, like her, has spent her life grieving at a bitter, unnecessary quarrel. ' "You shouldn't go on like that, then," Mrs Massey said, fretfully. But she, too, felt her eyes moistening. "Oh, dear, oh, dear." She tried bravely to smile, but it no longer seemed important that they had once quarrelled bitterly, or that her life had been full and Mary's quite barren—just that once they had been young together. A great deal of time had passed, and now they were both old.' But it is never a final revelation, never anything approaching a beatific vision, since it begins at once to be incorporated into a new system of ordinariness. It is this double disappointment which gives a raw reality to several of the short stories, like *Rigmarole* and *Magic Hat*, which have to do with marriage. First the wonder, then the routine, then the recognition, then the new situation and its new unsatisfactoriness, which is sometimes wholly exposed and sometimes merely promised.

Frequently the stroke of realisation brings out that the natural extension of a current state of affairs is, in fact, its contrary. This is so, for example, in *The White Pony*, in which a small boy, ecstatic at the thought of being allowed to attend a circus pony, is led on by a big, freckled, blue-eyed giant of a trainer to carry heavy pails filled with water-soaked sponges, but then brutally excluded when he has done his job.

'No kids in here,' the red-head said brusquely, taking the pails.
'Gee, Mister,' Tony cried. But the door had closed. Tony stood there

with his mouth open, feeling almost sick at his stomach, still seeing the
red-head's warm, magnificent smile. He couldn't understand, if the
red-head were like that, why the pony loved to swing its head to him.
Then he realised that the big fellow had simply used him, that that
was the kind of thing they took for granted in the world he had
wanted to grow into when he had glimpsed it from the garage
window.

'You big red-headed bum!' he screamed at the closed door. 'You
dirty, double-crossing, red-headed cheat!'

The same development by contrariety occurs in *The Shining Red
Apple*, in which the powerful, hairy Joe Cosentino, the green-
grocer, teases and lures the skinny kid who is hanging about waiting
to steal one of the big, juicy-looking apples. Every ounce of energy
and calculation is used to trap the boy, who is suddenly terrorised
as he grasps what is happening. He runs, and Joe is left desolated
that the boy will not succeed in stealing his apple. 'Joe stood on the
sidewalk, an awful eagerness growing in him as he stared at the
shiny red apple and wondered what would happen to the kid he
was sure he would never see again.'

There is a kind of dialectic in human feeling which makes it
swing violently from moment to moment into complete opposition. This movement brings a note of dramatic intensity into
Morley Callaghan's glum and narrow world, making its conflicts
domestic and intense. Turbulence in such a cramped, spiritual
universe—and, incidentally, in such a confined space (the stories
are hardly ever more than a few pages long)—conveys a sense of
unexpected energy: something one feels, too, in Morley Callaghan's
endless inventiveness inside such a limited medium. He has a
particular gift for defining the differing lines of family relationship
and the ugly knots which abruptly interrupt its continuity. There
are of course larger dimensions in his territory. He has a near
Marxist sense of grinding economic law and of the cage of poverty
and unemployment in which many of his subjects are trapped. The
passivity of the poor, an attitude bred by a careful accommodation
to external brutalities, is a favourite theme. At the same time he
shows a certain warmth and sweetness and directness of access to
human feeling which saves the stories from any diagrammatic
coldness.

This is particularly evident in his sensitive treatment of children, where his habit of making the explicit emotional comment appears more naturally than in the adult stories. In *The Little Business Man* the orphaned twelve-year-old Luke lives with his Uncle Henry in a house on the stream by a sawmill. Uncle Henry is a burly man who has mysterious pains which puzzle the doctors, and—fittingly, somehow—an obsessive concern with efficiency and practicality. He decides that the boy's eleven-year-old collie who can hardly see or eat should be put down, not maliciously but simply through motives of efficiency and the economic use of resources. There is nothing personal in his decision —which makes it even more dreadful to the child. The boy saves the dog from being drowned and, using the uncle's character against him, offers to earn and pay seventy-five cents a week for his keep. 'I want to make a practical proposition, Uncle Henry.' Uncle Henry tries desperately to turn his uneasiness and his shame at being weak when he agrees to the boy's keeping the dog into 'a bit of good useful common sense', and he accepts the proposition. ' "I am accepting it because I think you will learn something out of this," he went on ponderously.' The story poses in opposition, disinterested love and practical use, and the subtlety comes in the revelation of how the boy learns to defend the first by adopting the technique of the second. But this triumph is also in a sense an ironic comment on his education because it teaches him that 'love' must be flawed by 'use', and the intrinsic value if it is to be preserved in a world set to destroy it, cannot avoid being infected by the efficient means.

In another story of this kind, *A Cap for Steve*, Morley Callaghan again uses the child's ritualistic nature, the way in which his feelings coalesce overwhelmingly in an object, as the motive of the action. Steve, a games-loving boy, is given a cap by a famous athlete, and the sweaty thing is hallowed for him by an almost numinous glory. He is in despair when it is lost, and all his energy is concentrated on recovering it. When it is found in the possession of a rich man's son, Steve and his father visit the house to reclaim the cap. The scene here is beautifully played out: Steve avid for the cap, the father indignant on his son's behalf, the rich man shrewdly calculating the cost of keeping the cap for his own boy. His mounting offers of course trap Steve's father. The mutual resentment of father and child is developed with clarity and economy. The boy feels that *he* has been sold, the father that *he* has been caught through his son's fault in a web of another man's cunning and his own unfair poverty. The relationship of father and son has a remarkable depth and accuracy and it keeps in play a whole pattern of elements, their circumstances and attitudes, their aspirations and their limitations, their tentative, flinching hopes, their common feeling of betrayal, their fumbling efforts at reconciliation.

The capacity which could produce these clipped, significant stories is not very evident in the early novels, *Strange Fugitive* (1928), *It's Never Over* (1930) and *A Broken Journey* (1932) which are muddy in texture and melodramatic in action. It revealed itself first in *Such is My Beloved* (1934), a novel of which the whole air and idiom belong to the 'thirties, not, that is, the literary 'thirties, but the 'thirties of the depression, of insecurity, unemployment, malnutrition, meanness. Father Stephen Dowling is an assistant priest at a Cathedral—down-at-heel, North American Gothic in a district rapidly crumbling into slumdom. He shines with a special bloom of innocence, health and sincerity. He performs his priestly duties with an eager devotion. He is rapt at the altar, patient in the confessional, conscientious in visiting, eloquent in the pulpit. 'Last Sunday, for instance, at the ten o'clock mass, Father Dowling had preached a sermon on the inevitable separation between Christianity and the bourgeois world, and he spoke with a fierce warm conviction, standing in the pulpit and shaking his fist while his smooth black hair waved back from his wide white forehead and his cheeks were flushed from his glowing enthusiasm. After that sermon, Father Anglin had wanted to argue with the young priest, but he was afraid he would reveal too easily his own lack of faith in any social progress, so, instead of arguing, he merely stared at him with his pale blue eyes and shrugged his shoulders as a kind of warning.' But Father Dowling is also a priest of Irish extraction in a modern industrial society and he likes a good cigar, a ranging conversation with his agnostic friend, a well-cooked meal, a glass of wine, and bridge with the ladies of the parish.

The separation of the two worlds, Christian and bourgeois, is the initiating contrast of the novel. Father Dowling speaks of it in his sermon in a lofty, generalising way. The novel shows it becoming biting and personal—'inevitable' in this way—in his own life. For all his spiritual and social conviction, and in spite of his working-class origins, he himself, because of his education, his status, his looks, his popularity with the parishioners, has a recognised position in the bourgeoisie. Officially he is on the side of religion against bourgeois convention; in reality he has at least one foot in both camps. The point at which the antagonism of the two orders becomes incorporated into his own life, the point at which he starts to be harrowed by the necessity for deciding between them, comes when he meets the two young prostitutes, Ronnie and Midge. One winter night as he walks home from visiting the sick, the two girls solicit him, not realising what he is, and he hurries on in alarm and confusion. But his natural generosity turns him back. From this moment his life is entangled with that of the girls. He visits them in their seedy hotel, ignoring the leers of the proprietor, Mr H. C. Baer. He gives them money and clothes, he begs for them, he tries to find work for them. Above all he becomes their friend, and the girls after their first suspicions and their bewilderment at his motives, recognise his genuine concern and respond to his warmth and sincerity.

The girls' suspicions—the reaction of anyone in their rôle—correspond to Father Dowling's ostensible purpose—his official aim to convert them from their dissolute lives. But the relationship on both sides moves on from this stereotyped posture. Prostitution is only part of the girls' lives, their work, and hard, ill-paid, dirty, dangerous work at that. But it cannot, Father Dowling gropes to realise, be right to identify the person with the function and so to cancel out the girls' essential humanity. On his side, his professional concern with the girls' sinfulness, and his anxiety to redeem them from it, is, at its finest, his own interpretation of a more profoundly human preoccupation, his will to make a human presence available to them. The distinction between the religious and the bourgeois orders, which was implicit, but so ambiguously, in Father Dowling's consciousness at the beginning of the novel, is explored in the light of a similar perception. The point of religion is the expression and refinement of humanity. But many of its attitudes are only ritualistic endorsements of bourgeois prejudices. In the same way, the bourgeois world itself is seen to be larger than a system supported by middle-class morality and comfortable plushness. It stands, indeed, for what is worldly and immoral in a human sense and its membership is by no means limited to the middle classes. Its norm may be the wealthy parishioners Mr and Mrs Robison, its freer, more liberal side may exist in Father Dowling's friend, Charlie Stewart, but it also includes its formal spokesman in the conventional clergy, and a great range of others stretching from the more dubious functionaries necessary to sustain it, like Mr H. C. Baer, or the ghastly Lou, pimp and boy-friend of Ronnie, all the way up to its most eloquent voice, the subtle and impressive Bishop. Religion, during the course of the novel, becomes fined down to a single representative, Father Dowling, whereas the bourgeois world expands to include the proletariat and the aristocracy.

Immediately I write this I find myself, in trying to report on my response to the novel, wanting to correct what may give a misleading impression of neatness. The two worlds, religious and bourgeois, do not fall apart in this absolute way. The standard of human goodness embodied, or painfully achieved, in Father Dowling, is not totally separated from the grubby life of which it is the measure. Just as in Father Dowling himself there is, as I suggested, a clogging residue of bourgeois beliefs, so in the members of the bourgeoisie—in the larger sense—there lurk hints and distorted manifestations of the ideal which burns in Father Dowling. That this should be so, that there should be a distribution of quality over the whole human range, fits the manner of a novel which is governed not by natural law—certainly not that, nor by any Marxist dialectic—but by an economy of naturalness. The partial, uncertain life of the ideal, existing most fully in Father Dowling, may be glimpsed in the timid charity of the pompous Mr Robison, even in the puzzled uneasiness of Lou trying to see what lies behind the priest's actions; or it may be seen in the more complicated struggles of the Bishop's conscience and the irritability with which he applies his analytical intelligence to Father Dowling's situation.

N

'Father Dowling made a fool of himself. It became a kind of arrogance in him. Who does he think he is to win those girls over just by his presence?. . . . If I had it to do over again, I would face the problem in exactly the same way, he thought firmly. What on earth is bothering me then? He was an honest man who committed himself to a piece of folly that can't be tolerated, that's all there is to it.'

The economy of naturalness—which is a reconstruction of movement rather than a Zolaesque realism of detail—is best realised in the principal relationship of the novel, that between Father Dowling and the prostitutes. Its growth, like that of all complex human feeling, is checked, troubled, backsliding, never wholly smooth or continuous; and yet it moves irresistibly onward, obeying and balancing an inward initiative as well as outer circumstances. At first it is sympathetic but embarrassed on one side, suspect and then irritated on the other. 'Ronnie waved her long thin arm threateningly. "Look here. We've got our own way of living just as you've got yours." ' The girls see Father Dowling's intervention as a threat to a whole way of life. They are not persons aware of guilt but resentful of intrusion.

'Isn't it better to starve than lose your. . . .'
'If that's what's worrying you and if it will buck you up and make us seem like tin saints, we're just about starving now. Look around this dump. See all the silks and satins. What do you see? See that old brown coat of mine over there? I've been wearing it for three years. I have to take it off like it was tissue paper or it'll fall to pieces. Isn't this a lovely room? Don't you hate to put your wet boots on that lovely rug? It's filthy, filthy, filthy. But I'd rather be here than out there,' she said, pointing to the window. The little dark girl was pouring the words out of her as if she had become full of hate. 'We're not even high-class whores, see,' she said. 'We take what comes our way and mighty glad to get it.' She was speaking with all the fury of an indignant, respectable woman and the mingling of her strange humility and her passion was so convincing that Father Dowling began to feel doubtful, as if there might be many things he did not understand. He could see the twisted heels on Ronnie's shoes, the broken toe-cap, and the stockings with the sewn-up runs. A long time ago he had heard a Redemptorist priest preaching a sermon about the luxurious life of vice which was always a temptation to poor girls.

Somehow, he himself had always thought of vice as yielding to the delights of the flesh, as warmth and good soft living and laziness. But as he looked around this room and at these angry girls he felt close to a dreadful poverty that was without any dignity. He felt, too, that Ronnie and Midge worked far harder than almost any young women he knew.

As the priest begins to understand the economic forces beating on the young women ('. . . there was a whole economic background behind the wretched lives of these girls. They were not detached from the life around them. They had free will only when they were free'), his attention is less firmly concentrated on the rescue from prostitution and more on bringing a spontaneous human response from them. ' "Midge, would you do a small favour for me? Come around to the church some time. Just of an evening when the church is full. Will you do that?" "I guess so," she said, looking upset and a bit resentful. He loved to have this response and see that indignant expression. It made him feel there was a depth to her that could be touched, some kind of feeling, even if only resentment, and he was much encouraged. "There's passion still there," he thought.' He wants to come face to face with them as person to person instead of as physician to malfunction. But the girls are what they are, and it is hard for them not to believe that Father Dowling might actually be in love with them. They would encourage him, sit on his knee, put their arms around him, be puzzled when he pushed them away. They could not believe that sooner or later he would not want one or other of them. Father Dowling himself is a full-blooded man and there are moments when he feels the sensual attraction of the young women. 'I ought not to be ashamed of being tempted,' he thought. 'I am not a eunuch. The Church will not accept a eunuch for a priest. I'm a normal man and I wouldn't be normal if I wasn't tempted. But I'll never be tempted like this again.'

Father Dowling's estimate of himself is modest and accurate. He *is* a normal man with the customary ration of sensuality and other faults, but there is also a lambent quality in his nature, a glowing capacity for love, or for charity in theological terms, which slowly burns its way through his ordinary human shabbiness

to make its presence felt by others. Even the dim and the malicious
become aware of it, even the least sympathetic answer to it. It
shows itself not in any extreme spirituality or other-wordliness,
but in the power to enter into the lives of others. When he walked
about the streets on a mild evening with the snow nearly gone, and
freshness in the air 'he passed a young man and a girl walking very
close together and the girl's face was so full of eagerness and love
Father Dowling smiled'. And it is with Midge and Ronnie, the
extravagantly inappropriate whores, the ones at the remotest
distance from him, that this gift flowers. Its essential achievement
is not to 'save' the girls, who will, it is clear, never leave their
profession, not to mediate to them the grace of religion but more
miraculously still to communicate the grace of life. 'He felt very
happy to have thought of the dresses. It seemed that for a long
time he had been groping and scraping away at old reluctant
surfaces and suddenly there was a yielding life, there was a
quickening response. He sat there hardly smiling, looking very
peaceful.'

The contradiction between the donors and the deniers of life
is at the heart of *Such is My Beloved*. It is the conclusion to which
the original division between the religious and the bourgeois
worlds finally leads. Father Dowling in his efforts to be as richly
a donor as he can becomes a scandal to the deniers. The novel makes
it quite clear why; and not only clear but convincing. It has nothing
to do with any sentimental falsification of the girls or of prostitution. The angular Ronnie with her hopeless dependence on her
hideous lover, Lou, and the soft, neurotic Midge are thoroughly
credible, whether 'loafing or hunting'; and their mechanical
promiscuity appears as a flat denial of a fundamental law of life.
Father Dowling's offence is caused by a nature with a genius for
generosity which can be satisfied only with an immediate, personal
relationship with the prostitutes, and which, as a condition of that
relationship, acknowledges in the girls an uncrushable human
quality; and acknowledges it the more positively the more he gets
to know *them* rather than just their shiftless, disorganised lives. The
offence is to go outside the routes for treating with such people
sanctioned by the Church and the State. The approved institutional

modes are those of rescue, punishment, and, in the last resort, banishment. Their common note is one of detachment from an object, kindly or severe or even ruthless as the circumstances require. But Father Dowling's vocation by nature and profession is to personal engagement with a subject. By the end of the novel the two attitudes have been completely exposed and opposed in an angry antinomy. The resolution is uneventful and muted, a quiet, ordinary close to the agitation. A word from the Bishop to Mr Robison, and from Mr Robison to the authorities—all, it must be said, acting with a kind of social sincerity in defence of public propriety—and the police bring the girls before a tired, not in-human magistrate, who again with much sincerity and even a degree of kindliness, banishes them from the city. Father Dowling, too, suffers his own banishment. In his case it is an internal one, banishment from self and reason. He has a total mental collapse which leaves him only an occasional interval of sanity, and this he promises will be devoted to writing a commentary on *The Song of Songs*: a nice example, this, of a simplicity of character becoming an irony of situation.

As a composition *Such is My Beloved* has the benefit of several qualities not always evident in Morley Callaghan's work. It is a supple and articulate novel. Father Dowling's innocence is con-nected with spirituality and not with stupidity. He is an intelligent, eloquent man with a taste for analysing his problems. The two girls, Ronnie and Midge, have a quick, feminine expressiveness which makes them lively partners in conversation. So that the language of reflection is more refined, the dialogue nimbler and more vivid than we find either in the short stories or in several other novels. The idiom of this novel is more fluent, the movement less crabbed, and the density less oppressive than in the staple of his work. The minor characters are drawn with just, and no more than, that degree of depth required by a design strongly based on a single central figure and clear leading theme. If novels move between the poles of poetry and journalism, and if Morley Callaghan stands habitually nearer to the journalistic end, then this novel is the exception on the other side. I think this must be because of a natural consonance between talent and theme, because of the inwardness with which the nature of Father Dowling's dilemma is understood and because of the natural human significance which Morley Callaghan is able to extract from a system of religious reference. The religious conception, poetically treated, implicit in the structure of the novel is made to seem luminously relevant to the understanding —not the solution: there is no solution—of a permanent human predicament.

Poetry and religion have a universalising effect in *Such is My Beloved*, making it appear to the British reader more accessible and less off-puttingly embedded in alien ground than, say, *More Joy in Heaven* (1937), which wears an aspect—I can only put it like this— of continental parochialism. *More Joy in Heaven* is irremediably indigenous, North-American in a limiting way. It is the story of a paroled criminal's effort to re-enter the society which has first punished and then forgiven him. Behind it stands an ethos of violence and the myth of the heroic gangster. Its setting is the brutal North-American city, ugly and unhistorical and very much 'a machine for living', the sense of which is conveyed with confident incisiveness.

> The Coronet Hotel near the university was a four-storey, brick hotel used mainly by the second-class sporting trade. Across the street was a public dance hall. The hotel-keeper, Harvey Jenkins, wrestling and boxing promoter, had a string of wrestlers of his own. Squat, tin-eared, short-necked, heavy-shouldered men with bald heads were always going in and out of the Coronet. In the lounge there was always a group of young fellows gathered around some local light-weight who was promising to beat the ears off an imported punch-drunk third rater. During the racing season the hotel was crowded with men from far-away tracks with fine names like Blue Bonnets, Hialeah, and Tia Juana, who had been coming to the Coronet for years. Every day a special bus carried them out to the track and brought them to the hotel at night, or they could make their bets right in the hotel, for there was a wire direct to the track. With a dance hall just across the street, all the little tarts in town used to hang around there in the racing season.

The style of the characters is just what this *milieu* prepares one to expect: the local political boss, Senator McLean, 'investment banker, mining magnate', and his spoilt grasping daughter; the

central figure himself, Kip Caley, in whom there struggles some
Rousseauistic worth the progress of which is blocked, the novel
suggests, by an uncomprehending society; Caley's dying mother
and his prim lawyer brother who has changed his name in order not
to have his career destroyed by his relationship with a notorious
gunman and bank robber; two or three local gangsters and near-
criminals, including the fat, sinister hotel-keeper, a warm-hearted
all-in wrestler and a ferret-like Iago who is appalled by the idea of
Caley's falling for the good life and who hopes against hope that his
transformation is all a front; another rather dim good girl, Julia,
who is working as a waitress but is really a model resting—a
conventional combination of jobs, this; and inevitably 'the big,
raw-boned, sandy-haired prison chaplain'. One's expectations
about the characters in this novel comes not only from the *milieu*
but, one realises on reflection, from a succession of American films
of the 'thirties and 'forties. And how positive and important in
shaping expectations was the cinema for those growing up in this
period. Its images seemed to them to represent reality with a
peculiar point and fitness, its themes and situations to be exactly
level with their experience. The paradox of one's reaction to *More
Joy in Heaven* is that while its pure Americanism is so remote (it is,
it seems to me, markedly more American than Canadian, unlike
Such is My Beloved) its cinematic conception, technique, imagery
and characterisation are intimately familiar, part indeed of the
history of one's own life. So much so that it is impossible to think
about *More Joy in Heaven* without seeing it as a film and without
casting its characters from those familiar names: Victor McLaglen,
William Bendix, Janet Gaynor, Veronica Lake, Humphrey
Bogart, Richard Widmark, Sidney Greenstreet, Franchot Tone,
Edwin Arnold, Edward G. Robinson. *More Joy in Heaven* would
make—perhaps, for all I know, it has already made—a superb film
script. It begins abruptly with Kip Caley's release from prison, it
ends shockingly with his death after a battle with the police. In
between there are two distinct movements or sequences, one which
records his effort to re-enter the normal world, not just as a rescued
criminal but as a man with a new, positive function to interpret the
criminal to society and to ease his return to it; the other records the

process of Caley's realisation that society rejects his rôle as absurd and dangerous.

The clean-cut simplicity of design goes with an abundance of sharply photographed detail. The author maintains his customary unobtrusiveness. He is the registering camera, and the novel's effects are gained by swiftly tracking from point to point or by panning out over a wider prospect before focussing in to concentrate on a single feature. Here is an example of the latter tactic in a scene where Kip Caley watches the hard-up waitress Julie being cruelly teased by two young customers.

> 'Look, lady,' the fair boy said. He tossed the silver up and down. In spite of herself she half turned, her head down, watching the coins in his palm, and everything that Kip had ever wanted seemed at that moment to be held in the boy's palm, all the things he had wanted when he used to lie awake in his cell dreaming of nights of freedom when freight trains rumbled through the hills. And he whispered to himself, 'Go on, son. Give it to her.'

This concentration on a single, tiny, expressive area, in this case the hand tossing the coin, is an instance of an essentially cinematic technique. This is one variation that can be played against the base of the camera's gravely objective scrutiny. Another is to use its distorting power to produce a frantic nightmare unreality. There is a scene worked out in this manner when Kip Caley at a party at an ice-rink is suddenly appalled amid the metallic music and the capers on the ice, by the inhuman monkey-like curiosity of the company.

> When they shook hands with him, he became startled and backed away. Worried, he swung around, looking for a passage to the exit. But a little crowd had gathered in the aisle. They smiled and whispered. The tightness in him was becoming unbearable and spoiling this world for him. All their faces seemed to belong to the glistening ice, the violet lights, the stiffly jumping horses. These faces were bright masks. The Senator's mask was pink and white. Ellen had on a sharp, pretty little frozen-faced mask. Kip felt he was incredible. They gaped up at him as if he were a great crag of basalt.

This technique is supported by a characteristically American use of language in the cinema, by tersely rapping dialogue and by bare and bony speech for narrative, speech which seems to require the accompaniment of realistic acting if it is not to seem grimly thin and dry. The main relief, as in most American film speech, is the harsh wisecrack and the ethnically derived joke. As Kip enters the hotel, where as a famous converted criminal he is to be a draw, he calls out to the Senator:

'I saw the Mayor,' he said. 'He was swell. He wants me to go and see him. What do you know about that?'

'He wouldn't be smart if he didn't,' the Senator said. 'You're his whole social program walking around the streets.'

And then a round, rosy-faced Greek restaurateur with big black moustaches, bounces over to him shouting:

'Tomorrow I make a special sandwich. I call it the Kip Caley sandwich—a gesture for peace, freedom—international, see? How's that?' he asked grandly.

What Morley Callaghan's cinematic method is successful—in a qualified way—in doing in *More Joy in Heaven* is two things. One, to present characters, or rather one character, since Kip Caley's is the only one that counts, which can be felt by sympathy although not entered into by intelligence. The other is to convey a sense of life as energy, as an embodied force flowing this way or that. To point to this achievement is also to expose the essential and double problem of this novel which is both moral and artistic. Kip Caley's is a thick-set block of a character, one of a tribe of the nearly articulate, towards whom Callaghan feels a special sympathy. When Caley thinks or reflects or puzzles about his predicament, his mind creaks; the reader is aware of the clumsy stretching of unused muscles. Caley's thoughts are incapable of escaping from their deep immersion in his moods, from the euphoria with which he leaves prison on his mission to speak for the criminal to society, and from his despair when he finally grasps that in the eyes of society his rôle of interpreter is ridiculous and dangerous. He has the will to move to a moral level of existence without the capacity to make his will effective, or that lucidity of consciousness which is the condition of self-knowledge. Enfranchised from the Kingston Penitentiary Caley may be, but he remains caged in the prison of his own clogged nature.

I speak as though Caley's problem were a real historical event. But of course *this* problem, the inability of the protagonist to move in the direction which the formal transformation of his character requires, is an artistic problem. It is Callaghan's problem and an unsolved problem, too. It is the failure of the author to endow his protagonist with a dimension of possibility—the latent part of Caley's nature is too thin—and at the same time a fault in the author's eyesight which stops him from discerning this deficiency. Callaghan is asking from a character conceived in a certain mould more than it has in it to give. The moral problem in the novel is of a similar sort. It also comes from an uncritical or disproportionate expectation of what a given conception may be able to develop into. As with the character of Caley, so with the idea of experience implicit in the novel. Life is taken to be an expenditure of energy; some forms of it may be regrettable, others not. But it is judged in a pragmatic way solely by criteria within itself. It is impossible for life conceived of in this way, simply as energy, sometimes flowing, sometimes checked, to be the material of moral experience—which is what the author of *More Joy in Heaven* is asking of it in his fiction. Kip Caley's death in a welter of pointless violence is in keeping with the frantic, meaningless activity of his early life as a criminal. But it is also in keeping, it seems to me, with the interval, the period the novel deals with, during which he is, at first with the sympathy, and then against the hostility, of society, apparently undergoing a moral experience. It is in keeping because of the limitations imposed by the brutal convention in which the novel is written, where all human experiences, even as in this case the struggle for moral experience, appears as an outflow of force, another species of violence.

I have stressed what I take to be the essential failure in *More Joy in Heaven* but it remains a strong piece of work and an impressive example of its *genre*. It is solid, vigorous, lean and precise, the product of a serious mind. It has more weight than the documented but insubstantial study of a university institution, *The Varsity Story* (1949), more bite than the more vaguely organised *A Passion in Rome* (1961). *More Joy in Heaven* is a member of the group of novels which includes *Such is My Beloved*, *The Many Colored Coat* (1960),

and *The Loved and the Lost* (1951) to which I turn now. These
novels, different in theme and setting, have in common a preoccupation with what I should like to call self-preservation, as
long as I may remove from the term any hint of selfishness or
over-personal concern.

Morley Callaghan is fascinated by what Henry James in the
Preface to *What Maisie Knew* called a character's 'truth of resistance',
the gift or genius that some have for preserving intact the lineaments
of their nature. It is a power which has at its heart a certain insistent
simplicity: not self confidence but trust in self. In Father Dowling it
shows itself as a steady flame of goodness impervious even to the
most high-minded opposition, in Kip Caley as the persistent, and
finally desperate, thrust of an abrasively independent identity. In
The Loved and the Lost it is the girl Peggy Sanderson who possesses
this faculty. It reveals itself in conduct which ignores or evades—
rather than defies—the acceptable canons of behaviour in her world.
The well-disposed think her capricious, the suspicious perverse. Her
strangeness lies in her unpredictability, in her assumption that she is
not caught in the same net as everybody else. She is described by
his friend Foley to James McAlpine, a University teacher and
would-be newspaper columnist, who is our source of awareness
during this novel, in a fumbling conversation which tries to define
her strangeness, as a blue jay, a bird which flies off at crazy and
unpredictable angles.

The substance of the novel is the search for the true nature of the
girl's odd, disconcerting individuality. It is conducted against the
quietly insinuated but effectively established presence of Montreal.
In no other novel of Morley Callaghan is the city context so
significantly part of the story and—at least to a British reader—so
attractive. Incidentally, unobtrusively and, at every point, relev-
antly, the dimensions of the city appear, from the mountain with
wealth clustered round its sides, the river and the boats whistling
all night long, to the North-American towers and hotels, the
antique stone office buildings and the old French town and its
church steeples spreading eastwards, down to St Henri's along the
canal where Peggy Sanderson lives in a bare room in a run-down
apartment house, and St Antoine, the Negro quarter crammed

with tawdry taverns and cafés, pool parlours, delicatessen stores, cleaning establishments, railway yards. The detail carries with it a pure Canadian quality. One has a sense of a city, neither American nor European, with an authentically separate style of its own, of a place in which a complete human life can be lived and where an immense range of experience is available. It is the universal language with a unique accent. From a rapid touch here and there—there is little extended description—comes a sense of the form and condition of the place: space, snow, and air heavy with unbearable cold, the sound of church bells and sleigh bells, the varying manners of different races and nations and their tense relationships, the chime of different languages, the characteristic bluish winter light, the typical great occasion like the ice hockey match, the glimpses of a fastidious French-Canadian priest helping his sister from a taxi, a fat Jewish tavern keeper, Negro jazz players, a rich man contemplating his Renoir, a University professor with his marbles-in-the-mouth accent.

It is in the freshly realised setting of Montreal, then, that the search for a definition of the girl's identity is undertaken. There is a kind of symmetry between the exact notation of the city and the effort more and more precisely to reveal the quality of her individuality, although, I must add, the symmetry is unusual in that what is explicit and achieved on the side of the city, is suspended and enigmatic on the side of the girl. The instrument of exploration is the consciousness of James McAlpine which becomes, as the novel progresses, the mind and the approach of the reader. McAlpine is well suited to be the honest searcher and, in his normality, to stand for the engaged reader. He is open-minded, intelligent, sensitive and warm-hearted, with a rather obvious ambition to which he is consciously inclined to allow more weight than his fundamentally generous nature warrants. At first puzzled and then fascinated, and at last uneasily in love with Peggy, his feelings at each stage have in them an element of wonder at the girl's originality—an originality which is shown, ironically enough, to be no more than an intimate fidelity to her own nature. Other people in the novel live, as it were, at a distance from themselves, under the influence of principles, prejudices, conventions, formalities, imposed from outside. Most of their conduct and their feelings are imitated, not self-initiated: they are shown as activities and functions set in motion from the outside. But Peggy Sanderson has the strange power of being— herself. She is the standard, a mild, quiet, rather humble standard (remembered by her university teachers as merely a mediocre student) by which we judge the other characters; and so strong is the sense of general human truth in this novel, the standard by which we judge ourselves.

Peggy Sanderson lives directly from her own centre, and in a world where most live indirectly or deviously, this makes her an object of bewilderment and hostility, and since she is an attractive young woman, attitudes towards her are also clouded with sexual desire or sexual envy. The genuine goodness in her nature, hinted at in a variety of forms, and yet teasingly suspended as to certainty till the end of the book, leads her to seek out the poor in whom she feels the response her temperament naturally requires. The poorest in Montreal are the Negroes. She seeks them out not to do them good but simply to be with them. So that there hangs round her the dubious reputation of a woman with perverse sexual tastes, a reputation which is a projection of perverse white feelings, and all the stronger for being a matter of guess and inference. She has the same reputation among Negro men and women, too: among the men because they half-share the feelings of white society, among women because they see their men turning from them to her. Her Negro-haunting life costs her a respectable job—she is now working in a miserable textile factory and is known to James McAlpine as Peggy the Crimp—costs her as well her friends and reputation and ultimately her life. She is raped and murdered by a degenerate white man. The reasons for the shape of her life are partly that the Negroes are what they are in Montreal, and partly the events of her own past. She had loved, as the repressed child of a grim Methodist minister, a Negro family where the gaiety matched the poverty and where she had her chief experience of human warmth. She also had had her first sexual pang at the sight of a nude Negro boy. But these sociological and genetic circumstances, while their importance is recognised, are never offered by Morley Callaghan as total explanations or causes. They are occasions and conditions of spontaneous feeling. There is always in his account of the girl's motives a shaded ambiguity which, while it may be lacking in abstract logic, is, one feels, closely in correspondence with the complications of reality.

The last point suggests something of the technical achievement in *The Loved and the Lost*, Callaghan's success in treating a difficult and serious theme in a casually conversational medium. The writing has little local richness or intricacy; it is bare in metaphor and not at all remarkable in phrasing or wit. But it is always lucid and apt, it has an easy natural run, and the kind of subtlety of inflection more often found in the intimacy of speech. Not that Callaghan hasn't his own ways of using his low-toned medium to good effect: in particular, great skill in the sudden small shock of contrasting sequences, sometimes of personality, sometimes of location. In this novel he makes effective use of the contrast between the space of the city and vividly pictured interiors, between, for example, the rearing mountain and a brilliantly lit shop window showing a single carved leopard, or between the flowing expanse of the streets and the confined, nun-like severity of Peggy Sanderson's room, or a smoky ground-floor club occupied by rapturously intent jazz musicians. One notices even more the attitude of the writer, an air of relaxed restraint, which comes from his confidence in his capacity, certainly not to force, not even to persuade, but rather to allow, a profoundly significant theme to appear at critical moments and with complete naturalness from its immersion in the coolly observed detail.

It is this triple set of medium, theme and attitude, which distinguishes *The Many Colored Coat*, one of the finest of Morley Callaghan's novels, and the one I take to represent his latest, most developed work. The medium is in the same mode, quiet, unpretentious, close to speech in movement and with much of the flexibility and versatility of the spoken language. The medium, at once masculine and unpretentious, is in accord with Morley Callaghan's attitude, which is, characteristically, both self-effacing and positive. The theme of *The Many Colored Coat* is that of Joseph, the gifted and beloved young man. The novel rehearses the theme of the fortunes of the fortunate man. The biblical reference comes through, as the novel unfolds, without the least touch of impropriety or tactlessness, and it testifies to the steadiness Callaghan sees in human nature and to his perception of the permanent content of the varying crises it has to face. At the same time the pretentious absurdity of the hero's job, Public Relations man to a distillery, an ambassador of alcohol, in fact, has an almost clinically exact contemporary flavour, that of business modified to suit the entertainment industry and surrounded by a mist of dubious scientific management.

The novel has a pleasingly simple shape. It falls into two parts, each of which concludes in a critical and brilliantly conducted court scene. In the first we see Harry Lane as Joseph the blessed, blooming with health, beauty, riches, success, courage—he is modest about his fine war record—popularity and love. He deals with radio and television people, speaks at banquets, organises golfing tournaments, spends his employers' money right and left to sell whisky. Why then didn't all the phoniness rub off on him? It was because he radiated an essential air of well-being. People lived off him, but they loved to live off *him*. 'He had always had a talent for generosity . . . and his good natural talent was now flowering outlandishly. . . .' Scotty Bowman, a middle-aged, middle-class bank manager, a solid decent man, who is deeply drawn to him, notices two things about him: one, 'that unbelievable luck which was like a magical adjustment between himself and the world', and two, that he had, as Scotty said, '. . . a bad flaw. He's a kind of innocent guy.' Only the old or the twisted feel alien to him, like his girl's father Judge Morris, for whom his popularity was 'the whole corrupting essence of this thing', and for whom his attractiveness was terrible and criminal, 'his occupational weapon'; or Mike Kon, Scotty Bowman's friend, an ex-boxer with a passion for respectability, who is jealous of Harry's effect on the friend to whom he owes everything. To Kon, Harry is a smooth and superficial man. To Francis Ouimet, a Catholic lawyer with a spinsterish aloofness from any kind of self-indulgence, the grace and charm to which Harry's friends yield is 'the corrupting pressure of friendship'. The astonishing achievement of Callaghan's here is to make us feel the sweetness and wholesomeness, too easily accepted by Harry himself perhaps, but completely genuine, of the nature involved in this idiotic commercial confidence work. Callaghan can do this because he never sees the character as an abstraction, never takes it to be an arrangement of qualities but always a dense and complex pattern. He has an insight, which is both realist and mature, into the mixture of motives, the flawed surface and the clouded quality of human substance. There are discrepancies, aberrations, snags and twists in the material. But it impresses us always as real and not synthetic.

Harry's golden years are shattered when a friend, out of gratitude, offers him the chance of making a fortune in oil shares. He needs to borrow money to buy them and the banker, Scotty Bowman, persuades him to arrange a large loan at Bowman's bank. The consideration, the banker suggests, will be some shares for himself. The disconcerted Harry has brought home to him what has already been tellingly indicated to the reader, that Bowman has rapidly succumbed to the financial morality of the world around Harry. Harry agrees, the money is passed over, the shares turn out to be worthless, and the bank manager is tried for fraud since he had, although Harry had not realised this, insufficient cover for the loan. He is found guilty in a trial scene which has all the elegance of a ballet and the excitement of a film. The damage to Harry's reputation is done by Mike Kon, Bowman's devoted friend, whose testimony in defence of Bowman makes Harry out the chief though not legally responsible culprit. The disgust with which all his friends now look at Harry turns to horror when Bowman, who to all appearances was duped into committing a crime by the sophisticated Harry, kills himself in prison.

The second part of the novel traces, with an unemphatic, wandering but expressive line, the dissolution of personality worked in Harry Lane by his loss of reputation. The process, a passage from incredulous fury when his innocence is not recognised, through self-pity and disorientation to despair and revenge, is one partly of drift, a flinching accommodation to circumstances, partly of defiant self-destruction. Callaghan has the realist's talent for rendering the densely conditioned movements of life and their peculiar combination of limpness and drive. In *The Many Colored*

Coat the characteristically solid evocation is strengthened and filled out by a second parallel movement, the break-up of Mike Kon who in his truculent, dumber way, mimics the disintegration of Harry Lane. The finesse of the design lies particularly in the combined parallelism and friction of these two movements. Mike's decline, desertion by his friends, failure at work, a bad name, a disordered personal life, repeats Harry's; and yet each sees the other as the malevolent force which keeps the original cause of his disaster, Scottie Bowman's suicide (which means to Harry, Bowman's guilty silence, and to Mike his undeserved disgrace), continually operating as a malign influence in his own life. Each, once he is ousted from what he sees as his normal 'pre-lapsarian' state, has his own way of making the other suffer. Harry's is more consciously cruel, Mike's is more angrily bull-like.

The twisted logic of the novel's design fits the perverse will, itself the function of a distorted consciousness, which in each of the two men turns persecutor into victim, victim into persecutor, and makes punishment and crime change places. The irrational assumptions revealed in Harry's frantic conduct lead some to believe that his trauma has made him mad, 'You've changed,' his lover Molly says to him. 'Your whole personality has changed. This . . . this exploration of your innocence, I think you are out of your mind. . .' But a friend shrewdly comments on this, 'No, not mad at all. Harry Lane's thumbing his nose at the world.' What does become clear is that Harry's obsessive concentration on his suffering damages his capacity for human connection. 'When a man clings to his suffering,' Molly says to him again, 'he violates all human sympathy and without that human sympathy what he does has no meaning. All you're doing with your antics is cutting yourself off. . . .' The love between Harry and Molly becomes tense and finally impossible, and the same infection invades the devotion of his alter-ego, Mike, to his father, a paralysed old man, the whole of whose intelligence and affection is concentrated in his one good eye (both these relationships are realised with accurate, moving sympathy). Harry believes that he is carried along solely by the conviction of his own innocence. But what is even clearer is that his more constant feeling is one of 'a sense of foolish, endless humiliation'.

O

'Humiliation' is indeed the key word. Harry is fascinated by 'the blind and perfect selfishness of Bowman's despair that could let him make Harry his victim again. Oh, the monstrous egotism of despair, he thought, sighing.' But as an old mumbling priest, whose confessional he uneasily enters one night, not to confess but to ask for advice, points out as he complains of the injustice done to him, 'The more you suffer from injustice, the deeper the wound to your pride . . . a man killed himself, surely not to spite just you. What awful egotism of you to think so. . . .' Harry's bitter sense of injustice, his anguish at the guilt so unfairly imputed to him, turns out to be a disguise for the rage of wounded pride.

The importance attributed to pride, not in any doctrinal way but by suggestive, concrete pointing, is justified not only by the facts of the case in this novel and the intelligent psychological investigation of them, but by a certain habit of sensibility in Morley Callaghan himself. He has, as Edmund Wilson point out in a perceptive and sympathetic essay,[1] 'an intuitive sense of the meaning of Christianity'. 'Though [the novels] depend on no scaffolding of theology, though they embody an original vision, they have evidently somewhere behind them the tradition of the Catholic Church. This is not the acquired doctrine of the self-conscious Catholic convert—of Graham Greene or Evelyn Waugh.' The human vision of these novels depends on a Christian style of feeling, of a particular tradition of religious sensibility which is present not as dogma or metaphysic but as a mode of perception and reaction.

This Christian touch—it is as silent and precise as that—is present particularly in the quiet close of the novel. ('Climax' would be too heightened a word for work which, as Edmund Wilson in the same essay said, 'avoids convulsions and . . . allows itself no outbreak in tirades'.[2]) Mike Kon, maddened by Harry's harrassment and his refusal to back down, does serious violence to him, is arrested and put on trial in a scene which has all the acrid sharpness and the shaped definition of the earlier trial. Harry, who in hospital had

[1] Edmund Wilson, O Canada, London, 1967, p. 20
[2] Op. cit. p. 31

been calculating his revenge, unaccountably fails to appear to give evidence against Mike, and he is acquitted. With equal unpredicta-bility, Mike Kon suddenly admits in court that he was unjust to Harry Lane in his original testimony. There is a gratuitous, unprepared note in these two actions which corresponds to, or is the outcome of, the unforeseeable visitations of grace, the sense of which is the positive side in Callaghan's economy of Christian response, of his feeling for guilt and negation.

I speak of Callaghan's Christian response, but, of course, that response and the whole economy of feeling of which it is a part, are sunk deep in the constitution of the novelist. If Callaghan is a Christian novelist, this is the way in which he is one. He is not the spokesman of religion, but the artist who possesses it as part of his personal nervous equipment. This traditional steadiness blends in Callaghan with that acute feeling for contemporary society, which, to a European at least, seems very natural to an artist working in the New World, and the combination makes him a novelist of an impressively serious quality. The contemporary flavour appears everywhere in his work, in themes, situations, characters and pro-cedures. A single notable example of it in *The Many Colored Coat* is his treatment of the life of the streets. The street in a modern industrial society presents itself to him as an image of that society and its experience. His skill in rendering the flow of life through the street, the brutality and ugliness, the glimpses the street provides of other, less tangible experiences, the altercations, the moments of communication, show the street not only as a place but as the analogue of human vitality and representativeness. 'That night,' he writes of Harry Lane after his fall, 'he walked through the streets for hours feeling he was wandering through his own life.'

I end by quoting the concluding paragraphs of *The Many Colored Coat*, a novel which strikes one very much as a walk through the streets of life (and one, too, in which Callaghan allows himself the unaccustomed liberty of an explicit comment). It brings out, I think, the serenity and balance of a writer whose religious sense is part of his grip on reality, and the quality of one who, as he puts it, appreciate's people's capacity to 'handle their lives and be comfortable together' but who also sees the point of lives of a different sort, those who are 'alone, knowing the terror of their innocence'.

It was the hour when the neighborhood came alive for the night. People wandered along the boulevard seeking pleasure or excitement or just new sights, or new merchandise in the store windows. No one paid any attention to him. He was a stranger to them. Loafing along in the crowd he found himself looking with interest at the passing faces. A plain plump woman with her thin husband bumped against him. Three young men, hatless, their thick shiny black hair carefully combed, stared at him coldly. A taxi stopped at the curb and three men and three girls scrambled out and rushed at a doorway to a dance hall and went running and pushing each other up a long flight of stairs. He could hear the clatter of their footsteps and their laughter on the stairs. It was a fine clear evening. As he passed a dingy little candy store where the prostitutes were allowed to sit undisturbed, one of the girls smiled at him, then saw someone she knew on the street and got up eagerly. An old Jew with a beard and grave eyes passed by, then a tired old man, then a boyish-looking seminarian, plump-cheeked and clean, his eyes cast down, then a pretty girl with her stern watchful mother. An opulent fat man, a rich drug peddler who held court every night at a table by the dance floor in the biggest beer hall in the neighborhood, got out of a new car with three obsequious young fellows. The opulent-looking man had an evil face, Harry thought.

It was a tough neighborhood of ordinary people. Kids with long smooth hair and leather jackets, workmen, a lawyer taking a stroll, a serene-faced old man, girls in sweaters and short straight hair, and middle-aged men with pale hard faces and shifty eyes—they all brushed against him on the way to their cafés.

But on this wide crowded boulevard at that hour were all the faces of the world; some were evil, some pious, some greedy, some just didn't care, and some no doubt avowed their sins, suffering whatever torments. Yet they looked as if they could handle their lives and be comfortable together. There would be some though, he was sure, who would really be alone, knowing the terror of their innocence.

INDEX